Patrick Henry

A Biography

Patrick Henry. From a portrait by Thomas Sully.

Patrick Henry

A BIOGRAPHY

RICHARD R. BEEMAN

McGRAW-HILL BOOK COMPANY

New York   St. Louis   San Francisco

Düsseldorf   London   Mexico   Sydney   Toronto

Library of Congress Cataloging in Publication Data
Beeman, Richard R
   Patrick Henry; a biography.
   Includes bibliographic references.
   1. Henry, Patrick, 1736-1799. 2. Virginia—History—Revolution, 1775-1783.
E302.6.H5B44   973.3'092'4 [B]   74-11445
ISBN 0-07-004280-2

This book was set in Life by Cherry Hill Composition. It was printed and bound by Book Press. The designer was Elaine Gongora. The editors were Nancy Tressel, Laura Givner, and Phyllis McCord. Milton Heiberg supervised the production.
1 2 3 4 5 6 7 8 9 BP BP 7 9 8 7 6 5 4

For My Mother and Father

Contents

Illustrations

Frontispiece. Portrait of Henry by Thomas Sully.

Following page 57:

I. P. F. Rothermel portrait of the Stamp Act Speech.

II. The Stamp Act Resolves. From the original owned by the Colonial Williamsburg Foundation.

III. Henry's recollection of events surrounding the introduction of the Stamp Act Resolves. From the original owned by the Colonial Williamsburg Foundation.

IV. The House of Burgesses, Williamsburg, Virginia.

V. The Conference Room, Capitol Building, Williamsburg.

VI. Raleigh Tavern, Williamsburg.

VII. Portrait of Lord Dunmore by Sir Joshua Reynolds.

VIII. Patrick Henry's directive respecting slave security.

IX. Lord Dunmore's proclamation branding Henry an outlaw.

X. Edmund Pendleton's Resolutions for Independence published in *The Virginia Gazette* of May 18, 1776.

XI. Notice in *The Virginia Gazette,* July 5, 1776, of Henry's election as governor.

Preface

Patrick Henry has ever been a perplexing subject for biographers. In 1815, in the midst of his study of Henry, William Wirt exploded,

> It was all speaking, speaking, speaking. 'Tis true he could talk—Gods how he *could* talk! but there is no acting the while. . . . And then, to make the matter worse, from 1763 to 1789 . . . not one of his speeches lives in print, writing or memory. All that is told me is, that on such and such an occasion, he made a distinguished speech. . . . Again: there are some ugly traits in H's character, and some pretty nearly as ugly blanks. He was a blank military commander, a blank governor, and a blank politician, in all those useful points which depend on composition and detail. In short, it is, verily, as hopeless a subject as man could well desire.[1]

Undaunted, Wirt went on to complete his biography, inventing evidence when it proved impossible to fill in the blanks with verifiable facts. While the finished product too often omitted the "ugly traits," Wirt's portrait of Henry was phenomenally popular, going through twenty-five editions in the half-century that followed its publication in 1817. Wirt's Patrick Henry was the prototypical child of nature, reared without schooling in the backcountry of Virginia and rising to prominence by virtue of his natural abilities. For Wirt, Henry's triumph represented a victory for a natural aristocracy composed of men of talent and ability over an artificial aristocracy based on wealth and family ties.[2]

Of course, not all Wirt's contemporaries were happy with the book. Thomas Jefferson, hardly Henry's biggest booster, judged the biography "a poor book, written in bad taste," that "gives an imperfect idea of Patrick Henry." For Jefferson, the true Henry was not a natural aristocrat but rather "was avaritious & rotten hearted," a man whose legal training was "not worth a copper," and whose apostasy at the end of his career in the controversy over the Alien and Sedition Acts overshadowed any good that he might have achieved during the Revolution.[3]

Wirt's panegyric and Jefferson's bitter denunciations have hardly made things easier for those who have attempted to fill in still more of the blanks in Henry's life. Jefferson's comments were the product of personal pique and profound ideological disagreement dating from the early 1780s and continuing until Henry's death; as such, they are far from disinterested appraisals of Henry's worth as a Revolutionary statesman. Wirt's book presents an even more difficult problem. Because Wirt's writings had great literary flair, it has been difficult to resist the temptation to use his accounts of Henry when other evidence was lacking. Thus, Wirt's reconstruction has had a continuing, and on the whole pernicious, influence on subsequent studies of Henry. Although Henry's recent biographers have disputed the depiction of their subject as ill-educated and without social refinement, the basic picture—that of a frontier leader who adhered consistently to principles of liberty and republicanism—has remained. In the words of Robert D. Meade, Henry's most recent biographer, "Few of the great Americans of this and subsequent eras—not Thomas Jefferson or even Abraham Lincoln—seem to have got more beneficial results from their frontier environment. . . . The frontier, its distinctive customs and people, helped to make Patrick Henry a flaming apostle of American democracy."[4]

The time has come to wrest Henry from Wirt's grasp. It is not an easy task, and I suspect that other biographers before me may have started with the same vow. No amount of resolve, for example, will change the dismal state of the historical records relating to Henry's life; on that point Wirt's judgment was perfectly sound. What is not necessary, then, is another minutely detailed, day-by-day account of Henry's private and public lives; a thoroughly satisfactory account of that sort is unfortunately beyond the historian's grasp. There are other avenues of approach, however. Henry, more than any of his equally famous contemporaries, was in both his outward manner and mental outlook a product of the narrowly bounded society into which he was born. All the seemingly contradictory strains in his personality—his acquisitiveness and his occasional selflessness during the Revolution, his radicalism in the context of the struggle with Great Britain and his frequent conservatism on domestic issues within Virginia, his phenomenal popularity with lower- and middle-class Virginians and his reluctance to allow all those people a full voice in the political process—can best be explained not by sweeping generalizations respecting Henry's "liberalism" or his "love of liberty" but, rather, by an analysis of his actions in the context of the turbulent times in which he achieved his political power.

The pages that follow, then, may disappoint those who yearn to know more of Henry's private life. Some of the details are there, but I readily admit that others have done a more complete job than I of mining the meager supply of historical materials relating to the domestic side of the Revolutionary leader's life. What I hope the reader will gain from these pages instead is a more complete understanding of the society in which Henry operated; with that understanding will come, I think, a better comprehension of the pressures and principles, the opportunities and anxieties, that guided Patrick Henry's conduct during the Revolutionary era.

Acknowledgments

My interest in the history of Virginia during the Revolutionary era dates back to my undergraduate years; since it is well-nigh impossible to study the Revolution in Virginia without bumping into the figure of Patrick Henry along the way, it is at least technically accurate to say that the research for this biography has been in progress for over a decade. I must confess, however, that I have spent a good portion of that time either overlooking or misreading Henry's importance. I dealt with Henry in some detail in an earlier study of Virginia politics in the 1790s, but in retrospect I am most impressed by my failure to comprehend his extraordinary influence on the events of that period. Daniel J. Boorstin, who played an important role in guiding that earlier book, was the first to recognize both Henry's importance *and* my failure to explain adequately that importance. It was at his suggestion that I began work on Henry in earnest, and while there have been times when I have cursed him for setting me to work on a man who was so inconsiderate to leave such meager literary remains, I am now profoundly grateful for his advice and encouragement.

The research for this book and the writing have been facilitated by grants from the American Philosophical Society and the University of Pennsylvania. During the course of my research I have benefited from the assistance and courtesy of archivists at Colonial Williamsburg, Inc., the Virginia State Library, the Virginia Historical Society, the Valentine Museum, the Historical Society of Pennsylvania, and the staff of the library of the University of Pennsylvania.

Several of my colleagues in the historical profession have been kind enough to read various drafts of the manuscript and offer their suggestions. James C. Curtis of the University of Delaware, my editorial conscience for many years, offered his usual good advice. Thad Tate, director of the Institute of Early American History and Culture, saved me from several factual errors and also provided some important suggestions regarding the organization of the book. Finally, Rhys Isaac of La Trobe University, Australia, has proved to be a constant source of ideas on both Henry and the political style of eighteenth-century Virginia. I suspect that if Professor Isaac were to write a biography of Patrick Henry it would be substantially different from this one, but I hope that my work reflects at least a small portion of his considerable wisdom on the subject.

My wife Pamela and my two irrepressible children, Kristin and Joshua, are at the center of my life. All this would mean very little without them.

CHAPTER

1

Beginnings

"From birth he derived neither splendor nor opulence, but . . . he understood the condition of the Virginian planters and was completely embarked in their fate."[1] Thus wrote Edmund Randolph, a frequent foe, but also a man who, late in life, after partisan feelings had cooled, came to understand Patrick Henry's role in the struggle for independence better than any member of the Revolutionary generation.

Henry did not possess the illustrious family background of Randolph, the wide-ranging education and intellect of Thomas Jefferson, the extraordinary economic advantages of Landon Carter, or the manners and bearing of George Washington, but as Randolph's statement implies, he was no stranger to the gentry tradition. His family, if it did not rank with the First Families of Virginia, was nevertheless prosperous and growing more prosperous each year. Few of Patrick Henry's constituents would fully comprehend the intricacies of Jeffersonian thought and few would ever feel truly comfortable in the presence of men with the wealth and social prestige of the Randolphs and the Carters; rather, they were more inclined to identify with an aggressive, rising Virginia planter who still retained a vestige of the manners and habits of the yeomanry. It was both this commonness and the visible evidence that he was rapidly ascending the social and economic ladder of his region that would cause Virginians to find him so peculiarly representative of their own style of life and their own aspirations and fears.

★

Patrick Henry was born on May 29, 1736, on his father's plantation, Studley, in the still sparsely settled county of Hanover, situ-
ated on the eastern edge of Virginia's central Piedmont. His father,
Colonel John Henry, hardly a member of the humble yeomanry,
was born in Aberdeen, Scotland, of a family of at least middle-class
means. At the age of fourteen or fifteen, John Henry competed
successfully in a competition in Latin composition and won a
scholarship to Kings College at Aberdeen University.[2] Although the
precise details of his boyhood are uncertain, it seems reasonable to
assume that his family was both wealthy enough and cared enough
to secure for him the relatively costly education that enabled him
to win that competition. In this respect John Henry was unusual
among Scottish youth, as few had the time or the resources to
secure the equivalent of a secondary school education and even
fewer actually had the opportunity to continue that education in a
university.

John Henry spent four years at Kings College but never earned
his degree. Rather, he left the college, purchased a passage to Virginia, and set out to make his fortune in the New World. He arrived
in Virginia in February 1727 and for the next four years was the
guest of John Syme, a close friend of his family back in Aberdeen.
Syme was in a position to offer John Henry many of the advantages
of Virginia society. A colonel in the colonial militia, a large land-
owner, a member of the county court and of the House of Burgesses, Syme was firmly entrenched in the social and political elite
within his home county of Hanover.[3] John Henry's opportunities for
advancement were further enhanced in 1731, when Syme came to
an untimely death, leaving his attractive wife, Sarah Winston Syme,
a widow. According to William Byrd II, who visited her in the fall
of 1732, the young widow "seemed not to pine too much for the
death of her husband." In any case, Henry continued to live on the
plantation after Syme's death. Some time between January 1733
and September 1734, he took Sarah's hand—and her sizable estate
—in marriage.[4]

John Henry's new wife, considered by her contemporaries to be
both attractive and of pleasant disposition, was herself a daughter
of the Virginia provincial aristocracy. Her father, Isaac Winston,
was a prominent merchant and land speculator; her mother, Mary
Dabney, was a member of one of the most prominent families in the

Old Dominion. (The Dabneys had first come to Virginia in the early eighteenth century and ranked high in status even among the First Families of Virginia.) John Henry's new wife also brought him resources more tangible than a good name. Sarah Winston Henry was heir to at least 6,000 acres of land in Hanover County and this, added to the 1,200 acres patented by John Henry by the time of his marriage, left the couple in comfortable circumstances.[5]

His financial and social status significantly improved by his timely marriage, John Henry began to raise a family. There is no record of the date of birth of William, his first son, but we do know that on May 29, 1736, Patrick was born. By that time John Henry's landholdings had increased to at least 7,200 acres in Hanover County, a one-third interest in a 30,000-acre tract in Goochland County, a one-sixth interest in another 30,000-acre tract in the western Piedmont counties of Goochland and Amelia, at least 1,250 acres in Albemarle County, and another 4,850-acre speculative holding in Roundabout and Fork Creeks in Louisa County.[6]

John Henry continued to acquire land and children. After Patrick was born, Sarah Henry gave birth another nine times, to seven girls and two more boys. In addition to his steady accumulation of wealth, John Henry also began his ascent in the social and political structure of his community; during his career he served as chief justice of the Hanover County Court, surveyor of the county (an ideal position for an aggressive land speculator), vestryman of the Church of England, and colonel of the militia. In short, Colonel John Henry had become a "gentleman freeholder" and had been fully accepted by even the most prestigious members of his wife's socially conscious family. By 1752, when Patrick was only sixteen years old, six of the twelve justices of the Hanover County Court, including Patrick's half-brother John Syme, Jr., were close relatives.[7]

We find, then, that Patrick Henry hardly suffered from a "disadvantaged youth." His father had married into a prominent family, had quickly proved his worth, and had ascended rapidly in the social and political hierarchy of his county. Although his manners were slightly less refined, his family lineage less imposing, and his plantation less splendorous than those of the leaders of Virginia's planter aristocracy, John Henry was, in the context of eighteenth-century Hanover County, a powerful and respected man.

John Henry's wealth and power notwithstanding, the cultural and educational opportunities open to a young man growing up in Hanover were severely limited. Virginians would not think seriously about erecting a system of public education until the mid-nineteenth century, and as a result educational opportunity was limited to those who could afford to send their sons to a private academy or to hire a tutor. And the quality of both the academies and the tutors of Virginia was questionable. Even in the prosperous and populous Tidewater, there were frequent complaints about the scarcity of competent schoolmasters; in Hanover County, which was underpopulated and closer to the·frontier, the wealth of the relatively few prominent families in the area was often not enough to support a decent academy or to pay the salaries of more than a few capable tutors.[8]

Colonel Samuel Meredith, later Henry's brother-in-law, has left us with the only surviving description of Henry's academic training:

> He was sent to a common English school until about the age of ten years, where he learned to read and write, and acquired some little knowledge of arithmetic. He never went to any other school, public or private, but remained with his father, who was his only tutor. With him he acquired a knowledge of the Latin language and a smattering of Greek. He became well-acquainted with Mathematics, of which he was very fond. At the age of 15 he was well versed in both ancient and modern history.[9]

Although this description seems to belie William Wirt's rather harsh judgment that Henry's "aversion to study [was] invincible, and his faculties almost benumbed by indolence," neither does it foretell the emergence of one of the revolutionary era's greatest orator-statesmen. The "common English schools" in the central Piedmont of Virginia were not of the level designed to produce a polished, erudite ten-year-old. And while John Henry was himself better educated than most fathers in Virginia, the fact that he was increasingly preoccupied with the development and management of an ever-growing estate precluded any possibility of rigorous, sustained training at home. It seems more likely that Patrick Henry's early years were spent in a manner much like that of his youthful contemporaries. Mastery of the classics or fluency in Latin and Greek was hardly a preparation for managing a plantation in western

Virginia. Rather, it is more likely that he indulged, at least until the age of fifteen, in the kinds of activities that occupied the time of most of the sons of prosperous plantation owners. Colonel Meredith commented on Patrick's fondness for guns, and nearly all of his contemporaries in his later life noted his passion for hunting.[10]

In a real sense, however, Patrick Henry's boyhood ended at age fifteen. At that age, in 1751, he was sent out to work as a clerk to a small merchant in Hanover County. Although some historians have argued that this decision was reached because his family could not afford to give him a college education at either William and Mary or in England, this does not appear to be an altogether satisfactory explanation for Henry's decision to forsake college for business.[11] By 1751 John Henry was a prominent man of considerable and ever-increasing wealth. Some of Henry's contemporaries —Thomas Jefferson and John Marshall, for example—came from families of approximately the same means, yet those families were able to bear the financial burden of Jefferson's and Marshall's matriculation at the College of William and Mary. It would seem more likely that John Henry saw little need for further formal education for his son. And Patrick, both during the years of his formal schooling and during the subsequent five years of informal tutoring, seemed to show neither enough aptitude for nor interest in his studies to warrant a further investment in a college education.

The decision to send Patrick into the world as a store clerk rather than enroll him in college was probably dictated less by monetary considerations than by the desire to help the young man find a practical trade that would be useful to him in later life. The job of clerk in a county store was, in effect, an apprenticeship which served as a substitute for a continuing, formal education. It was, in addition, a logical way for the Henry family to begin to extend its influence on the economic life of the region.

Patrick must have fared tolerably well in his apprenticeship. The next year John Henry purchased the goods necessary to set his older brother and him up in business for themselves. Perhaps in some mysterious way this new mercantile venture prepared Patrick for his future role as statesman and orator, but an entrepreneur he was not. Patrick's and William's initial business venture on their own was a flop. According to Colonel Meredith, the Henry brothers "did not continue business longer than one year, when it was found necessary to abandon it, as they had injured themselves by granting too extensive credit."[12]

Within a year after liquidating his store, Patrick, with few tangible resources and with little of the training that would promise him future success, decided to assume the responsibilities of marriage. His wife, Sarah Shelton, was only sixteen. At that time only eighteen himself, Patrick was undoubtedly viewed by his neighbors as very young for his new role, as the average age of marriage for males in eighteenth-century Virginia was probably at least twenty-one. Although Sarah has usually been described as coming from humble origins, her family was actually on much the same social and economic level as John Henry's family. In fact, when it became obvious that the impetuous young couple would need outside assistance in order to provide for themselves, it was Sarah's family that contributed the greater share. Her father, John Shelton—like John Henry a rising member of the planter class, a land speculator, and also owner of a tavern in the county—gave the newlyweds a 300-acre tract of land adjoining his plantation and six slaves. Although the land was not the most fertile in Hanover County, William Wirt definitely exaggerated when he gave this description of the hardships endured by the young husband:

> It [was] curious to contemplate this great genius, destined to guide the councils of a mighty nation . . . encumbered, at the early age of eighteen, with the cares of a family; obscure, unknown and almost unpitied; digging with wearied limbs and with an aching heart, a small spot of barren earth, for bread, and blessing the hour which relieved him from toil.[13]

It is likely, of course, that most of the toil fell on the shoulders of the black slaves, not on Patrick himself. Wirt was correct, however, in describing the farm as unproductive, as the only thing that the Henrys proved successful in producing was children—the first less than a year after they were married and a steady procession of them thereafter. The marriage between Patrick and Sarah yielded six offspring, and Patrick's subsequent marriage to Dorothea Dandridge, in 1777, led to the birth of ten more.

Henry's career as a farmer lasted little longer than his career as a storekeeper. In the spring of 1757, Pine Slash caught fire; Henry's house and most of his possessions were destroyed. He and his family took temporary shelter in a tolerable but hardly comfortable cabin that adjoined their burnt out estate and lived there until the fall, when they moved in with Sarah's family. Henry soon thereafter sold most of his slaves and, obviously disgusted with the life of a farmer, used the money from the sale of the slaves to buy another stock of goods to start a second country store.[14]

The second storekeeping venture followed the pattern of the first; it was an unmitigated disaster. The account book for the store, which seems to have been conscientiously kept up to date (although judging from the handwriting, by someone other than Patrick), indicates that Henry remained either unwilling or unable to collect from his customers the necessary cash receipts to keep the business going. Although he did not formally close his store until July 1760, he had for all practical purposes ceased to do business by the end of 1759.[15]

After the failure of his business, Henry sought to earn his keep at his father-in-law's tavern in Hanover County, which served as the temporary residence of the financially distressed young family. His conduct while living at that tavern has become a major and probably unnecessary source of controversy. Both Thomas Jefferson and Nathaniel Pope, Jr., in letters to William Wirt in 1805, asserted that Henry acted as a part-time barkeeper for his father-in-law. Pope was informed by Henry's cousin William Winston that the future hero of the Revolution was at that time rudely clothed, barefoot, and occasionally accustomed to playing his violin for the amusement of the guests at the tavern. Evidently some of Henry's nineteenth- and twentieth-century admirers have been offended by the suggestion that one of the nation's founding fathers began his career as a bartender, but there hardly seems much reason for alarm. It was after all only fitting that Henry help to earn his keep at Shelton's tavern by aiding in the principal business of that establishment. There is no evidence that anyone in the eighteenth century thought less of Henry for his brief excursion into the tavern-keeping business; Jefferson and Pope certainly did not report the event in such a way as to indicate that they saw anything wrong with it. In fact, Jefferson believed Henry's fondness for "fiddling, dancing, and pleasantry" to be a major cause for his later popularity with the Virginia gentry. The planter class of Virginia placed a high value on conviviality, and Henry seemed to possess that attribute in extraordinary abundance.[16]

In the spring of 1760 Patrick left the tavern to begin an entirely new career. By what chain of reasoning Patrick Henry decided to enter the legal profession, after failing in a number of other, presumably less demanding, careers, and how he managed to prepare himself on such short notice for that profession are questions that must remain unanswered. We are left only with the statement of Judge Edmund Winston that Henry was "a virtuous young man . . . in very narrow circumstances, making a last effort to supply the wants of his family."[17] There was some logic to the decision. He had tried farming and storekeeping and had met misfortune in both. The practice of law was one of the few remaining avenues open to a young man of reasonable intelligence and social standing in Virginia. And while it may seem surprising to us that a man of such undistinguished previous educational attainment should dare aspire to that profession, the decision would not have appeared startling to those familiar with eighteenth-century Virginia legal procedures. The "unspecialized lawyer" of the eighteenth century, to use historian Daniel J. Boorstin's term, was markedly more lackadaisically trained than his English counterpart. For the members of the Virginia planter aristocracy the law was an eminently practical profession; the year or so of study generally necessary to qualify for the bar—a process loosely administered by other planter-lawyers—was extremely useful to those Virginia gentrymen whose careers so often embraced farming, commerce, and politics.[18]

Henry arrived in Williamsburg in 1760, sometime around the first of April, to take the examination that would determine whether he would be allowed to practice law in the colony of Virginia. The panel of lawyers that was to examine him—Robert Carter Nicholas, John Randolph, Peyton Randolph, and George Wythe—must have looked on the young applicant with some measure of horror. Even by the abysmally low formal requirements of the Virginia legal profession, Patrick Henry's ignorance of the law was notable. George Wythe, though he had little academic legal training, was one of the finest legal minds in Virginia and perhaps in all America. John Randolph, the attorney general of the colony of Virginia, and Peyton Randolph, who would become the speaker of the House of

Burgesses, had both trained at the Middle Temple in London. Robert Nicholas, a man who was considered by many to be the leader of the provincial bar, had studied at William and Mary. Henry, by contrast, had spent somewhere between one month and nine months, depending on which account one accepts, preparing for his legal career. The most commonly accepted figure, given by both Henry's close friend Edmund Winston, and Thomas Jefferson, a not-so-close friend, was six weeks.[19]

We can be sure, at any rate, that as Patrick Henry walked down the streets of Williamsburg in 1760, he must have had at least some sense of his inadequacy as a legal scholar. And that inadequacy did not escape the notice of his examining committee. Although the accounts of the proceedings of his examination differ, all agree that it was a close call. Jefferson, reminiscing in 1814, stated:

> Two of the examiners . . . , Peyton and John Randolph, men of great facility of temper, signed his license with as much reluctance as their dispositions would permit them to show. Mr. Wythe absolutely refused. Robert C. Nicholas refused also at first, but on repeated importunity and promises of future reading, he signed. These facts I have afterward from the gentlemen themselves, the two Randolphs acknowledging he was very ignorant of law, but that they perceived him to be a young man of genius and did not doubt that he would soon qualify himself.[20]

John Randolph, in his portion of the examination, found that Henry knew very little law, but that his power of "natural reason" was quite remarkable. According to Judge John Tyler, to whom Henry gave an account of the proceedings, Randolph closed the examination by escorting him to his law office and admonishing him: "You have never seen these books, nor this principle of the law; yet you are right and I am wrong. And from the lesson which you have given me . . . I will never trust to appearances again. Mr. Henry, if your industry be only half equal to your genius, I augur that you will do well, and become an ornament and an honor to your profession."[21]

Although the entire sequence of events by which Henry—young, ill trained, and with little apparent direction—came to be admitted to the bar is almost inconceivable to the modern reader, Henry would in fact ultimately achieve fame as well as honor in his new profession. He would, in the coming years, show an energy—his enemies would attribute it to greed—that had previously not been evident in his behavior. His principal assets, a quickness of mind and phenomenal oratorical gifts, would be of far greater value in his new career than in either of his previous two. And of course, those gifts would be developed and come to have their greatest impact in the midst of one of the major events in modern Western history.

2

The Road to Power

It must have been difficult for those who had witnessed Henry's previous failures to mask their skepticism about his new career. Henry immediately set about to wipe that skepticism away, however. He was issued his license to practice law in Goochland County in 1760 and plunged headlong into his work. For the remainder of that year his account book shows that sixty clients were served in 197 cases. In all probability his caseload was even greater than the records indicate, as the first page of his fee book is missing. The next year his practice remained on about the same level. He took on some 185 cases, collecting £54.6.7 out of the more than £200 owed to him in fees. By 1763 his business had doubled, growing to the point where his caseload reached 374 and his accounts receivable rose to over £600. That year seems to have been a difficult one for his clients, however, as Henry managed to collect only about a third of that total.[1] Nevertheless, it amounted to a promising start for the young lawyer, particularly impressive when one considers his earlier efforts at farming and storekeeping.

Henry's success in his law practice is not altogether incomprehensible. First, there seems to be no question that he had finally found an occupation which he genuinely enjoyed. And although Jefferson had maintained that he was "totally unqualified for anything but mere jury causes" and never undertook to do any legal research himself, the record clearly shows that Henry was both well organized and hardworking.[2] As befitted a lawyer of his position, Henry proved eager to take on any case he could get. In addition to acting on behalf of clients in many of the ordinary civil suits that were so common among litigious Virginians, he appeared in damage suits, defended debtors, represented creditors, and drafted countless wills at fees ranging from roughly 7 to 15 shillings. He even represented his cousin John Winston in a slander suit against a man named Spender, where "said Spender did utter, publish, and declare aloud" that Winston was a hog stealer. Winston claimed that he had "Suffer'd much in quietude and undergone much contempt and Danger," and therefore asked for £500 in damages. Evidently Winston's good name was not quite that highly valued in the community. After four years of on and off litigation, Henry finally managed to win a £20 judgment for his client.[3]

Henry proved willing to travel great distances to attract clients. Although his base of operations remained a room in John Shelton's tavern in Hanover County, he traveled to neighboring Goochland County, to Louisa, Albemarle, and Chesterfield Counties, and even to Cumberland County—a full day's ride—to try many of his cases.

Hard work alone was not responsible for the expansion of Henry's practice. His increasing prosperity was also the result of the indirect and occasionally active intervention of prominent members of the Syme, Henry, and Shelton families. In addition to the case of his cousin John Winston (which may have been more of a burden than a blessing because of the time it consumed), Henry accepted cases from his father-in-law; his uncle William Winston; his brother-in-law William Shelton; Isaac Winston, another uncle; and Isaac Winston, Sr., his wife's grandfather.[4] These cases were not particularly important in themselves, but when these people in turn sent their clients and friends to Henry—people from prominent families such as the Dabneys and the Coles—the network of clients open to the young lawyer was significantly expanded.

This system of family influence, which pervaded all the social, political, and economic affairs of the Old Dominion, obviously worked against those who were not blessed with the social connections of a Patrick Henry or, more strikingly, of a Lee or a Randolph; but neither was that system a guarantee of success to those possessing important family connections. The social and economic structure of eighteenth-century Virginia, although hierarchical and oligarchic, was nevertheless generally efficient. Although membership in at least the lower orders of the provincial elite was usually a prerequisite for rapid social or economic advancement, membership in the elite was not in itself sufficient. There were countless Virginia aristocrats who were given the opportunity to improve their fortunes but who, because of either a lack of ability or a disinclination to work at it, did not. Patrick Henry, a member of the outer fringes of the Virginia aristocracy, a young man with neither the polish nor the extensive network of prominent friends and relatives that so many of his contemporaries in the Revolutionary movement in Virginia possessed, had finally found a profession in which he was capable of using his social status effectively.

The law profession would also serve as the vehicle through which Henry entered into the political life of eighteenth-century Virginia. In fact, it would propel him into a position of prominence at a very early stage in the conflict between Great Britain and America. Henry's role in the celebrated case of the "Parsons' Cause" would serve to establish his reputation as an exceedingly effective courtroom lawyer and as an early defender of colonial rights.

The Parsons' Cause was precipitated by the passage of the Two Penny Act by the Virginia General Assembly in 1758; the bill was designed as a temporary statute to be in effect for just one year and calculated to allow Virginia taxpayers to fulfill their obligations to support the Anglican clergy by paying each of their ministers their annual stipends of 16,000 pounds of tobacco in currency at the rate of twopence per pound of tobacco, rather than at the prevailing, inflated market price of roughly fourpence per pound. The members of the House of Burgesses, suffering from the effects of the drought which had been the cause of the inflation in tobacco prices and hard pressed by a heavy tax burden resulting from the costs of the French and Indian War, were of course eager to see such an act passed. Moreover, while relatively few of the burgesses intended to undermine either the authority of the established Anglican church or British imperial prerogative in America by passing the Two Penny Act, there are clear indications that the act was at least in part an expression of the gentry's widespread personal disdain for many of the members of the Anglican ministry in Virginia. Stemming both from a contempt for the pretensions of a class of clergymen whom the Virginia gentry believed to be their social inferiors and from a conviction that the financial demands of the clergymen were excessively avaricious in the first place, the Two Penny Act served the dual purpose of protecting the interests of all Virginia

taxpayers at a time of economic crisis and of striking at an unpopular minority within the population. Within Henry's home county of
Hanover there would be yet additional support for any act striking
at the Anglican clergy; a center of activity for New Side Presby-
terians beginning in the 1740s, Hanover was the home of many
citizens who—still a decided minority throughout the colony at
large—would welcome any measure resulting in the diminution of
Anglican authority in the Old Dominion.[5]

Francis Fauquier, the Royal Governor of Virginia, was anxious
to stay on good terms with the provincial leaders in the legislature
and allowed the act to take effect despite a provision in his instructions from the King explicitly ordering that any revenue measure
passed by the colonial legislature first be approved by the Privy
Council before going into operation. Fauquier's letter to the Board
of Trade defending his acquiescence is worth quoting at length, as it
embodies virtually all the reasons for the decline of royal authority
in America during the eighteenth century:

> As the Bill was a temporary Law to ease the people from a burthen
> which the Country thought too great for them to bear, for one year
> only, a Suspending Clause would have been to all Intents and pur-
> poses the same as rejecting it. A Bill of the same Nature in a like
> Time of Scarity of Tobacco had been passed without such a Clause,
> in the late Governor's Time and he incurred no Censure for having
> pass'd it. The Country were intent upon it, and both the Council
> and the House of Burgesses were almost unanimous in their press-
> ing it. And I conceived it would be a very wrong step for me to take
> who was an entire Stranger to the Distresses of the Country, to set
> my Face against the whole colony by refusing a Bill which I had a
> precedent for Passing. Whatever may be the Case now, I am per-
> suaded that if I had refused it, I must have despaired of ever gain-
> ing any Influence either in the Council or House of Burgesses.[6]

Fauquier was obviously genuine in his defense of the interests of
the provincial leaders who had passed the acts. As men of wealth,
prestige, and some cultural attainment, they were the people upon
whom Fauquier depended for social intercourse during his term of
office in Virginia. To act directly counter to the interests of that
class would virtually guarantee him a contentious and unpleasant
stay in Virginia; moreover, the resulting recriminations might very
well hinder his later career in the royal bureaucracy. As Fauquier,

and royal officials like him, developed close ties to the provincial elite, they tended to think not in terms of the royal officials in London but rather to adopt the perspective of the provincial leaders. From that perspective the operation of the suspending clause, which would have halted operation of the Two Penny Act until the Privy Council approved it, was tantamount to defeating the law, since that law was only an emergency measure intended to meet a temporary crisis caused by the dramatic rise in price and decline of supply of tobacco. Finally, as in most cases of leniency by royal governors, Fauquier could point to a precedent that would allow him to protect himself against the charge of laxness.

In most cases of this sort the Privy Council, once it had found time to review the act, would probably have let it stand. In this case, however, a militant Anglican clergyman, Reverend Mr. John Camm, a former professor of divinity at the College of William and Mary and rector of Yorkhampton Parish in York County, determined to fight for full payment, at the market rate of tobacco, of his clerical salary. Camm, who was upset with a number of aspects of the relationship between colonists and clergy in Virginia—the appointment of lay vestrymen, the increased secular control of the College of William and Mary, the decline in the influence of the Commissary, the Bishop of London's representative in Virginia—fought his battle on several fronts. In a convention of Anglican clergy of the colony, in petitions to the Privy Council, in newspaper articles and pamphlets, and finally, in a series of law suits, Camm and a faction of Anglican ministers lobbied vigorously to have the Two Penny Act declared null and void. Camm initially failed in his efforts, but undaunted, he sailed to England himself sometime in late 1758 or early 1759 to present the clergy's case before the Privy Council.

At this stage the dispute is best seen as a purely local one between colonial clergymen and colonial taxpayers, but other factors began to enter into the Privy Council's decision. In London Reverend Camm enlisted the support of the Archbishop of Canterbury, and, when he appeared before the Board of Trade sometime in early 1759, he was successful in persuading them to believe that the Two Penny Act was not merely a temporary response to a local problem but rather that it was only one more step in the systematic diminution of both royal prerogative and the authority of the Anglican church. At Camm's urging, the Bishop of London, Thomas Sherlock, wrote a letter to the Board of Trade, which was then forwarded to the Privy Council, claiming that the Virginians enacted the Two Penny Act out of a desire to weaken the power of both Crown and clergy in the colony.

The Bishop of London was wholly misinformed and, in fact, a careful student of colonial Virginia politics has concluded that the eighteenth-century House of Burgesses, instead of moving to weaken the Anglican church, had actually adopted legislation over the years designed to strength it. Once the Bishop had spoken on the subject, however, the Board of Trade felt obliged to give Camm's petition a more sympathetic hearing and accordingly, on July 4, 1759, it recommended to the King and Privy Council that the Two Penny Act of 1758, along with its predecessors of 1753 and 1755, be disallowed. On August 10 the King and Privy Council concurred, at that same time sternly rebuking Governor Fauquier for his laxity. Thus, the Virginia Anglican clergy had won a victory in its local contest with the provincial leaders and the Crown had reasserted a prerogative, often neglected in the past, regarding the limitations in the power of colonial assemblies.[7]

The victory came a bit late, however, as by August 1759 the Two Penny Act of 1758 had already served its purpose and had naturally expired after being in operation for its stipulated twelve months. Reverend Camm and the Anglican clergymen were not willing to settle for a moral victory alone and insisted on instituting another round of litigation in the courts. Camm, who filed the first suit, and four other clergymen who followed him hoped to prove that the Privy Council's disallowance of the act was effective retroactively to the date on which the act was first passed.

The case of Alexander White in King William County was the first to come to trial, in August 1762. The county court justices of King William, entirely unsympathetic toward the claims of the clergy, ruled that the Two Penny Act was valid until the date on which the Privy Council had officially disallowed it, thus rejecting the claim of the Reverend Mr. White. The next case, that filed by Thomas Warrington of Elizabeth City, had a similar outcome.[8]

The third case was instituted by Reverend Mr. James Maury of Louisa County against the lay vestry of the church of that county, which had, on March 24, 1761, explicitly rejected Maury's plea for "the overplus due him for his salary." Maury chose to have his suit against the Louisa vestry tried in neighboring Hanover County, where the political influence of the Louisa vestry was less in evidence, but in so doing he brought his case into a county where dissenting religious sects were particularly strong. Moreover, he brought his case into the sphere of influence of a young lawyer by the name of Patrick Henry.

Maury began proceedings on April 1, 1762, lodging his complaint against the collectors of taxes for Louisa County. His counsel, Peter Lyons, was an exceptionally capable lawyer who later became President of the Virginia General Court. John Lewis, a Hanover lawyer, was initially secured to prepare the defense. When the case was first heard in November 1763, the presiding judge, a devout Anglican and none other than Patrick's father Colonel John Henry, departed from the previous decisions and ruled that the Two Penny Act was null and void from its inception. Thus, the only discretion left for the jury was to determine the amount of salary due to Maury—that amount presumably representing the difference between the market price for the tobacco due him and the twopence per pound actually paid to him.

John Henry's ruling probably surprised some present, as the trend in previous cases had definitely been in favor of the Virginia taxpayers and against the clergy. On the other hand, the Henry family had always been closely allied with the Anglican church. John Henry was himself a vestryman of the Hanover Church and his brother, the Reverend Mr. Patrick Henry, who had immigrated to Virginia some five or six years after John Henry had made the move, was rector of St. Paul's Church in Hanover County. In fact, Reverend Mr. Henry had a similar suit pending against the citizens of Hanover. It is in this context that counsel for the defense turned over the case to young Patrick Henry. Although John Henry's earlier ruling seemed to have dashed all hopes of repudiating the claims of the clergy, it probably seemed wise to yield to someone who might have enough influence with the court to obtain a reversal of the previous ruling.[9]

It was against this backdrop that Patrick Henry, on December 1, 1763, entered public life. And what a world of interwoven and oft-conflicting interests he had entered. It was peculiarly typical of Virginia public life that Patrick would plead a case in a courtroom presided over by his father, while his uncle, a directly interested party, was ardently rooting for the other side.

According to Maury, who wrote a lengthy letter to John Camm describing the trial, the sheriff in charge of selecting the jury abandoned any attempt at impartiality. Even after one allows for Maury's pique, it is clear that there was considerable truth to his charge. After excusing two men from service whose involvement in the case was particularly apparent, the sheriff then proceeded to select the jurors from what Maury termed "the vulgar herd." Included in the jury were at least three members of dissenting sects—George Dabney, Roger Shackleford, and Samuel Morris—all of whom had a vested interest in undermining the power and authority of the Anglican establishment. Dabney was also a close friend and relative of Patrick Henry and was thus a particularly unsuitable selection from Maury's standpoint. There were a few jurors who possessed considerable wealth and social position—John Thornton and John Wingfield, for example—but most of the others, if not representative of the "vulgar herd," were at least of relatively low social and economic status. It is, however, difficult to see how social class per se would have affected the outcome, as a wealthy planter was every bit as likely as a lowly yeoman farmer to want to avoid paying the clergy more money. More important, it was dissenters like George Dabney, who happened to be a man of wealth and prestige in his county, who constituted the biggest obstacle to an impartial verdict.[10]

Patrick Henry, in answer to Maury's protests, "insisted they [the prospective jurors] were honest men, and, therefore, unexceptionable, [and] they were immediately called to the book and sworn." Following the swearing in of the jurors, Lyons called the two largest tobacco dealers in Hanover County to testify as to the price of tobacco in the county during 1759. They established that the market price at that time was roughly 50 shillings per 100 pounds of tobacco. The only evidence that Henry introduced was a receipt indicating that Maury had already been paid £144.[11] It would seem that with these two pieces of evidence before the jury—the one introduced by Lyons indicating that the 16,000 pounds of tobacco due Maury would have been worth some £400 at the market price and the other indicating that Maury had been paid only a fraction of that amount—it should not have taken much mental effort to calculate the exact amount in back salary due to the Anglican minister.

It was precisely at this stage, however, that Patrick made his oratorical debut. There are a number of reminiscences of that event, some occurring shortly after the fact and others written as much as forty years later. One of the most oft-quoted of these claims that those who heard the speech were

> taken captive; and so delighted with their captivity, that they followed implicitly, whithersoever he led them; that, at his bidding their tears flowed from pity, and their cheeks flushed with indignation; that when it was over, they felt as if they had just been awaked from some ecstatic dream, of which they were unable to recall or connect the particulars.[12]

As tempting as it may be to rely on colorful recollections such as this, it is perhaps safer to use James Maury's account, which was written immediately after the event. Although Maury was admittedly hostile to Henry and termed his address to the jury a "harangue," he nevertheless found it important enough to the eventual outcome of the case to devote most of his December 12 letter to John Camm to an analysis of it.

The main thrust of Henry's argument according to Maury was that the "act of 1758 had every characteristic of a good law; that it was a law of general utility, and could not, consistently with what he called the original compact between King and people, stipulating protection on the one hand and obedience on the other, be annulled." Henry then proceeded to infer that "a King, by disallowing Acts of this salutary nature, from being the father of his people, degenerates into a Tyrant, and forfeits all right to his subjects' obedience." Peter Lyons, on hearing these words, "called out aloud, and with an honest warmth . . . that the gentleman had spoken treason." Lyons's cry was echoed by others in the courtroom, but Henry was undaunted. He had in fact gone straight to the heart of the matter, invoking the compact theory of government and implying that the King's subjects were freed from obeying their sovereign when that sovereign did not fulfill his part of the compact. This was heady rhetoric, the sort of rhetoric that would not come into common use until the eve of independence. Nor did Henry confine his remarks to the King alone; referring to the Anglican clergy of

Virginia, he claimed that "they had most notoriously counteracted those great ends of their institution; that therefore, instead of useful members of the state, they ought to be considered as enemies of the community."[13]

Maury was amazed that such incautious statements should be tolerated by the court; yet Henry was allowed to proceed "in the same treasonable and licentious strain, without interruption from the Bench, nay, even without receiving the least exterior notice of disapprobation." Maury himself had no doubts about Henry's motives; he called him a "little petty-fogging attorney" and was convinced that his speech to the jury was self-consciously demagogic. He even claimed that Henry had confessed to him after the trial that "his sole view in engaging the cause, and in saying what he had, was to render himself popular." What Henry actually said to Maury is not known, but it is clear that, at least from the jury's standpoint, he had taken up a popular cause. After deliberating less than five minutes, the jury brought in a verdict ordering the tax collectors of Louisa County to pay James Maury a total of 1 penny in damages.[14]

The verdict amounted to a virtual repudiation of Colonel John Henry's earlier ruling. Peter Lyons was furious, arguing that the verdict was contrary to the evidence presented and irreconcilable with Judge Henry's ruling on the point of law. All of Lyons's pleas for a resubmission of evidence and a retrial were quickly rejected by the court, however, and Patrick Henry had won his first major case. He would receive a fee of 15 shillings for his efforts, and, in fact, would have to wait nearly five years before collecting that paltry sum, but he had gained more than a few shillings by his participation in the case.[15] He had taken the first step toward building a reputation as an orator and defender of colonial rights against the claims of the Crown and clergy of England, a reputation that would propel him into the spotlight in Williamsburg and beyond.

The furor over the Parsons' Cause did not die immediately after Maury's case was decided. Henry's uncle, the Reverend Patrick Henry, still had a suit pending against the tax collectors of Hanover County, and John Camm was continuing his suit in York County. Camm was also conducting a minor pamphlet war with Richard Bland and Landon Carter, two prominent members of the House of Burgesses and leading Anglicans themselves. After having his claims either rejected or evaded by every agency of government from the county court to the Privy Council, he would finally give up his quest for the vindication of the rights of the Virginia clergy. The Reverend Mr. Henry, his suit postponed until the outcome of Camm's was decided, would ultimately be disappointed as well.[16]

There has been a tendency among historians, their imagination captured by the drama of Henry's courtroom arguments denouncing King and clergy, to view the Parsons' Cause as the opening round of the struggle that would lead to the wholesale denial of royal authority in Virginia. It was certainly not isolated from the currents of thought that would ultimately lead Virginians to revolution, but it would be misleading to locate the event at the center of the early movement for independence. That aspect of the Parsons' Cause controversy which took place in the Hanover County courthouse was first and foremost a local event, with all the complexities, conflicting interests, and dimly perceived motives that so often characterize local, factional, political behavior. John Camm, in charging that Henry's "sole view . . . was to render himself popular," was no doubt somewhat uncharitable in his assessment of Henry's motives for accepting the case, but there is little question that Henry had made a decision calculated to enhance his career within his county. The personal hostility of the Anglican gentry toward the Anglican clergy and the more generalized hostility of the Hanover County dissenters toward the entire Anglican establishment made the case a desirable one for any lawyer with an eye toward political advancement. The motives for John Henry's reversal in the case are less clear, although one cannot discount the simple fact of his son's presence as counsel for the defense as a primary factor in his sudden change of heart. Moreover, as a politically sensitive member of the county court John Henry may have belatedly come to recognize the full strength of his constituents' opposition to the claims of the clergy and, ignoring the pressures exerted by his brother, the Reverend Mr. Patrick Henry, sided with the majority sentiment in his county.

In its larger content the Parsons' Cause was one of many disputes between royal and provincial authority occurring throughout the eighteenth century. As in virtually all those disputes, the colonists came out on top. Although the Privy Council had succeeded in officially disallowing the Two Penny Act, the colonial courts had

systematically refused to take the action that would have transformed the Privy Council's decision from a legalistic one to a meaningful defense of royal power in America. It was not that the citizens of Virginia were determined to undermine the influence of the
established church or the royal government (although there is some
evidence indicating that they were growing increasingly impatient
with a considerable number of the Anglican ministers in Virginia),
but, rather, that they quite naturally wished to avoid being taxed in
almost any circumstance. This consistent desire to avoid taxation,
of which the Parsons' Cause was only one example, did not signify
that the residents of the Old Dominion were ripe for revolution so
much as it indicated a constant readiness to reap the benefits of
colonial status while avoiding the burdens.

--- ★ ---

Henry's involvement in the Parsons' Cause would prove a distinct
advantage when he decided to step directly into the political arena
a few years later. In fact, his performance was probably one of the
factors causing the leaders of Hanover County to select him to fill
a vacant seat in the House of Burgesses in 1765, but the more
immediate effect of his involvement in the case would be to enhance
his law practice in his home region.

Henry's fee book illustrates the upward movement of his law
career. From 1764 to 1768, still relying on relatively small fees
accruing primarily from cases within the counties of Hanover,
Goochland, and Louisa, he collected fees in some 2,200 civil cases
totaling over £2,500. The criminal cases that he handled, which are
not recorded in the fee books, undoubtedly provided considerable
additional income, since much of Henry's reputation stemmed from
his courtroom successes in criminal cases.[17]

In 1769 Henry took another upward step by gaining admittance
to practice before the General Court, the supreme legal tribunal of
the colony. The court, composed of the Royal Governor and the
Governor's Council sitting as a body, was one of the many colonial
institutions where the functions of the executive, legislative, and
judicial branches were not kept separate. Since Virginia statute
made it illegal to practice before the General Court while at the
same time carrying on a local practice before the county courts,

Henry's decision to practice before the General Court temporarily ended his career as an aggressive county lawyer. It did not hurt his pocketbook, however. His caseload per year declined by about half after 1767, but his income improved dramatically. In 1769 his earnings amounted to £538, in 1770 £957, and in 1771, even though his caseload had declined from 554 in 1767 to only 102, his income rose to £1,300.[18]

The advantages of practicing before the General Court were not confined to high fees. That practice also gave Henry an opportunity to work with and against prestigious lawyer-politicians like Attorney General John Randolph, Robert Carter Nicholas, George Wythe, and Edmund Pendleton. Henry, in fact, impressed Robert Carter Nicholas enough with his legal skill that Nicholas turned over his practice to him in 1773, when he found that the duties of being treasurer for the colony were too burdensome to allow him to continue his legal practice. Before offering his practice to Henry, he first offered it to another and perhaps slightly more polished young lawyer, Thomas Jefferson.[19] Although Henry's thoughts on being second choice behind Jefferson in this instance are not recorded, it is not unlikely that he felt a twinge of jealousy, as the two men, even at this early stage in their careers, often found themselves in competition for popularity and favor in both their public and private lives. And it was particularly in the private affairs of the Virginia aristocracy—affairs such as the disposition of Robert Carter Nicholas's law practice—that the better-connected and better-educated Jefferson held an advantage.

Henry and Jefferson were generally able to cooperate with each other at this stage in their careers, however. A public statement, signed by Henry, Jefferson, and four other colleagues—Pendleton, John Randolph, James Mercer, and Gustavus Scott—gives some indication of Henry's own interests and connections during the pre-Revolutionary period. The six lawyers, all of whom practiced before the General Court, complained in the pages of the *Virginia Gazette* in May 1773 that "the fees allowed by law, if regularly paid, would barely compensate our incessant labors . . . , yet even these rewards, confessedly moderate, are witheld from us in a great proportion, by the unworthy part of our clients." The lawyers resolved not to accept any cases "but on payment of the whole fee" in advance. They closed by expressing the hope that "no person whatever may think of applying to us in any other way." The signers of the statement, most of them leaders in the fight against the "tyranny" of Great Britain, evidently were less willing to be flexible in donating their professional time to citizens who needed their services.[20]

Clearly Henry had not yet completely given himself over to the struggle against Great Britain if his mind was focused on such mundane matters as legal fees. Nor does it seem, despite his involvement in such highly publicized debtor-creditor cases as the Parsons' Cause, that Henry was recognized as a defender of the debtor classes. A substantial portion of his practice in Hanover County before 1769 was devoted to securing the collection of back debts for merchants. Between 1766 and 1770, Henry collected sixty-five fees from Hanover County merchant Alexander Donald and forty-four fees from Geddes Winston, another merchant and distant relative.

According to his account books, Henry's legal practice did begin to decline sometime around 1771, however. His fee book for 1772 records only forty-three cases, for 1773 merely seven, and for 1774 none.[21] This decline was perhaps due to his growing involvement with the political struggles with England, but it is also likely that it is exaggerated by the fee book. Henry's records were always somewhat haphazard, and it is possible that he simply allowed his recordkeeping to lapse during the hectic years preceding independence.

Whatever personal decisions Henry might have made regarding the time he was willing to devote to his practice during the years leading up to the break with England, it is clear that he had won a considerable reputation in his own right as a courtroom lawyer by 1776 and that it was this reputation, as much as the influence of his friends and family on his behalf, that was responsbile for the steady increase in his income. He was reckoned to be a particularly good criminal lawyer, a fact which probably stemmed from a combination of his own particular gifts and the deficiencies of the legal profession in Virginia at the time. One student of Henry's legal career has concluded that the Virginia county justices, themselves virtually ignorant of the intricacies of criminal law, were more likely to be swayed by the undeniable power of Henry's oratory and by his "natural reasoning" and frequently ruled in favor of Henry's clients in spite of the existence of legal precedents that should have dictated a contrary verdict.[22]

Nearly everyone who witnessed Henry in the courtroom was impressed by his forensic skills. St. George Tucker, a student at the College of William and Mary during the years that Henry practiced before the General Court and later to become one of the Old Dominion's ablest jurists himself, recalled that Henry's manner

> in debate . . . was so earnest and impressive . . . as to give to his countenance a severity sometimes bordering on the appearance of anger or contempt suppressed, while his language and gesture exhibited nothing but what was perfectly decorous. He was emphatic, without vehemence or declamation; animated, but never boisterous; nervous, without recourse to intemperate language; and clear, though not always methodical.[23]

Spencer Roane, reminiscing about Henry's style, commented: "He was perfect master of the passions of his auditory, whether in the tragic or the comic line. The tones of his voice, to say nothing of his matter and gesture, were insinuated into the feeling of his hearers, in a manner that baffled all descriptions."[24] Neither Tucker nor Roane dwelt on the state of Henry's legal knowledge in their commentaries on his courtroom manner. It was not that they judged Henry to be deficient in legal skills, but rather that Henry's courtroom presence and his oratorical abilities so overshadowed whatever technical, legal skills he may have possessed. Judge Peter Lyons, the counsel for James Maury during the Parsons' Cause case, later recalled: "I could write a letter or draw a declamation or plea at the bar with as much accuracy as I could in my office, under all circumstances, *except* when Patrick rose. . . I was obliged to lay down my pen and could not write another word until the speech was finished."[25]

Henry's increasing prominence in the public life of Virginia did not rest merely on his reputation as a lawyer. Like nearly all of Virginia's prominent citizens, he was by the time of the Revolution a "gentlemen freeholder" of substantial proportions. In 1765, at the age of twenty-nine, Henry received from his father a 1,700-acre tract of land called "Roundabout" in Louisa County in repayment for a loan that he had made to his father sometime previously.

Henry's house in Roundabout was hardly a rival to the great mansions of the Byrds, Carters, or Randolphs; rather, it was a simple story-and-a-half building with three rooms downstairs and one room above.[26]

But it was a beginning. Henry would live at Roundabout for just six years, but in that short space he would add appreciably to his holdings. John Henry had begun speculating in western lands almost immediately after his marriage to Sarah Winston, and his son Patrick would have the same impulse. In 1766, discovering that his father-in-law was on the verge of bankruptcy because of his overextension in mercantile and western land speculation, Patrick purchased from John Shelton 1,400 acres of land on the Moccasin Creek and 1,935 acres of land on the Holston River, both tracts located in the southwest corner of the colony. It is unlikely that Henry was too generous in his terms with his father-in-law. Shelton had a number of debts outstanding to Patrick at the time, and Henry was not one to forget a debt, even one owed by a close relative. In fact, Henry had noted in his account book that his father-in-law had promised to give him 400 acres of land and ten Negroes upon his marriage to Sarah, but that he had actually turned over only 300 acres and six Negroes. He calculated that "the deficiency will greatly over ballance any claim against me," and thus, with this display of familial affection, he started his career as a land speculator by canceling the debts owed him by John Shelton in return for the claims to the land on the Moccasin and Holston Rivers. It initially appeared that Henry had made a bad bargain, as he was able to locate only one of the tracts in a survey trip that he made to the site of the lands shortly after his purchase, and he soon discovered that nearly all the land had also been claimed by the Cherokee Indians. But this was a common annoyance for any land speculator; Henry held on to his claims, and after he and other speculators succeeded in getting the government to alter the treaty line which had initially given the Cherokees the right to the land, he ultimately acquired a clear title to nearly all the land he had purchased from Shelton.[27] It was in this manner that Henry, and scores of men like him, would enhance their fortunes; in the process, they would push the Indians of Virginia and the north and southwest off their lands and into virtual extinction.

In 1767, a year after he initiated the purchase of the Moccasin and Holston River lands, Henry purchased yet another mortgage from his father-in-law, this one to six tracts of land somewhere, vaguely noted in Henry's account book, "on the waters of the Mississippi." By 1769 Henry had become an important figure in the newly formed Ohio Company, which in that year petitioned the Crown to grant it 50,000 acres on the Ohio below the New River. The petition, which included the names of people like Thomas Jefferson, Patrick's brother William Henry, his brother-in-law William Christian, and Samuel Meredith, another brother-in-law, would be a long time in settlement, but it would ultimately prove to be one of the many speculations that would bring wealth to Patrick.[28]

Henry's acquisitive tastes were not confined solely to undeveloped western lands. In 1771 he purchased from John Payne, a Quaker and the father of Dolly Madison, a part of a tract called "Scotchtown" in Hanover County. That tract had originally belonged to Colonel John Chiswell, a planter-aristocrat who had in turn sold it to his son-in-law, John Robinson, the speaker of the House of Burgesses and treasurer of the colony. When Robinson died in 1766, the estate was divided and sold by his executors. John Payne had purchased the 960-acre section of the estate, upon which was built the principal dwelling. It was to this 960-acre tract, which included a mansion that was generally considered to be one of the finest in the Piedmont, that Patrick Henry moved his family in 1771.[29] There must have been some irony to the move, as Henry, by settling on Robinson's former estate, was moving to the residence of one of the richest and most politically powerful men in the colony, a man who had quickly become a political opponent during Robinson's last and Henry's very first term in the Assembly.

The £600 that he had paid for the plantation seemed a very small price to pay for such a prestigious tract. The main house contained sixteen rooms, four times as many as his previous residence. It was, in short, precisely the kind of dwelling that was the mark of the planter-aristocrats who so dominated the provincial elite in eighteenth-century Virginia. Henry, with each year, was asserting ever-larger claims to a place in the upper levels of that elite.

Henry's western land speculation continued after he moved into Scotchtown. In 1773 he purchased 5,000 acres in Botetourt County, the home of his sister Anne and his brother-in-law and frequent partner in speculation William Christian. And according to Thomas Perkins Abernathy, Henry, during the years immediately preceding the Revolution, did not allow the impending struggle with the mother country to divert his interests in western lands. In addition to his partnership with several prominent Virginians—including William Byrd III and William Fleming—to purchase acreage in Kentucky, Henry seems to have been involved in the largest speculative enterprise of the pre-Revolutionary years, the Vandalia Company. Not content to stop there, he became a part of the Transylvania Company in 1774, an enterprise which sought to obtain vast tracts of land in the Carolinas from the Cherokee Indians.[30]

As Henry's land interests grew, so too did his slaveholdings. These holdings offer the most convincing evidence that Henry was not merely a lawyer whose principal holdings consisted of vacant western lands; rather, it is clear that Henry was becoming a substantial planter in his own right.[31] Although he would occasionally issue laments regarding the injustices of the slave system and would bemoan the fate of the African, neither his frequent slave purchases nor any of the known facts about his treatment of slaves indicates that his concern about slavery was, even by eighteenth-century standards, more than perfunctory.

Patrick Henry's enhanced economic position was an important key to his rise in the social and political structure of pre-Revolutionary Virginia, but it was not the only ingredient. Equally important, Henry's own relatives, by hard work which enabled them to move up the economic ladder by themselves and by timely marriages among leading families of the Virginia aristocracy, began to improve their claims to distinctive social status. And Henry was then able to use the influence and prestige of those relatives for his own advancement up the social and political ladder. John Henry, by the time of his son's public debut in the Parsons' Cause case, had risen to be a justice of the Hanover County Court and, as we have seen, was actually the presiding justice when Patrick made his famous argument in that case. Moreover, members of Sarah Shelton's family, if anything more prestigious than the Henrys, were also represented among the justices of the county. Indeed, the Dabneys and the Winstons had dominated the legal and political affairs of their county for generations, and Henry, connected to that family not only by marriage but also by occupation, could hardly help but profit from their influence. In fact, George Dabney, a Dissenter and a close friend and relative, served on the jury in the Parsons' Cause case, a fact which hardly could have been comforting to those who supported the claims of the Anglican clergy.

Henry's economic fortunes would also be aided by the timely marriages of his sisters. Anne Henry married William Christian, who, in addition to his involvement with Henry in land speculation, was a member of the House of Burgesses and a prominent merchant. Christian's political influence in his home county of Augusta would prove extremely helpful to his brother-in-law, who would increasingly depend on the support of western counties like Augusta for his political power in the House of Burgesses. His sister Mary was wedded to another Augusta County oligarch whose family would also aid Henry in both his speculative dealings and his political career in the west. And yet another sister, Jane, would marry Colonel Samuel Meredith, a man who would prove to be one of Henry's closest friends and allies during the Revolution.[32]

Probably the most obvious sign of Henry's rise within the provincial elite was his growing political prominence. In colonial Virginia wealth and social prestige were nearly indispensable requirements for, although not a guarantee of, political success. Since the Virginia provincial aristocracy was relatively large—a fact which is best explained by both the high birthrate in the colony and by the abundance of land which allowed families like the Henrys to expand their holdings and buy their way into the aristocracy— wealth and social prestige did not automatically entitle a man to political power.

The first step on the road to political power was usually the county court, whose members were theoretically appointed by the Royal Governor but who in actuality were selected by the sitting members of the county court themselves and rubber-stamped by the Governor. These county court justices, although originally expected to serve only for five years, gradually extended their terms to life. The duties of the county court were in some ways of more immediate importance to Virginia residents than those of the colonial legislature or even of the Royal Governor. The court, often acting in a legislative and executive capacity as well as in its judicial role, gradually assumed responsibility for the collection of taxes, the maintenance and often the actual construction of public works, the licensing of all public utilities, and the supervision of charities. It was of course also the court of first instance for all civil and criminal suits.

If a son of the provincial elite had an inclination to try his hand at public service, the chances were reasonably good that he would be appointed to a position on the county court in order to test his interest in and aptitude for political life. County court service was, for most of Virginia's political leaders, an apprenticeship, a way of testing a man's merit to see whether he deserved to be sent to Williamsburg to serve in the House of Burgesses. Indeed, most of Virginia's Revolutionary heroes—Washington, Jefferson, James Monroe, George Mason—had all spent a portion of the early years of their public careers serving on the county court.[33]

Patrick Henry was one of the few prominent eighteenth-century Virginians to violate this tradition by leaping directly from private life to the House of Burgesses, bypassing service as a justice on the county court. When the 1765 session of the House of Burgesses convened—a momentous session indeed, as that session would mark the beginning of an opposition movement that would ultimately lead to independence—the duly elected delegate from Louisa County, William Johnson, resigned his post to accept the office of coroner. In a special election to fill that vacant seat, William Venable, an influential citizen of Louisa, put up Patrick Henry's name for the office, even though Henry lived in neighboring Hanover County and not in Louisa. This seemingly unusual procedure was in fact quite common in eighteenth-century Virginia, as Henry owned land in Louisa and it was a perfectly accepted practice among the ruling oligarchy for a freeholder to serve a county even when he did not live there. In any case, the residents of Louisa County, their numbers bolstered by forty-one residents of Hanover who also held freeholds in Louisa and who traveled to the Louisa County courthouse on that day, elected Henry to replace William Johnson in the House of Burgesses.[34]

Unfortunately there is little evidence to explain why Henry was elected to such an important office at this juncture, without first having served on the court. At least one of Henry's biographers has claimed that the citizens of Louisa were deliberately seeking a man who would lead the opposition to the Stamp Act in the House of Burgesses, but since news of the act had not even reached Virginia by the time of Henry's election, this explanation seems doubtful.[35] Rather, it is more likely that Henry's influence in the affairs of a more strictly local concern was steadily increasing in his region. Charles Campbell, in his history of Virginia, written in 1860 but compiled by a man whose family had intimate ties with all the leading personalities of the Revolutionary period, maintained that William Johnson and his brother Thomas, also a burgess from Louisa, were themselves supporters of Henry.[36] If this was the case, then it is not difficult to see how Henry won his seat, as Virginians, who were accustomed to paying deference to the members of the ruling provincial elite, were unlikely to vote against the wishes of their sitting and retiring representatives in the legislature unless there were compelling reasons for doing so. And of course, there was little reason for rejecting the advice of their representatives in this case, as Henry was no longer an obscure country lawyer. His participation in the Parsons' Cause case; his subsequent performance in the Dandridge-Littlepage contested election case, where he failed to uphold the election of his client Nathaniel Dandridge but impressed many of the members of the House of Burgesses nevertheless; and his steadily increasing caseload made him a genuinely important lawyer in his region. In addition to these professional achievements, he was the owner of a respectable plantation in Louisa and would soon be moving his family there.

Henry's political prominence would, in the course of the years 1765 to 1776, increase dramatically. The rise in power and stature would be not due so much to the size of his law practice or of his landholdings or to the subtle influence of family ties. It is clear that Henry's own considerable gifts—his talent for oratory and his incisive way of making legalistic, constitutional problems assume an immediacy to those around him—were principally responsible for his eventual accession to the highest levels of political life in the Old Dominion. But it is equally certain that Henry owed much of his initial start in political life to factors other than his still unproved oratorical and theatrical skills. For Patrick Henry, although he was to become a spokesman for American rights on an international level and for the rights of the western counties on the provincial scene, was still a member of a privileged class of western Virginia planters and lawyers and owed much of his early political success to his membership in that class.

CHAPTER

3

Challenge to Authority

When Henry walked into the House of Burgesses on May 20, 1765, to take his seat, he joined a group of men who were keenly aware of their own status and prerogatives. They had reached the pinnacle of their society in nearly every respect; there was a nearly direct correspondence between their extraordinary wealth, education, and family connections and their considerable political power.

The median landholding of the burgesses at that time was approximately 1,800 acres, the median slaveholding, forty slaves. Moreover, between five-sixths and seven-eighths of the burgesses had inherited property rather than purchased it themselves, a sure sign that family ties were an important ingredient in both economic and political power. The smaller group of men who assumed primary responsibility for the transaction of the daily business of the House —men like Speaker of the House and treasurer John Robinson, Edmund Pendleton, and Richard Bland—were even more strikingly wealthy and well connected. Jack P. Greene, in his study of the leadership of the Virginia House of Burgesses between 1720 and 1776, has discovered that of the 630 men serving in the House during those years, some 110 could be classed as distinctly more powerful than their fellow members by dint of their service on and chairmanship of important committees in the House. Greene has found that nearly three-fourths of these exceptionally powerful men possessed landholdings in excess of 10,000 acres, a sizable holding even for agrarian Virginia. And of course, the holdings of some were even larger; John Robinson, for example, owned more than 40,000 acres and 300 slaves.[1]

Half of the leaders of the House of Burgesses during those years were related either by birth or marriage to the handful of truly prestigious families in Virginia. The Randolphs, Carters, Beverlys, and Lees provided eleven, nine, eight, and six leaders respectively. Equally striking was the high educational level achieved by the leaders in the Assembly. In a society where public education at even the lowest levels was lacking, nearly half of the leaders had attained a college or university education, with about forty attending the College of William and Mary and most of the others obtaining their schooling in England. This, of course, was one obvious way in which the ill-educated Henry would differ from most of his new colleagues.

The vast majority of the leaders of the House of Burgesses had served a political apprenticeship in their respective counties; over four-fifths of them had served as justices of the peace before entering the legislature.[2] In this instance too Henry would deviate from the traditional road to power in his colony.

This group of generally wealthy and well-born men constituted a remarkably stable and homogeneous leadership for the House from the beginning of the eighteenth century up until at least the time that Henry entered the chamber. Of similar wealth, family background, and educational and social attainment, they ruled the internal affairs of the colony with little evidence of serious opposition from either their colleagues in the House or from their constituents at home. Though there was often disagreement among them over single issues, there did not exist any permanent divisions within their ranks.

Patrick Henry's earliest biographer, William Wirt, was merely the first of many historians to look for bitter divisions in the House of Burgesses between "aristocrats" and "democrats" in order to depict Patrick as the leader of an insurgent faction fighting the wealthy and entrenched aristocrats; but St. George Tucker, who was a frequent observer of the proceedings of the House about the time Henry made his debut, assured Wirt that the differences among the burgesses were "only such as different men, coming from different parts of our extensive Country, might be well expected to entertain." There did not exist, Tucker affirmed, anything like organized or cohesive parties. And modern scholars, utilizing quantitative techniques in analyzing voting behavior in the House of Burgesses, have confirmed Tucker's observation. This is an extraordinarily important fact to remember, for it contradicts the contention of nearly all of Henry's biographers, who have tried to place their subject at the head of a "liberal," "democratic" insurgency group representing the "humble yeomanry" of the frontier.[3] In some respects Henry's rise to power in the House would mark a gradual shift in the gentlemanly way in which business was conducted and would signify the beginning of discernible factionalism in the affairs of the House, but the divisions among the burgesses, as we will see in later chapters, were never between permanently defined groups of "liberals" and "conservatives," nor was Henry always identified with the forces for "democracy" or with the "humble yeomanry."

On May 29, 1765, nine days after he entered the Chamber and on the day of his twenty-ninth birthday, Henry introduced a series of resolutions into the House of Burgesses protesting the recent enactment by Parliament of a stamp duty to be levied on the American colonies. It would be, in Henry's own judgment, one of the most important actions of his life. Although notoriously careless about preserving those personal papers relating either to his public or private life, Henry carefully left a copy of his Stamp Act Resolves and a brief account of the circumstances surrounding them with his last will and testament. By Henry's own account:

> I had been for the first time elected a Burgess a few days before, was young, inexperienced, unacquainted with the forms of the House and the members that composed it. Finding the men of weight averse to opposition, and the commencement of the tax at hand, and that no person was likely to step forth, I determined to venture, and alone, unadvised, and unassisted, on a blank leaf of an old law book, wrote the [Stamp Act Resolves].[4]

There is some uncertainty as to precisely how many resolutions he introduced. Henry's own copy of the resolutions lists five; the Journal of the House of Burgesses lists four. They read:

> Resolved, That the first Adventurers and Settlers of this his Majesties Colony and Dominion brought with them and transmitted to their posterity and all other his Majesties Subjects since inhabiting in this his Majesties said Colony all the Privileges, Franchises, & Immunities that have at any Time been held, enjoyed, & possessed by the people of Great Britain.

Resolved, That by two royal Charters granted by King James the first the Colonists aforesaid are declared intituled to all the Privileges, Liberties & Immunities of Denizens and natural born Subjects to all Intents and Purposes as if they had been abiding and born within the Realm of England.

Resolved, That the Taxation of the People by themselves or by Persons Chosen by themselves to represent them who can only know what Taxes the People are able to bear and the easiest Mode of raising them and are equally affected by such Taxes themselves is the distinguishing Characteristic of British Freedom and without which the ancient Constitution cannot subsist.

Resolved, That his Majesties liege People of this most ancient Colony have uninterruptedly enjoyed the Right of being thus governed by their own assembly in the article of their Taxes and internal Police, and that the same hath never been forfeited or any other way given up but hath been constantly recognized by the Kings & people of Great Britain.[5]

The resolutions are in themselves a significant though not particularly radical assertion of colonial rights. The first two resolutions essentially reaffirmed the long-standing assumption that the citizens of Virginia were entitled to the same rights and privileges as residents of England, and the third and fourth asserted the principle of "no taxation without representation," a principle which had been laid down by the House of Burgesses the previous year in its discussion of the attempt by England to levy a tax on molasses imported into the colonies. In fact, the wording of all of the first four resolutions was similar to that of the resolutions passed by the House the previous spring.[6]

But Henry also presented a fifth resolution, one possessing more fire than the previous four. It read:

Resolved, therefore, that the General Assembly of this Colony have the *only* and *sole exclusive* Right and Power to lay Taxes & Impositions upon the Inhabitants of this Colony and that every Attempt to vest such power in any Person or Persons, whatsoever other than the General Assembly Aforesaid has a manifest Tendency to destroy *British* as well as *American* freedom.

Here was more than an abstract assertion of colonial rights; it was nothing less than an explicit denial of English authority to tax the colonies and an implicit but nevertheless vigorous denunciation of the Stamp Act.[7] According to Henry's own recollections, "upon offering them [the resolutions] to the House violent debates ensued. Many threats were uttered, and much abuse cast on me by the party for submission." Henry was not prepared for submission, and in his speech before the House defending the resolutions he supposedly exclaimed, according to popular legend, "Tarquin and Caesar had each his Brutus, Charles the First his Cromwell, and George the Third. . . ." This phrase was reportedly interrupted by the cry of "Treason! Treason!" from the Speaker of the House, John Robinson, a charge that was echoed by a substantial number of the burgesses. According to Paul Carrington, a member of the House that year who had not, however, taken his seat by the time of the speech, Henry stared the speaker of the House in the eye and finished his sentence with: ". . . may profit by their example! If this be treason, make the most of it!"[8]

Carrington described the event, an occasion which he had not even witnessed, in 1815, long after Henry's reputation as a dramatic orator had been established. Although there are a few other accounts that lend some credence to Carrington's recollections, they too were gathered long after the fact. Thomas Jefferson, for example, who was standing in the hallway of the House of Burgesses at the time Henry gave the speech, wrote William Wirt some forty years later: "I well remember the cry of treason, the pause of Mr. Henry at the name of George III, and the presence of mind with which he closed the sentence and baffled the charge vociferated."[9] There was, however, only one person who actually heard the speech and then immediately wrote down his impressions of it. In the diary of an unknown French traveler, who had stood with Jefferson in the hallways of the House of Burgesses and listened to Henry's performances on May 30 and May 31, is a full account of the speech:

> Shortly after I came in one of the members stood up and said he had read that in former times tarquin and Jules had their Brutus, Charles had his Cromwell, and he did not doubt but some good american would stand up, in favour of his Country, but (says he) in a more moderate manner and was going to continue, when the speaker of the House rose and Said, he, the last that had stood up had spoken traison, and was sorey to see that not one of the mem-

bers of the house was loyal Enough to stop him, before he had gone so far. Upon which the same member stood up again (his name is henery) and said that if he had afronted the speaker or the house he was ready to ask pardon, and he would shew his loyalty to his majesty King G. the third at the Expence of the last Drop of his blood, but what he had said must be atributed to the Interest of his Countrys Dying liberty which he had at heart and the heart of passion might have lead him to have said something more than he intended, but, again, if he had said anything wrong, he beged the speaker and the houses pardon.[10]

The account, from someone who presumably had no special interests to serve, corresponds with nearly everyone's description of the first part of the speech, but his testimony respecting the remainder of Henry's oration does much to call into question the commonly accepted version of Henry's defiant answer to the charges of treason. Although this account may not be as satisfying to our desire for drama as Carrington's, it seems wise to give it more weight, as it is the only one not clouded by the passage of time or the construction of myth.

It seems pointless to quibble over just one sentence in Henry's oration on that day, for even the French traveler was impressed by the force and vigor of Henry's words. As late as January 6, traveling through Newcastle, Virginia, the Frenchman again felt compelled to mention the speech, reporting that there was "a great deal said about the Noble Patriot Mr. henery, who lives in this county, the whole inhabitants say publicly that if the least Injury was offered to him they'd stand by him to the last Drop of their blood."[11] Henry's fame had indeed spread quickly, and his words before the House of Burgesses, whatever their exact phraseology, had done much to awaken the people's interest in the constitutional controversy with England.

The House, on May 30, voted on Henry's resolutions. Only 39 of the 116 members of the House were present, and many of those who were missing were precisely those most likely to have opposed Henry's resolves. When the vote was taken, the first four resolves were passed by small but respectable majorities. The fifth one caused the most controversy; it was narrowly passed, causing Peyton Randolph, an opponent of the resolutions, to exclaim after the vote, "By God, I would have given 500 guineas for a single vote."[12]

One more negative vote would have caused a tie, which would have allowed Speaker of the House John Robinson to cast the deciding vote against the resolution.

The bitter opposition to Henry's resolutions is only partially explicable. It seems clear that the more cautious members of the House were genuinely shocked by the strident tone of the fifth resolution and sincerely opposed it, but their opposition to the first four resolutions, which were similar in tone to some passed by the House the previous year protesting the Sugar Act, is less understandable. Edmund S. and Helen M. Morgan, two careful scholars who have investigated the details of the Stamp Act crisis, have concluded that the objections to the resolutions were perhaps not substantive ones but rather stemmed from the hostility of the established members of the House toward an upstart like Henry, who they believed was deviating from the standards of decorum for newly elected members of the House.[13]

On May 31, the day after the vote on the Stamp Act Resolves, Peter Randolph, a member of the Governor's Council and a cousin of Peyton Randolph, was busily searching for precedents that would allow him to initiate proceedings to reverse the action of the previous day. Although the Journal for May 31 makes no mention of any debate or action on the Stamp Act, testimony from a number of other sources indicates that a faction of "cautious patriots" in the House of Burgesses succeeded in pushing through a motion to expunge Henry's fifth resolution.[14] They had won only a partial victory, however, as the newspapers in most of the American colonies, apparently unaware that the Virginia House had reversed itself, continued to report that all five resolutions had been passed.

Some newspapers actually printed six, and a few even seven, resolutions. The sixth explicitly stated that Virginians were "not bound to yield obedience to any Law or Ordinance whatsoever, designed to impose any Taxation upon them, other than the Laws or Ordinances of the General Assembly . . ." and a seventh ordered that anyone who upheld Parliament's claim to tax the colony would be "Deemed AN ENEMY TO THIS HIS MAJESTY'S COLONY." Both of these, of course, went far beyond even the fifth resolution, as they called not only for a redress of grievances but also outright resistance.[15]

These additional resolves were likely drafted by John Fleming of Cumberland County and George Johnston of Fairfax, the only two men to whom Henry had shown his original five resolutions. The two resolutions were evidently kept aside, to be put before the House if the climate of opinion seemed favorable. The climate, judging from the closeness of the vote on the first five, was decidedly not favorable to them and there is some doubt as to whether they were ever offered or not. Governor Fauquier, writing to the Board of Trade on June 5, reported that Henry and his supporters had two more resolutions "in their pocket, but finding the difficulty they had in carrying the 5th . . . and knowing them to be more virulent and inflammatory; they did not produce them."[16] Apparently some members of the House did at least know of their content, as the French traveler who has furnished us with our only eyewitness account of the proceedings reported that "one of the resolves . . . was that any person that would offer to sustain the parlement of Eng'd had a right to impose or lay any tax . . . should be looked upon as a traitor, and Deemed an Enemy to his Country."[17] Again, what was important was not the precise sequence of events in the House but that the sixth and seventh resolutions did find their way into the public prints. The Newport, Rhode Island, *Mercury* printed the sixth and seventh resolutions, for some reason omitting the third, and the *Maryland Gazette* printed all seven.[18] And of course, most people who read them, learning also of Henry's daring speeches supporting them, would assume that all of the resolutions were his handiwork.

The Stamp Act Resolves, in nearly all their different forms, would mark a major departure in Anglo-American relations. Nearly every colony in America would use them as the basis for similar resolutions of their own. Rhode Island even went so far as to endorse the sixth resolution advocating resistance to the tax, and even those colonies that had not gone so far as Rhode Island went on record, with the example of Virginia before them, opposing parliamentary taxation without the colonies' consent.

In October 1765 a Congress of eight American colonies would convene to protest the Stamp Act with a united voice. The first truly successful intercolonial gathering, it would further sharpen America's constitutional position with respect to the limits of parliamentary authority. Virginia, along with Maryland, North Carolina, and Georgia, would be prevented from sending delegates to the

Congress because of her Governor's refusal to convene the House of Burgesses in order to allow it to elect delegates. In fact, the Royal Governor of Virginia had dissolved the Assembly on May 31 as a way of signaling his disapproval of its actions.[19] It was of course entirely within his prerogative to do this, but it was something that was resorted to only rarely, as royal governors and provincial leaders had usually managed to sustain generally amicable relations in the past. But new issues and new personalities were complicating the traditional order of political life in Virginia, and it would be difficult for the leaders of the Assembly to remain on good terms with royal officials if they hoped to stay in step with an increasingly popular figure like Henry.

Henry, for his part, had "gone quietly into the upper parts of the country," back to Hanover County. He had gone there, according to William Robinson, Commissary for Virginia and a man who thoroughly disapproved of what had passed, "to recommend himself to his constituents by spreading treason, and enforcing firm resolutions against the authority of the British Parliament."[20] But he would return to the House of Burgesses the next year and every year after that for the next decade to continue to speak his mind.

★

Henry's conduct in the years following the Stamp Act crisis, though it would ultimately cause him to become the rallying point for those anxious to see America place herself in bold opposition to England, was not always consistent. The thought and actions of some Virginians from 1765 to 1776 would fall nicely in line with the constitutional orthodoxy that had been laid down during the Stamp Act crisis, but not so with Henry. Sporadic in his attendance to the business of the House of Burgesses, erratic in the quality of his performance in that body, he nevertheless continued to gain influence until, by 1776, he was recognized as the principal spokesman for the Revolution in the Old Dominion, a man who by his prescience would cause men initially antagonistic to him ultimately to join ranks with him.

Although Henry made his debut in the House of Burgesses as a bold defender of the constitutional rights of Virginians, he nevertheless did not possess at any time during that struggle a clear or consistent view of the proper division of authority between Crown and colony or between government officials and their constituents. The only constant theme in his attack on royal authority was his defense of purely local, particularistic interests. This attachment to localism was not accompanied by a consciously articulated doctrine pitting "centralized power" against virtuous, local units of government. The local interests that Henry sought to protect were not abstract constitutionalisms but rather concrete interests, to be protected in specific instances and by whatever devices necessary. We find, therefore, Henry denouncing the notion of centralized power in some circumstances but embracing it in those cases where he saw in that power a way to protect the interests of his own region. We also find, on some occasions, Henry rising to genuine ferocity in his attacks on royal government and, on others—when the provocation is equally great but when other, private matters intervene—that he is notable by his absence from the public stage.

In spite of these vacillations Henry was the rallying point for those who were to lead Virginia into the Revolution. That he played such a central role is explained by two facts. First, and least startling, he was, as many discovered during his defense of the Stamp Act Resolves, an orator of unbelievable skill. It is this quality that is most difficult to convey on the printed page. His speeches, or rather, the purported texts of those speeches, are impressive enough on paper, but judging from the testimony of virtually all of Henry's contemporaries, friend and foe, the drama and impact of his oratory must have been far greater than the twentieth-century reader can ever comprehend. This fact, which has been emphasized by everyone from the authors of grade-school readers to Henry's most recent biographer, is the starting point for understanding Henry's role in the Revolution. It is difficult to quantify and analyze its import, but there is ample evidence attesting to his ability to rally people to his cause by the force and effect of his words.

There was a second factor, however, that lent some substance to his oratory. Those people who were most captivated by his speeches tended to be those whose own circumstances were most similar to Henry's. Residents of the Piedmont or transmontane West, wealthy, but still not recognized as the equals of the Randolphs or the Pendletons, sharing Henry's particularistic view of the interests of their constituents, these Virginians were much more likely to identify with a rising planter-aristocrat like Henry than they were with the leaders of the Tidewater elite.

——————— ★ ———————

Virginians, like the residents of every colony in America except Georgia, which had cooperated with the distributing of the stamps, put up a nearly united front in refusing to allow the Stamp Act to be implemented. Although the usually friendly Governor Fauquier had refused to call the House of Burgesses into session for fear that it would be used as a base for further opposition, the county courts took up the slack, with many of the local justices refusing to call the courts into session so long as the Stamp Act was in force. And the citizens of Virginia made it plainly apparent to the newly appointed stamp distributor, Colonel Hugh Mercer, that he would have a most unpleasant life in Virginia should he try to carry out his duties. Mercer had been in England when the act was passed and was out of touch with the temper of Virginians on the subject; on his return to Virginia to take up his duties, he was greeted by an angry mob of people who threatened to seize him unless he resigned his commission as stamp distributor. The "mob," in Governor Fauquier's words, "was chiefly if not altogether Composed of Gentlemen of Property in the Colony—some of them at the Head of their respective Counties, and the Merchants of the Country. . . ." Mercer would have probably been disconcerted by the threat of violence from any mob, but when that mob was principally composed of his own peers in Virginia society, the wisdom of a speedy resignation as stamp distributor became immediately clear to him.[21]

After the repeal of the Stamp Act in March 1766—which was brought about by a combination of the colonial agitation against the act, pressure from British merchants in London, and a change in the political winds in Parliament which caused George Grenville to be replaced by the more conciliatory Marquis of Rockingham—Virginians were quite well prepared to drop their strident rhetoric of the previous months.[22] Neither Patrick Henry of Virginia nor Sam Adams of Massachusetts made any public utterances denouncing the rider to the repeal of the Stamp Act, the Declaratory Act, which asserted Parliament's right to legislate for the

American colonies in "all cases whatsoever." Since most members of Parliament had always insisted that there was no legal distinction between *taxation* and *legislation*, the Declaratory Act represented, from the point of view of Parliament, an important statement of constitutional principle. But Americans, happy to have won the immediate battle over the Stamp Act, allowed the abstract danger presented by the Declaratory Act to pass without substantive opposition in either the colonial legislatures or in town and county meetings.

This attitude of temporary acquiescence, which typified the response of nearly all Americans, was particularly in keeping with Henry's bent of mind. With the notable exception of his opposition to the United States Constitution, Henry never showed any inclination to act until the dangers involved in a measure were manifest in concrete form.

When the Virginia House of Burgesses met on November 6, 1766, after sitting idle for a year and five months because of Governor Fauquier's unwillingness to convene it, Henry was once again a representative from Louisa. It was clear that in the year and five months that had elapsed since the last meeting the Assembly had adopted a more conciliatory attitude toward royal authority. Whereas in May 1765 the Assembly had denounced Parliament, it now passed a bill to erect a statute to the King to commemorate his role in bringing about the repeal of the Stamp Act.[23]

English politicians in Parliament, however, were at that same time contriving to diminish this renewed spirit of goodwill. One of these, Charles Townshend, the new Chancellor of the Exchequer in England, was described by Horace Walpole as having "almost every great talent . . . if he had had but common trust, common sincerity, common honesty, common modesty, common steadiness, common courage, and common sense." When Townshend persuaded Parliament that he could make America submit to a program of taxation where others before him had failed, the debate over England's right to tax the colonies was revived. In a speech before Parliament, Townshend advocated taxing America on a wide variety of commodities and, in fact, maintained that Parliament had the right to levy internal taxes such as the stamp duty as well as external taxes on colonial trade. After stating this position Townshend looked up to that part of the gallery in Parliament where the various colonial agents usually sat and asserted: "I speak this aloud, that all you who are in the galleries may hear me; and after this I do not expect to have my statue erected in America." The rhetorical flourish was an effective one and the members of Parliament, with a lingering resentment over the violence in America over the Stamp Act, passed, in May 1767, a series of duties on wine, fruits, glass, paper, lead, and tea entering America, together with an act further tightening the enforcement of the customs laws.[24]

If the American colonies had been fully prepared to back up their earlier stand against all forms of parliamentary taxation, internal or external, the Townshend Acts would have met the same hostile reception that the Stamp Act faced two years earlier. And in some areas of the country the reception was similar. Massachusetts, for example, once again took the lead by drafting a strongly worded remonstrance to Parliament, at the same time sending a circular letter to her sister colonies asking for a boycott of British goods until the acts were repealed. New York and Pennsylvania, on the other hand, were unwilling to risk the commercial prosperity they were enjoying for the constitutional principles they had so recently formulated and hesitated about adopting the Massachusetts proposals. The Virginia House of Burgesses did not meet until March 1768, nearly a year after the passage of the Townshend Acts, and its proceedings were delayed still another month by the death of Governor Fauquier, a man genuinely admired by the provincial leaders. Finally the House, on April 2 and 4, heard petitions from the citizens of Chesterfield, Henrico, Dinwiddie, Amelia, Westmoreland, and Prince William Counties denouncing the Townshend duties. On April 14 the House agreed to send a remonstrance to both the King and Parliament. The communications, which were typical of those drafted by colonial legislatures at this early stage of the controversy, expressed the Virginians' devotion to the principles of the English Constitution, reiterated their affection for the King, and firmly stated their commitment to the principle of "no taxation without representation." Both the address to the King and to the House of Commons, along with another to the House of Lords, were passed unanimously, and on April 15, the House, again with no dissent, agreed to send a message of support to the Massachusetts legislature, applauding their

"Attention to American liberty" and pledging their help in securing repeal of the Townshend duties.[25] The burgesses did not, however, indicate that they would support Sam Adams's suggested boycott.

One would perhaps expect that Henry, having distinguished
himself during the debate on the Stamp Act, would have played
an important role in the Assembly's response to the Townshend
Acts. In fact, he was not even present during the March and April
session. Although reelected to represent Louisa County during that
session, he was sufficiently engrossed in his own personal business
not even to put in an appearance in Williamsburg. Henry was not
alone in his apathy; over half of the elected burgesses did not
attend the session. Most of them were probably inconvenienced
by the repeated postponements caused by the death of the Governor and had made other plans by the time the Assembly actually
met.[26] In Henry's case this likely meant that he was surveying the
western lands that he had recently purchased from his father-in-
law. And as we shall see in later chapters, Henry's acquisitive urge
for amassing ever larger landholdings would command at least
equal priority with his commitment to public service for the
remainder of his life. This continued pursuit of private wealth was
thoroughly in keeping with the ethos of the squirearchy of which
Henry was so rapidly becoming a prominent member. The building
up of an estate was important on at least two counts: an estate was
a visible symbol of the common interests of the Virginia provincial
ruling class as well as a necessary patrimony for one's descendants.

A spirit of relative calm prevailed in Virginia for at least a year
after the Virginia legislature took its mild stand on the Townshend Acts. In November 1768, Norborne Berkeley, the Baron of
Botetourt, arrived in Virginia to fill the vacant post of Royal Governor. He seemed determined to avoid conflict with the provincial
leaders, but by May 1769, due mainly to events out of his own
control, he too was placed in a position of direct opposition to the
burgesses. Responding to the British Ministry's order that the
colonial legislatures disregard the Massachusetts Circular Letter
or else face dissolution, John Blair, on May 16, reported a series
of four resolutions, the first reiterating the right of no taxation
without representation, the second upholding the right of the Massachusetts Assembly to issue its circular letter, the third criticizing

a recent British act aimed at extending liability under treason laws to the American colonies, and the fourth requesting that a new remonstrance to the King be drafted. Those resolutions were passed unanimously and subsequently printed in the *Virginia Gazette.* On May 17 the address, which asked the King to intervene and end Parliament's abuse of power, was passed unanimously. On that same day, however, the Governor, who had by then read the resolves of the previous day, sent a message to the Assembly stating simply: "I have heard of your Resolves, and augur ill of their Effect. You have made it my duty to dissolve you; and you are dissolved accordingly."[27]

The burgesses, possibly by prearrangement, immediately walked down Duke of Gloucester Street and held a rump meeting at the Raleigh Tavern. At that meeting they adopted a nonimportation agreement extending to all British goods. Thus the "radicals" of Massachusetts, who had been unable to arouse meaningful opposition in the months immediately following the passage of the Townshend Acts, were able, two years after the passage of the acts and with the help of the overreaction of the British, finally to enlist the aid of other colonies like Virginia.[28]

There were few outward signs of division among the Virginia provincial leaders over these measures. The older, established leaders in the House of Burgesses such as Peyton Randolph, Carter Braxton, and Edmund Pendleton were in favor of both the remonstrance to the King and nonimportation; the younger and supposedly more radical burgesses—people like Henry and the first-term burgess from Albemarle County, Thomas Jefferson—were content to limit their protests to those measures as well. Henry seems to have played no special role in the matter. He was simply one of the eighty-nine burgesses who agreed that a boycott of British goods was the next logical step necessary to convince England that the American colonies were willing to make sacrifices in order to uphold their right to be taxed only with their consent. He, like most other burgesses, was prepared to defend the constitutional rights of the American colonies against British encroachments now that those encroachments affected not only the citizens of Boston but his own political prerogatives as well.

In Virginia the boycott had the effect of greatly weakening the resolve of royal officials. In November 1769 Lord Botetourt called the burgesses back into session and assured them that most of the Townshend duties would be repealed. The response of the burgesses to this news is indicative of the up-and-down relationship between Governor and Assembly. In spite of the fact that Botetourt had made it clear that the Crown would continue to levy taxes on at least a few items, the burgesses, pleased with the prospect of a lighter burden of taxes, passed a friendly address to the Governor, concurring in his call for a resumption of amicable relations between Crown and colony. Thus Virginians, with Henry voting with the majority, had decided to drop temporarily their protests against parliamentary taxation so long as the costs of acquiescence were smaller than those of continued resistance.[29]

In April 1770, when Lord North, the new head of the British Ministry, fulfilled Botetourt's promise to the Virginians by persuading Parliament to repeal all the Townshend duties except that on tea, the Virginians continued to moderate their position. Although the Assembly did take steps to enforce the existing nonimportation agreements when it convened in late May, the agreements became increasingly ineffective throughout the year. Moreover, the burgesses remained silent on the subject of the Boston Massacre, the news of which had undoubtedly reached them by the time they convened. There is little indication that Henry was unhappy with what was occurring; rather, in the face of another calm in Anglo-American relations, he seems once again to have devoted most of his attention to his private affairs.[30]

Although the popular Botetourt died in October 1770 and was replaced by John Murray, Earl of Dunmore—a man who would eventually earn the enmity of nearly every white Virginian—relations between royal and provincial leaders remained cordial, with the Virginians continuing to submit to the duty on tea in theory while drinking smuggled tea from Holland. The next two assembly sessions—a short and ill-attended one in July 1771 and a long and productive one in the winter and spring of 1772—produced no serious attempt to define further the limits of English authority in America. The burgesses, occupied with such pressing local concerns as the provision of aid to those people whose fortunes had been threatened by heavy flooding of most of the principal Virginia rivers in 1771, simply did not seem to have time to worry about the future of Anglo-American relations. During most of that time

Patrick Henry did not even find the time to attend the Assembly. He seems to have attended the July 1771 session only briefly and left for home on March 23, 1772, a full three weeks before the 1772 session came to a close.[31]

When the burgesses met again in March 1773, there had still been no major altercation between Great Britain and America since the repeal of the nonimportation agreements in 1770. Yet the political climate was subtly becoming more tense. The new Royal Governor and the Assembly, although they had not confronted each other directly on issues affecting broad questions of British colonial policy, had nevertheless developed a mutual antipathy for each other stemming from a series of minor local disagreements. Moreover, relations between England and several other American colonies were once again severely strained, a fact which would ultimately have its effect in Virginia. The burning of the customs ship *Gaspee* by colonists in Rhode Island and the subsequent royal investigation of the incident, the continuing hostility between Royal Governor and Assembly in Massachusetts, and the increasing determination of all royal officials to use their prerogatives more forcefully in order to thwart the expansion of the power of the colonial assemblies—these all undoubtedly had an effect on the proceedings of the Virginia General Assembly when it convened in the spring of 1773. And Henry would be among those who roused themselves from their lethargy.

Following the lead of Sam Adams and the Massachusetts legislature, Dabney Carr, a young but influential burgess, introduced into the House in March 1773 a resolution calling for the establishment of a Committee of Correspondence "whose business it shall be to obtain the most early and authentic intelligence of all such acts and resolutions of the British Parliament . . . as may relate to or affect the British colonies in America." The committee that was appointed was nearly evenly divided between conciliatory and deliberate men like Peyton Randolph, Edmund Pendleton, and Archibald Carey and younger, somewhat more impatient men like Henry, Jefferson, and Carr.[32] Judging from the testimony of Jefferson, a small clique of men including himself, Henry, Carr, Richard Henry Lee, and Francis Lee was largely responsible for the move to establish the Committee of Correspondence. Some time previous to March, those men, "not thinking our old and leading members up to the point of forwardness and zeal which the times required," met in a private room of the Raleigh Tavern, drafted the resolutions, and entrusted Carr with the responsibility of introducing them into the House.[33] On the day the resolutions were presented, young St. George Tucker, a student at William and Mary, was in the gallery. Tucker was actually more impressed on that particular day with Richard Henry Lee's oratorical performance than with Henry's, but a number of Tucker's classmates, who had witnessed Henry speak on the previous day on the same subject, maintained that Henry did indeed deserve to be considered the finest orator in the House. Tucker, although not quite willing to give credence to the observations of his fellow collegians, remarked that "if his [Lee's] speech was excelled by Mr. Henry's, the latter must have been excellent indeed."[34]

After the resolutions were adopted, they were sent by the newly formed Committee of Correspondence to other colonial legislatures, which in turn joined Massachusetts and Virginia in setting up similar committees. These committees would serve as a transition between the ill-organized and loosely coordinated colonial opposition prior to 1773 and the Continental Congresses, which would first convene in the fall of 1774.

Lord Dunmore, displeased both by the establishment of the Committee of Correspondence and by the Assembly's subtle rebuke of the way in which he had handled a criminal case in the southern Piedmont County of Pittsylvania, prorogued the Assembly after it had been in session only eleven days.[35] Relations between Governor and Assembly became still worse the next month, when Parliament passed the Tea Act. Although in fact intended as a device to bail out the ill-managed and financially tottering East India Company and not to antagonize the colonies further, the Tea Act would prove of little value to the East India Company and would serve to inflame colonial opinion to a degree that had not been reached since the Stamp Act crisis.

By the terms of the act, the East India Company was to be allowed to export tea directly to America, avoiding all duties in England and paying only the threepence per pound duty still in force in America. This would serve to lower the price of tea in America substantially, thus allowing the East India Company to undersell those merchants importing smuggled tea from Holland.

The North Ministry was reasonably confident of the wisdom of the plan, as the actual effect of the act in the colonies would lower prices, not raise them. But North miscalculated. The colonists, because they realized that the Tea Act was in part designed to induce them to accept the principle of parliamentary taxation and because many of the leaders of the commercial colonies were precisely those people whose businesses would be damaged if the Dutch tea trade were undercut by a monopolistic trading company, suddenly regained their commitment to constitutional principle. The result of course, was the famous Boston Tea Party, an event which, though deplored in Virginia as well as in London, seemed to signify the end of attempts at peacefully petitioning Parliament for a redress of grievances.[36] And the members of Parliament also seemed to recognize that Anglo-American relations had entered a new phase. Even men like Edmund Burke and William Pitt came to blame the colonists for their wanton disregard for the rights of property. Nearly everyone in Parliament, however, was inclined to place special blame on the Boston "radicals" and tended to feel that if those radicals were punished swiftly and firmly, the provincial leaders in other colonies, having observed their example, would quiet their opposition. Accordingly, on March 25, the Boston Port Bill passed Parliament, closing the port of Boston until the value of the lost tea had been recovered.[37] When the Virginia General Assembly convened on May 6, 1774, the Port Bill was almost the sole topic of conversation. Governor Dunmore, recognizing the agitated state of colonial opinion, would undoubtedly have preferred to avoid calling the Assembly into session at that time, but the press of purely local business—the Governor needed the Assembly's cooperation in settling a boundary dispute with Pennsylvania—made it necessary that the burgesses meet for at least a short time.

By the time the House began its deliberations, Patrick Henry had cast off any of his previous apathy toward the recent differences between America and England and was prepared to resume his bold stance of the Stamp Act crisis. According to George Mason, soon to become a principal participant himself, there was a great deal of activity going on behind the scenes during the opening days of the session, with Henry playing the leading role. The general plan was to delay a discussion of measures opposing the recent parliamentary action until the close of the session, presumably so that the House could complete its regular business before being prorogued by the Governor, who, judging from his recent attitude, was not likely to take kindly to any statement of colonial rights from the burgesses.[38]

Two-and-a-half weeks after the House convened, and after most of the important local business had been dispatched, the leaders of the "younger" wing of the Assembly began to implement their plan. According to Jefferson, the younger members "cooked up a resolution . . . appointing the first day of June, in which the Port Bill was to commence, for a day of fasting, humiliation and prayer." This resolution, when presented on May 24, was immediately adopted. Although it was actually an extremely mild form of protest, Governor Dunmore nevertheless interpreted it to be "conceived in such terms as to reflect highly upon his Majesty and the Parliament of Great Britain," and accordingly, he dissolved the Assembly.[39]

The dissolution was only a minor annoyance, as the members of the Assembly simply moved their deliberations to the Raleigh Tavern. In the meeting at the Raleigh Tavern the burgesses entered into an "association," agreeing to boycott British goods. Although the nonimportation resolution is often interpreted as a total boycott of all British goods, it was in fact only a partial boycott affecting only the products from East India except saltpeter and spices. Other goods from England were still to be allowed into the colony. The burgesses rationalized this half measure by maintaining that "a tender regard for the interests of our fellow subjects, the merchants and manufacturers of Great Britain, prevents us from going further at this time." This was in some ways logical, as many Americans looked on the English merchants as allies in their constitutional struggle with Parliament, but it is likely that some of the "younger" members of the Assembly might have wished for a more thoroughgoing boycott. The partial boycott did, however, permit the burgesses to put up a united front; it was unanimously adopted by the rump session of the burgesses, with such cautious leaders as Peyton Randolph and Edmund Pendleton supporting the measure.[40]

The Committee of Correspondence, meeting separately, worked to reinforce the actions of the House of Burgesses. On May 28 it drafted a resolution to be sent to the other American colonies expressing approval of a plan, put forward by the New York Committee of 51, for a "general Congress" of all the American colonies. And on May 31 the committee issued a call for a convention to meet in Williamsburg in August, composed of delegates from each of Virginia's counties, to discuss the state of affairs with England and to appoint representatives to the general congress.[41] This convention was undoubtedly intended to serve as a substitute for the House of Burgesses, which, subject to the whim of the Governor for its time and place of meeting, was no longer a reliable forum for business of any kind.

Although the public journals say little about Henry's precise role in the adoption of any of these measures, at least some of his colleagues in the House placed him at center stage. George Mason, commenting on the proceedings of that session, noted:

> I had an opportunity of conversing with Mr. Henry, and knowing his sentiments; as well as hearing him speak in the house since on different occasions. He is by far the most powerful speaker I ever heard. Every word he says not only engages, but commands the attention; and your passions are no longer your own when he addresses them. But his eloquence is the smallest part of his merit. He is in my opinion, the first man upon this continent, as well in abilities as public virtue.[42]

There must have been many men—like Pendleton and Peyton Randolph—who would have disputed that extravagant assessment, for Henry's activities at this stage were viewed as dangerous by the established leaders in the House of Burgesses for a number of reasons. At the most obvious and self-interested level, Henry's growing popularity represented a real threat to their preeminence in the affairs of the colony; men like Pendleton and Randolph were increasingly concerned that Henry's espousal of bold opposition to Great Britain might serve as the platform which would propel him, over their heads, to a position of leadership in the daily affairs of the House. Secondly, men like Pendleton and Randolph genuinely believed that Henry's oratory, although impressive in its eloquence, was calculated to make a peaceful and honorable settlement with England more difficult, a settlement which they, more than Henry and his followers, earnestly desired.

It was not that the Pendletons and Randolphs were pusillanimous and timid while Henry was bold and farsighted. Rather, Henry's experience and perspective were vastly different from that of his older and better-connected colleagues. Edmund Pendleton, for example, had by 1774 served in the House of Burgesses for twenty-two consecutive years; he had known and worked harmoniously with royal officials for a good portion of that time. He was understandably reluctant to move toward a confrontation with royal authority until every avenue toward a restoration of the former, peaceful relations between Crown and colony had been explored. Henry, on the other hand, had not even come in contact with royal authority in any direct way until 1765. And how things had changed by 1765! From the moment he entered the House of Burgesses the harmony that had existed between provincial and royal officials in the past was interrupted almost yearly by strife. It is no wonder that, from his own perspective, Henry could see little to be gained from conciliation and compromise.

These two different perspectives would, of course, make Henry seem "radical" and Pendleton "conservative" in the context of the struggle with England. In Henry's case, however, the label is a poor guide to the direction and intensity of his social and political thought. Henry's attitude toward the struggle with England was the product of his very particular situation and experience. There would be a number of occasions after the crisis over royal authority had passed when Henry's attitude would hardly seem radical. As in so many cases during the Revolutionary era, radicalism in the particular context of the imperial crisis did not always lead to a radical view of the need for social reform at home.

Both the Royal Governor and the British Ministry were surprised and alarmed by the turn of events in Virginia. Lord Dartmouth, writing to Dunmore on July 6, 1774, recollected that at the time of the passage of the Boston Port Bill "there was reason to hope, from appearances in other colonies, that the extravagant proportion of the people of Boston would have been everywhere disregarded." He added, however, that "it may now be well doubted whether the extraordinary conduct of the Burgesses of Virginia, both before and after their dissolution as a House, may not become (as it already has become in other instances) an example to the other colonies."[43]

By July news of a series of new parliamentary acts reached the colonies. They were again aimed primarily at Massachusetts but indirectly threatened all the colonies. Titled by foes the "Intolerable Acts," they included the Boston Port Bill; the Massachusetts Government Act, drastically weakening the powers of the provincial government; the Administration of Justice Act, allowing British officials accused of crimes in Massachusetts to be tried in England; and an amendment to the Quartering Act, requiring that Americans quarter British troops in their homes whenever and wherever necessary.[44]

These new acts produced an outpouring of petitions and resolves from nearly all of Virginia's counties. The citizens of Hanover, at a meeting at the courthouse on July 20, expressed their views to Henry and John Syme, Henry's half-brother and fellow burgess. After appointing Henry and Syme as their delegates to the Williamsburg Convention in August, the citizens of Hanover expressed their sentiments on the current crisis in imperial relations. Beginning with a statement asserting their claim to the same constitutional rights enjoyed by Englishmen living in England, they then affirmed the principle which had started the conflict in the first place—the principle embodied in the statement: "We will never be taxed but by our own representatives." The Hanover residents then turned to the recent events in Boston and, characteristically, while not approving of the behavior of the "radical" Bostonians, nevertheless deplored the punitive measures applied by the British to their sister colony, claiming that "if our sister colony of Massachusetts is enslaved, we cannot long remain free." The remonstrance concluded with recommendations for a firmer intercolonial union and a more inclusive boycott of British goods as means of achieving repeal of the Intolerable Acts.[45]

It is difficult to evaluate the importance of these county meetings in the Revolutionary struggle. They were certainly a novelty in a society where the elected representatives and the appointed members of the county court were accustomed to acting on their own initiative, with little concern for the views of their constituents on particular matters of public policy. The Hanover County meeting, and others like it, represented a step away from this oligarchic and authoritarian political style toward a mode of political discourse where the constituent power meant something. It is quite possible,

however, that at this early stage the shift amounted only to a super-
ficial change of form and not substance. If the Hanover meeting
was conducted like most of those occurring in Virginia at this time,
then a few politically powerful individuals—most likely Henry and
Syme themselves—stage-managed the whole affair, drawing up
resolutions ahead of time and simply allowing the Hanover residents to ratify their proposals. It seems particularly likely that this
was the case in Hanover, as the resolutions calling for a more drastic boycott of English goods and for greater efforts at intercolonial
unity represented exactly Henry's sentiments on both of those questions, sentiments that were slightly more radical than those of the
majority of provincial leaders at the time.

The resolutions, even if they were dictated by Henry and Syme,
would nevertheless have important future implications. Once politicians came to rely on these public forums as a means to rally support to their causes, the people assembled at those meetings would
gradually become more assertive about their right to guide the
actual formulation of public policy. No longer content to let their
representative do their thinking for them, they would begin to
think of him merely as their attorney, bound to reflect their views
and represent their interests. This would, however, be a slow
process in Virginia, with its long tradition of an oligarchic and deferential style of politics.

In Williamsburg the ultimate confrontation between royal and
provincial authority was rapidly moving nearer. The Convention
met on August 1, and in the six days that it was in session agreed
to a thoroughgoing boycott of all English goods and, interestingly,
vowed to import no more slaves into America after that date.[46] The
Convention also appointed Peyton Randolph, Richard Henry Lee,
George Washington, Patrick Henry, Richard Bland, Benjamin Harrison, and Edmund Pendleton delegates to the First Continental
Congress to be held in Philadelphia in September. The delegation
represented most shades of opinion within the ruling elite, with
Henry and Richard Henry Lee being the most outspoken advocates
of stern resistance against England, Peyton Randolph, Harrison,
and Pendleton representing the more conciliatory leadership in the
old House of Burgesses, and Washington and Bland—the former
by his manner and the latter by a series of influential pamphlets
written in 1766—occupying moderate positions and winning the

respect of both groups.[47] A contemporary, Roger Atkinson, described the delegation in this manner: Randolph was a "venerable man," with "knowledge, temper, experience, judgment—above all integrity." Atkinson had little to say of Lee other than that he liked him; moving on to Washington he opined: "He is a soldier, a warrior; he is a modest man; sensible; speaks little; in action cool, like a Bishop at his prayers." Bland, although he had "something of the look of old must parchments, which he handleth and studieth much," was a "wary, old experienced veteran at the bar and in the senate." Of Henry: "He is a real half Quaker . . . moderate and mild, and in religious matters a saint; but the very d - - - l in politics—a son of thunder. He will shake the Senate." Concluding his assessment with Pendleton, who was destined to be nearly always in at least mild opposition to Henry in the coming months, Atkinson simply noted, "the last and best."[48]

Henry, when he journeyed to Philadelphia to take his seat in the Continental Congress, would be moving to a very different scene of action, with new personalities and new issues often demanding different talents. It would be the first opportunity that the representatives of the other American colonies would have to gauge the caliber of political leadership in Virginia. Henry would no longer be judged simply by the standards of provincial Virginia but by those of the wider world. In many cases, alas, the judgment would at best be mixed.

Opposite: Portrait of Patrick Henry delivering the Stamp Act Speech by P. F. Rothermel. This nineteenth-century artist, like the writers of popular histories, was inclined to romanticize Henry's speech defending the Stamp Act Resolves.

Below: Patrick Henry's Stamp Act Resolves. The handwriting is probably not his own, the wording is drawn heavily from a previous set of resolutions passed by the House of Burgesses in December 1764, but the impact of the Resolves was nevertheless profound.

Colonial Williamsburg Photograph

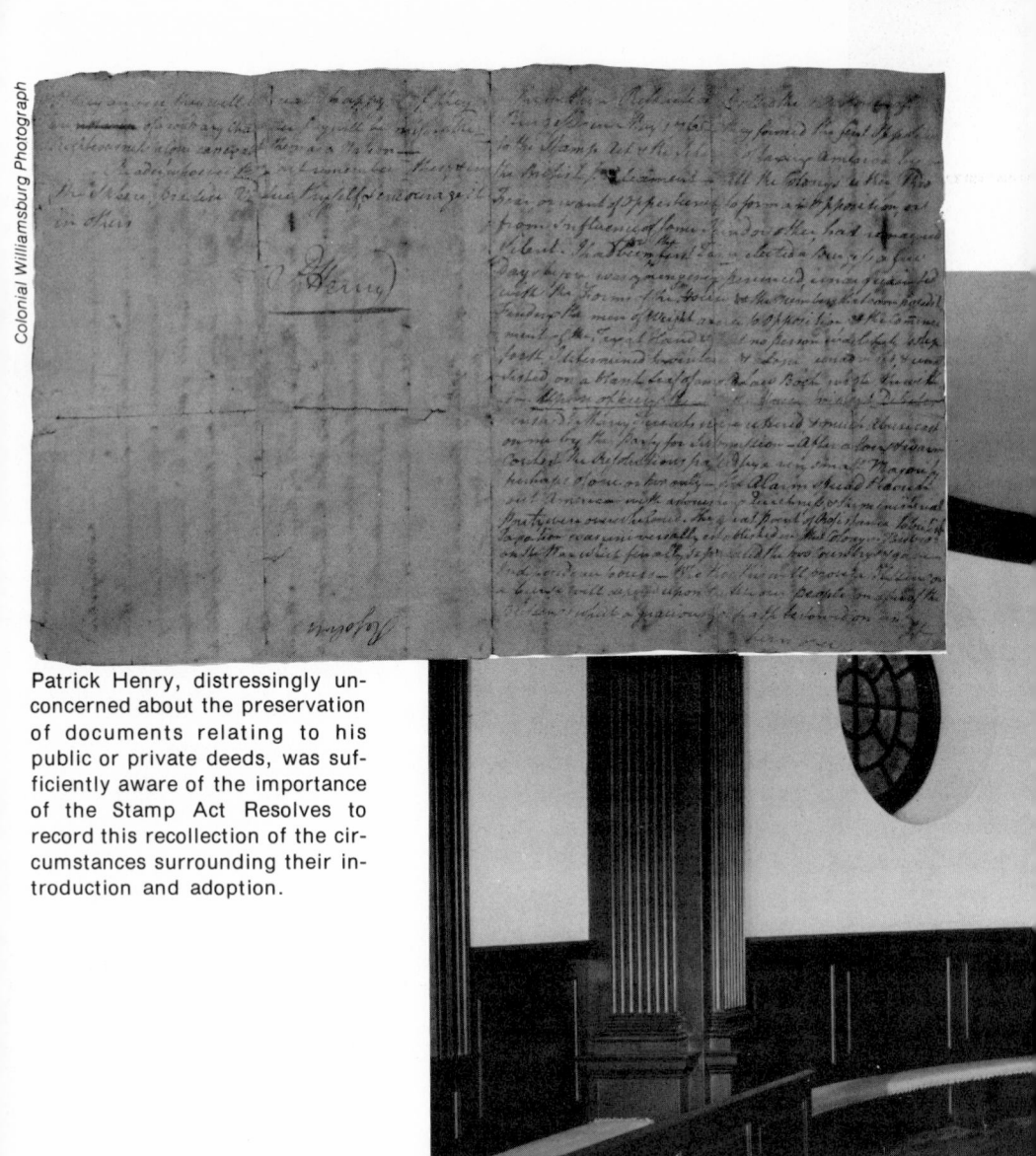

Patrick Henry, distressingly unconcerned about the preservation of documents relating to his public or private deeds, was sufficiently aware of the importance of the Stamp Act Resolves to record this recollection of the circumstances surrounding their introduction and adoption.

The Virginia House of Burgesses, Williamsburg. This was the principal meeting place of the Virginia provincial elite.

Above: The Conference Room, Capitol Building, Williamsburg, Virginia. In what would undoubtedly have seemed grand irony to the three gentlemen, the portraits of Edmund Pendleton, John Robinson, and Patrick Henry hang together in the reconstructed conference room. This may constitute the only condition in which Henry could associate with Pendleton and Robinson and not find himself involved in conflict.

Opposite: The Raleigh Tavern. Frequent dissolutions by Governor Dunmore in the years immediately preceding independence caused the members of the House of Burgesses to use the tavern as a site for their meetings.

Opposite: Portrait of John Murray, Earl of Dunmore, by Sir Joshua Reynolds. In conflict with provincial leaders almost from the moment of his arrival in Virginia in 1771, Dunmore inadvertently pushed even cautious Virginians into the patriot camp by his proclamation offering freedom to slaves who deserted their masters and fought on the side of the British.

Below: Patrick Henry's directive respecting slave security. This was Colonel Henry's response to Lord Dunmore's proclamation.

SIR,

*A*S the Committee of Safety is not fitting, I take the Liberty to enclose you a Copy of the Proclamation issued by Lord **Dunmore**; the Design and Tendency of which, you will observe, is fatal to the publick Safety. An early and unremitting Attention to the Government of the S L A V E S may, I hope, counteract this dangerous Attempt. Constant, and well directed Patrols, seem indispensably necessary. I doubt not of every possible Exertion, in your Power, for the publick Good; and have the Honour to be, Sir,

Your most obedient and very humble Servant,

P. HENRY.

HEAD QUARTERS, WILLIAMSBURG,

November 20, 1775.

By the **LION** & **UNICORN**, Dieu & mon droit, *their Lieutenant-Generals, Governours, Vice Admirals, &c. &c. &c. &c.*

A HUE & CRY.

WHEREAS I have been informed, from undoubted authority, that a certain **PATRICK HENRY**, of the county of Hanover, and a number of *deluded followers*, have taken up arms, chosen their officers, and, ftyling themfelves an *independent company*, have marched out of their county, encamped, and put themfelves in a pofture of war; and have written and defpatched letters to divers parts of the country, exciting the people to join in thefe *outrageous* and *rebellious* practices, to the *great terrour* of all his Majefty's *faithful* fubjects, and in *open defiance* of *law* and *government ;* and have *committed other acts of violence,* particularly in *extorting* from his Majefty's *Receiver-General* the fum of 330 l. under *pretence of replacing the powder* I *thought proper* to order from the magazine; whence it undeniably appears, there is *no longer* the leaft fecurity for the *life* or *property* of any man: Wherefore, I have *thought proper,* *with the advice of his Majefty's Council,* and *in his Majefty's name,* to iffue this *my* proclamation, ftrictly charging *all perfons,* upon their *allegiance,* not to *aid, abet,* or *give countenance* to the faid **PATRICK HENRY**, or *any other perfons* concerned in *fuch unwarrantable combinations;* but, on the contrary, to oppofe *them,* and *their defigns,* by *every means,* which defigns muft otherwife inevitably involve the *whole country* in the *moft direful calamity,* as they will call for the *vengeance* of *offended Majefty,* and the *infulted laws,* to be *exerted here,* to vindicate the *conftitutional* authority of government.

Given, &c. this 6th day of May, 1775.

D * * * *.

G * * d * * * the P * * * *.

Above: Lord Dunmore's proclamation branding Henry an outlaw.

Opposite: Edmund Pendleton's Resolutions for Independence. Excessively wordy, lacking in literary grace, the Resolves had the important virtue of uniting representatives of widely varying temperaments and ideologies on the question of independence.

IN CONVENTION.

PRESENT one Hundred and twelve MEMBERS.

WEDNESDAY, MAY 15, 1776.

FORASMUCH as all the endeavours of the United Colonies, by the most decent representations and petitions to the King and Parliament of Great Britain, to restore peace and security to America under the British government, and a re-union with that people upon just and liberal terms, instead of a redress of grievances, have produced, from an imperious and vindictive Administration, increased insult, oppression, and a vigorous attempt to effect our total destruction. By a late act, all these colonies are declared to be in rebellion, and out of the protection of the British Crown, our properties subjected to confiscation, our people, when captivated, compelled to join in the murder and plunder of their relations and countrymen, and all former rapine and oppression of Americans declared legal and just. Fleets and armies are raised, and the aid of foreign troops engaged to assist these destructive purposes: The King's representative in this colony hath not only withheld all the powers of government from operating for our safety, but, having retired on board an armed ship, is carrying on a piratical and savage war against us, tempting our slaves, by every artifice, to resort to him, and training and employing them against their masters. In this state of extreme danger, we have no alternative left but an abject submission to the will of those over-bearing tyrants, or a total separation from the Crown and Government of Great Britain, uniting and exerting the strength of all America for defence, and forming alliances with foreign powers for commerce and aid in war: Wherefore, appealing to the SEARCHER OF HEARTS for the sincerity of former declarations, expressing our desire to preserve the connection with that nation, and that we are driven from that inclination by their wicked councils, and the eternal laws of self-preservation,

RESOLVED UNANIMOUSLY, that the delegates appointed to represent this colony in General Congress be instructed to propose to that respectable body to declare the United Colonies free and independent states, absolved from all allegiance to, or dependence upon, the Crown or Parliament of Great Britain; and that they give the assent of this colony to such declaration, and to whatever measures may be thought proper and necessary by the Congress for forming foreign alliances, and a confederation of the colonies, at such time, and in the manner, as to them shall seem best: Provided, that the power of forming government for, and the regulations of the internal concerns of each colony, be left to the respective colonial legislatures.

RESOLVED UNANIMOUSLY, that a committee be appointed to prepare a DECLARATION of RIGHTS, and such a plan of government as will be most likely to maintain peace and order in this colony, and secure substantial and equal liberty to the people.

EDMUND PENDLETON, *President.*
JOHN TAZEWELL, *Clerk of the Conv.*

WILLIAMSBURG.

SATURDAY, JUNE 29, 1776.

THIS day PATRICK HENRY, Efq; was chofen Governor of this country, and a committee appointed to acquaint him therewith; to which he returned the following anfwer to the Convention.

To the Honourable the PRESIDENT *and* HOUSE *of* CONVENTION.

GENTLEMEN,

THE vote of this day, appointing me Governor of this Commonwealth, has been notified to me in the moft polite and obliging manner, by George Mafon, Henry Lee, Dudley Digges, John Blair, and Bartholomew Dandrige, Efquires.

A fenfe of the high and unmerited honour conferred upon me by the Convention fills my heart with gratitude, which I truft my whole life will manifeft. I take this earlieft opportunity to exprefs my thanks, which I wifh to convey to you, Gentlemen, in the ftrongeft terms of acknowledgment.

When I reflect that the tyranny of the Britifh King and Parliament hath kindled a formidable war, now raging throughout this wide extended continent, and in the operations of which this Commonwealth muft bear fo great a part; and that, from the events of this war, the lafting happinefs, or mifery, of a great proportion of the human fpecies will finally refult; that, in order to preferve this Commonwealth from anarchy, and its attendant ruin, and to give vigour to our councils, and effect to all our meafures, government hath been neceffarily affumed, and new-modelled; that it is expofed to numberlefs hazards and perils in its infantine ftate; that it can never attain to maturity, or ripen into firmnefs, unlefs it is guarded by affectionate affiduity, and managed by great abilities; I lament my want of talents; I feel my mind filled with anxiety and uneafinefs to find myfelf fo unequal to the duties of that important ftation to which I am called by favour of my fellow citizens, at this truly critical conjuncture. The errors of my conduct fhall be atoned for, fo far as I am able, by unwearied endeavours to fecure the freedom and happinefs of our common country.

I fhall enter upon the duties of my office whenever you, Gentlemen, fhall be pleafed to direct; relying upon the known wifdom and virtue of your Honourable Houfe to fupply my defects, and to give permanency and fuccefs to that fyftem of government which you have formed, and which is fo wifely calculated to fecure equal liberty, and advance human happinefs. I have the honour to be,

WILLIAMSBURG,   Gentlemen, your moft obedient,
June 29, 1776.   And very humble fervant,
                                        P. HENRY, Jun.

Notice in *The Virginia Gazette* of Henry's election as governor. A new constitution, a new independent commonwealth, and a new governor.

4

Rebellion

On August 30 Henry and Pendleton journeyed together to George Washington's plantation at Mount Vernon, there to join Washington for the ride to Philadelphia. For Henry the journey would be only his second political mission outside the colony (in 1770 he had traveled to New York to an unsuccessful intercolonial meeting on the regulation of the Indian trade).[1] The trio of Washington, Pendleton, and Henry, after arriving in Philadelphia, were fed at the City Tavern and then entertained at the home of William Shippen, a Philadelphia physician who had married the sister of Richard Henry Lee.[2] John Adams, looking over the Virginia delegation, called it the "most spirited and consistent" of any. Of the individuals, Adams's judgment ranged from "an insolent, luxurious, heavy gentleman, of no use in Congress or committee, but a great embarrassment to both"—Benjamin Harrison—to "he is a masterly man"—Richard Henry Lee. His opinion of Henry was not yet formed, but he had been told that he was "the Demosthenes of the age."[3]

The Congress, after waiting five days until a quorum of the delegates had arrived, began its deliberations on September 5, 1774. Almost immediately after the commission of each individual delegate was read, an issue arose—unrelated to the struggle with Great Britian—that threatened to renew intercolonial rivalries and endanger the harmony of the Congress. That issue, which would recur during the debates on both the Articles of Confederation and the federal Constitution, concerned the question of representation in the Continental Congress, with delegates from the most

populous colonies quite naturally desiring representation apportioned according to population and those from smaller colonies
such as Delaware and Rhode Island asking that each colony receive
an equal voice.

It was on this question that Patrick Henry first exhibited his
oratorical skills to an intercolonial audience. According to Charles
Thomson, Secretary of the Congress, Henry more clearly resembled
"a Presbyterian clergyman, used to haranguing the people" than a
Virginia planter-aristocrat. In that first speech before the Congress,
which seems not to have been one of any great distinction, Henry
simply took the reasonable position, for a Virginian, that it was
unfair for a small colony to carry the same weight in the deliberations of the Congress as a large one.[4] The next day Henry continued his argument, and this time he used his forensic skills more
fully. According to a synopsis of the speech made by John Adams,
Henry maintained that "Government is dissolved" and that the
American colonies were back in a "state of nature." He was not
pursuing this radical line of reasoning—a line that would ultimately serve to justify independence in 1776—in order to persuade
his fellow delegates to break ties with England immediately, but
rather was merely using it as a device to persuade the representatives to cease thinking about individual colonies as separate entities
and instead begin to think of them as units of population, each to
be given representation in the Continental Congress in proportion
to its population. It was in this specific context that Henry uttered
the famous words: "The distinctions between Virginians, Pennsyl-
vanians, New Yorkers and New Englanders are no more. I am not
a Virginian, but an American."[5] This was hardly a rejection of provincial attachments and an adoption of a continental view. In fact,
it was precisely the opposite. Henry, defending the special interests of Virginia in the matter of representation in the Continental
Congress, was merely using a tactical argument, with nationalistic
overtones to be sure, to advance those interests. There was perhaps
no prominent man in the Continental Congress who would remain
more of a spokesman for localism, for "Virginian" rather than
"American" interests, than Patrick Henry; to misread this oft-
quoted statement is to ignore one of the few consistent aspects of his
political life—the attachment to local and provincial interests, an

attachment that was born of the fact that nearly all of his political experience and popular support lay at the local level.

Henry was to lose the argument. His colleagues from Virginia, Richard Bland and Richard Henry Lee, and one of the delegates from New York, John Jay, all pointed to the practical difficulties of apportioning representation by population. Bland and Lee, noting that there were as yet no reliable figures to make apportionment of representatives anything more than guesswork, maintained that apportionment would merely amount to the same kind of arbitrary use of power for which the Americans were presently condemning the British. And Jay, alarmed by Henry's assumption that the bonds of government had already been dissolved, asked that the Congress continue to operate for the moment with each colony being given an equal weight and with the understanding that the decision was only tentative and should not serve as a precedent for the future. A motion to that effect was then adopted, with Henry bowing to the wishes of the majority.[6]

The first important step taken by the Congress came on September 17, when Sam Adams introduced into the Congress a set of resolutions passed in Suffolk County, Massachusetts. The resolves, which were ultimately adopted by the Congress, committed America, against the wishes of many of the more hesitant delegates, to a course that drastically increased the chances of armed conflict with the mother country. They explicitly called for resistance to the Coercive Acts, ordered that all public monies be withheld from the Crown, and asked for complete commercial nonintercourse with Great Britain.[7]

All these deliberations took somewhat longer than they might have, for, in John Adams's words, the "Assembly is like no other that ever existed. Every man in it . . . must show his oratory, his criticism, and his political abilities." He ventured that if a motion was made saying that three plus two made five, "we should be entertained with logic and rhetoric, history, politics and mathematics" in the discussion of the motion.[8] Given Henry's fondness for public speaking, it is almost inconceivable that he was not one of the offenders.

The next item to come before the Congress was a plan for a "Proposed Union between Great Britain and the Colonies" presented by Joseph Galloway of Pennsylvania, perhaps the most conservative member of the Congress. The more militant members of the Congress, by a scant one-vote margin, turned aside Galloway's proposal for a joint English-American council to decide questions of imperial policy relating to America, thus ending the hopes of those who saw in the Continental Congress a means of diverting the colonies from their course toward revolution.

It was now up to the "violent party" in the Congress—Sam and John Adams, Richard Henry Lee, and Henry were all generally included in this category—to regain the initiative and implement the principles of the Suffolk Resolves. To that effect a committee was appointed to set up the enforcement machinery for the non-importation agreement and a smaller committee appointed to draft an address to the King defending the colonists' position. This committee—composed of Richard Henry Lee, John Adams, Thomas Johnson of Maryland, John Rutledge of South Carolina, and Henry —was considered at the time to have had the most delicate task of all. Henry, presumably because of his reputation as a staunch and articulate defender of colonial rights, was selected as the man who would prepare the first draft of the address. Unfortunately, Henry did not prove as adept a penman as an orator, and he was replaced by John Dickinson, the author of the widely respected *Letters from a Pennsylvania Farmer*. The petition, as drafted by Dickinson, was overwhelmingly approved by the Congress on October 25.[9]

The Congress also appointed a committee to draft an address to the people of England, vesting Richard Henry Lee with the responsibility for the actual composition of the document. Like Henry, Lee was more impressive as a public speaker than as a writer of prose, and when Lee presented his draft before the committee "every countenance fell and a dead silence ensued for many minutes." This time John Jay stepped in and drafted another version, which was immediately adopted.

This was the extent of Henry's contribution to the First Continental Congress. On October 26, after a committee headed by John Adams drafted a declaration of American rights and grievances explicitly denying to Parliament the right to legislate for the colonies in any way other than the normal regulation of trade, the intercolonial body adjourned.[10] It had taken some fateful steps. By denying all parliamentary authority except in matters of the regulation of trade, the delegates had moved closer to a total denial of English authority in America, extending their prohibition of English power from taxation to nearly all legislation. The activities of the "Association" set up by the Congress to enforce the nonimportation agreements would serve notice on the British that the militance of the colonies was not confined to vague constitutional pronouncements alone. As nonintercourse was enforced—and it was sometimes enforced in a zestful manner indeed—the British would soon realize that the opposition in America was not confined merely to Sam Adams and a handful of Boston radicals.[11]

Patrick Henry's role in this, his first and one of his last important intercolonial gatherings, was somewhat less than decisive. On the positive side, his oratory unquestionably impressed many of the delegates present. Silas Deane of Connecticut, writing immediately after the debate on the Suffolk Resolves, remarked: "Mr. Henry is . . . the compleatest speaker I ever heard. If his future speeches are equal to the small samples he has hitherto given us, they will be worth preserving."[12] Yet when he left Philadelphia for Hanover on October 23, three days before the Congress adjourned, Henry must have felt some sense of disappointment about his performance there. Aside from his occasional oratorical displays, his contributions to the day-to-day work of the Congress had been minimal.

Henry's achievements in the Virginia House of Burgesses had been impressive. He had gone a long way toward gaining the admiration and respect of the members of that body and he would continue to grow in influence and prestige within his home colony. But in the Continental Congress Henry was only one able man among many exceptional men and a relatively inexperienced one at that, a situation that must have constituted something of a surprise to the provincial Virginian from Hanover County.

By November 1774 Henry was back home overseeing the organization of a volunteer militia company in Hanover, one of the first of its kind in America.[13] In addition to his duties as the political and military leader of his home county, Henry was also occupied with extraordinarily difficult personal problems during the months between his arrival in Hanover and his departure for the second session of the Virginia Convention in March 1775. Although the evidence is fragmentary, it seems likely that his wife Sarah had reached a state of insanity by 1774. It apparently was not a mild disorder, for it was necessary to confine her. Although there was a mental hospital in Williamsburg, few would have considered that a suitable place for her, given the eighteenth-century view of mental illness, which looked on such disorders as criminal, sinful, or both. Instead, Henry kept her in the basement of his Scotchtown plantation, probably entrusting her care to a female slave.[14] It is not difficult to imagine the sheer horror evoked by the situation, and Henry, no doubt touched both with pity for his wife and not a little guilt over relegating her to the basement, never referred to his wife again after her death sometime in early 1775. His inability to discuss the matter would prove typical of his dealings with most of the members of his immediate family. When tragedy touched a member of his family, as it frequently did during the years after the Revolution, Henry would most often be absorbed either in affairs of state or in his own legal career.

It was, then, probably with a mixture of anticipation, grief, and guilt that Henry took his seat as one of the representatives from Hanover County to the second session of the Virginia Convention on March 20, 1775. The Convention met in St. John's Church in Richmond, a building reputed to be the largest in the town, although contemporary testimony indicates that it was nonetheless too small for a gathering the size of the Convention. The decision to move to Richmond was prompted by the fear that Governor Dunmore might try to break up the proceedings if they were held in Williamsburg. Moreover, Richmond was fast becoming an important commercial center, geographically more convenient to most delegates than Williamsburg. That it was selected as the site is an indication of the gradual shift in power away from the older, established Tidewater toward the Piedmont.

On the opening day of the session, Peyton Randolph, long-time speaker of the House of Burgesses and president of the first session of the Convention, was reelected president of the second session by unanimous vote. Although generally allied with the more cautious Tidewater wing of planters, Randolph continued to command the respect of enough burgesses to make an open challenge to his position by insurgents extremely difficult.[15]

On March 23, the fourth day of the Convention, Pendleton, who was undoubtedly fearful that some members of the body would force the colony into an extreme position, introduced a petition to the King, dated December 28, 1774, from the Jamaican General Assembly. In many ways the petition reflected precisely Pendleton's views toward the dispute with England. The petition, which had been published in Purdie and Dixon's *Virginia Gazette* the week before and therefore was generally known to most of the delegates before it was introduced, was in part a vigorous defense of American colonial rights, but it also specifically repudiated the notion of forceful resistance to Great Britain and, moreover, postulated the theory that American rights rested on grants from the Crown, not on the fundamental principles of the British Constitution. But if one ignored these two portions of the Jamaican petition, it amounted to a spirited though essentially moderate defense of American rights. Pendleton therefore introduced a resolution into the Convention extending the "unfeigned thanks" of the body to the Jamaican Assembly for its support and expressing "the most ardent wish of this colony . . . to see a speedy return to those halcyon days when we lived a free and happy people."[16]

Pendleton's motion was not permitted to go unchallenged. Henry rose to present some resolutions of his own, resolutions that he had obviously prepared well in advance. The first resolution might have seemed harmless enough in another context; it simply affirmed that "a well-regulated militia, composed of gentlemen and yeomen, is the natural strength and security of a free government." The second resolution, stating that "the establishment of such a militia is, at this time, peculiarly necessary," was more pointed. And the third resolution, asking that the colony immediately be put in a state of defense, left no one uncertain of Henry's frame of mind.[17]

Many members of the Convention, including even some moderates like Richard Bland, thought that Henry's resolutions were unnecessarily provocative. Although they were not opposed to discreet efforts to strengthen the colony's defenses, they believed that a public resolution calling for military preparations was irresponsible and calculated only to hinder any efforts at reconcilation. If one accepts their premise—that some settlement with England was desirable—they were undoubtedly correct. But Henry, who had never appreciated the benefits of conciliation between royal and provincial authorities and who by 1775 had probably determined in his own mind that some form of armed resistance was inevitable, viewed their moderation as weakness. It was at this stage, in answer to the arguments of the cautious patriots, that Henry delivered his most famous oration.

The speech was so powerful that virtually everyone who heard it carried a recollection of it long after the event. And while each listener's reconstruction of the oration varied, it is clear from all the accounts that Henry's performance was unequaled in the long and forensically illustrious history of the House of Burgesses. Thomas Marshall, a delegate to the Convention and the father of the future Chief Justice of the Supreme Court, remembered the speech "as one of the most bold, vehement, and animated pieces of eloquence that had ever been delivered."[18] And Edward Carrington, who was standing near a window outside the church when the speech was given, is supposed to have exclaimed, "Let me be buried at this spot!"—a wish that was actually fulfilled at his death in 1810.[19]

William Wirt's account is, predictably, the most dramatic. With St. John's Church crowded past capacity, yet the assembled burgesses hushed to catch every word, Henry closed his speech:

> Gentlemen may cry peace, peace—but there is no peace. The war is actually begun! The next gale that sweeps the north will bring to our ears the clash of resounding arms. Our brethren are already in the field! Why stand we here idle? What is it the gentlemen wish? What would they have? Is life so dear, or peace so sweet, as to be purchased at the price of chains and slavery? Forbid it, almighty God! I know not what course others may take; but as for me . . . give me liberty or give me death![20]

We need not accept the precise text of Writ's reconstruction in order to be impressed with the force of Henry's words. Edmund Randolph, not always an admirer of Henry's, looked back on the event and recalled:

> Henry was his pure self. . . . It [his oratory] blazed so as to warm the coldest heart. In the sacred place of the meeting, the church, the imagination had no difficulty to conceive . . . that the British King was lying prostrate from the thunder of heaven. Henry was

thought in his attitude to resemble St. David, while preaching at Athens, and to speak as man was never known to speak before.

Randolph placed a high value on the gift of oratory as an essential part of the Virginia gentry's claim to political leadership. As the wealthy but unpopular Landon Carter would discover to his dismay, it was through the techniques of persuasion by means of logic, reason, and good sense as much as through wealth and family heritage that the Virginia gentry earned the respect of the electorate. And Henry's oratory was simply unmatched. His closest rival, Richard Henry Lee, possessed elegance; Jefferson was without peer in his grasp of republican theory; but it was Henry, "without the advantages of literature," who was capable of "rousing the genius of his country and binding a band of patriots together to hurl defiance at the tyranny of so formidable a nation as Great Britain."[21]

The burgesses, moved both by Henry's argumentation and by the not insignificant fact that they were already disposed to favor the substance if not the tone of his proposals, adopted the resolutions and appointed a committee, with Henry as chairman, to implement the plans for arming the colony. Significantly, Henry was not given a blank check by the House; also serving on the committee were such cautious patriots as Pendleton, Robert Carter Nicholas, and Benjamin Harrison.[22]

Shortly after that committee had returned a report recommending that each county raise one or more voluntary militia companies, the Convention proceeded to the business of electing delegates to the Second Continental Congress. All seven men who served in the first Congress, with the additional election of Thomas Jefferson as an alternate in case Peyton Randolph found that his duties as President of the Virginia Convention made it impossible for him to attend the Congress, were reelected. The vote tabulation for the seven is shown in the accompanying table.[23]

Peyton Randolph	107	Benjamin Harrison	94
George Washington	106	Richard Bland	90
Patrick Henry	105	Thomas Jefferson	18
Richard Henry Lee	103	Thomas Nelson	14
Edmund Pendleton	100	Others	8

That those seven should be reelected, demonstrating among them a balance among all degrees of militancy toward Great Britain, is testimony to the continued desire of Virginia's provincial leaders to do everything possible to harmonize interests and to prevent factionalism within the elite. Thomas Jefferson, reminiscing long after the event, caught this spirit of conciliation:

> These [Pendleton, Randolph, et al.] were honest and able men, who had begun the opposition on the same ground, but with a moderation more adapted to their age and experience. Subsequent events favored the bolder spirits of Henry, the Lees, Pages, Mason, etc., with whom I went in all points. Sensible, however, of the importance of unanimity among our constituents, although we often wished to have gone faster, we slackened our pace, that our less ardent colleagues might keep up with us; and they, on their part, differing nothing from us in principle, quickened their gait somewhat beyond that which prudence might of itself have advised.[24]

This desire to preserve harmony would influence the outcome of the Revolution in Virginia enormously. In colonies like Pennsylvania, the established leaders of the provincial elite, unwilling to "quicken their gait," would ultimately find themselves dislodged from their traditional positions of political power by those citizens desiring bolder action. In Virginia, the Randolphs, Pendletons, and Nicholases, by their willingness to at least move with the tide created by bolder members like Henry, would find that they, though often forced to yield some of their power to the insurgents, would nevertheless be able to retain their influential position within the political system once the Revolution actually commenced.

★

It did not take the royal government long to react to this new boldness on the part of the provincial leaders. Lord Dunmore, motivated by the same policy considerations that caused General Gage to send troops to Lexington and Concord, determined on April 20, 1775, to lessen the military threat to royal government in Virginia by seizing the supply of gunpowder in the public magazine in Williamsburg. News of Dunmore's action spread quickly. Peyton Randolph and Robert Carter Nicholas, anxious to avoid a violent confrontation with royal authorities, personally interceded to dissuade the citizens of Williamsburg from taking drastic action should Dunmore not return the powder. In Fredericksburg, volunteer militia companies were also threatening to march on Williamsburg and capture the Governor. Dunmore succeeded in further inflaming the situation by making known his intention of arming his own slaves to protect himself and of emancipating all slaves who would fight with him.[25] This latter action, perhaps more than any other taken by royal officials in Virginia, would drive previously conservative Virginians closer to those advocating radical action.

The slave system was the cornerstone of social and economic power in Virginia. It provided Virginia planters with the wealth and property that were the essential ingredients of social status in their colony, and it made possible the leisure that allowed them to devote their time to being "gentlemen-statesmen." But it nevertheless constituted a glaring contradiction in the virtuous republican society which they believed they had created. There is no doubt that many Virginians felt genuinely troubled by the effects of slavery on the condition of the black man, but it is likely that still more were disturbed by the danger slavery posed to white society. In spite of a repressive slave code that forbade blacks to wander anywhere off the plantation without written passes from their masters or to congregate at any time in large groups, the fear of slave rebellion remained uppermost in the minds of nearly all the members of the provincial elite. That such a rebellion should now receive the encouragement of the Royal Governor himself was, in their minds, the most destructive act imaginable. If final proof were needed of the intent of the Crown to impose tyranny on white Virginians, Dunmore's appeal to the slave population, an appeal which was later issued as a formal proclamation, surely provided it.[26]

Randolph, again wishing to avert armed conflict, assured a messenger from the Fredericksburg militia company that the situation was well in hand and implored the troops not to march on Williamsburg. When the Fredericksburg troops, which were now some 600 strong, got Randolph's message, many wanted to continue the march anyway. But finally, much to the relief of Pendleton and Randolph, who were indirectly negotiating with Dunmore throughout the crisis, the Fredericksburg troops disbanded.[27]

The disbanding of the Fredericksburg militia marked only a temporary lull, as Patrick Henry, on May 2, got news of the Battle of Lexington and Concord and began efforts to lead the Hanover County militia company to Williamsburg in search of gunpowder. Dunmore's actions, in combination with the news of Lexington and Concord, were just what Henry needed to rouse public opinion, and he obviously wanted to make the most of it. According to his cousin George Dabney, however, he was pushing his fellow citizens a bit too fast, and his proposal was considered by many to be "imprudent and impolitic." But Henry, through his control over the Hanover County committee, which included not only several of his political supporters but his half-brother and cousin as well, was able to override most of the opposition to the plan. Once the committee had approved the plan, Henry was elected captain of the expeditionary force. He then dispatched some of his men to neighboring King William County, where they demanded £330 from Colonel Richard Corbin, the King's Surveyor General, as compensation for the "stolen" gunpowder. The Hanover militia company, with Henry in the lead, next set out for Williamsburg. On the way they stopped at Doncastle's Ordinary, where they met Carter Braxton, who had been sent by the Governor to promise payment of the £330. Henry then sent Braxton's written promise of payment to Robert Carter Nicholas, the treasurer of the colony, offering him the services of his militia company should he feel that the public monies, like the public arsenal, were unsafe in Williamsburg. Nicholas, who was one of the provincial leaders who was not at all happy with the drastic steps which Henry had taken, replied that "he had no apprehension of the necessity or propriety" of Henry's services and let it be known that, contrary to Henry's expectations, the citizens of Williamsburg had pretty well quieted their opposition to the Governor.[28]

With the promise of payment from the Royal Governor and with the clear message from Nicholas that his help was not needed, Henry and his company of soldiers had nothing to do but to return to Hanover. Just a few days later Dunmore issued a proclamation condemning "a certain Patrick Henry, of the county of Hanover, and a number of his deluded followers," and threatened to punish them severely if such an occurrence were repeated in the future. And in private Dunmore expressed the same concern about Henry's conduct, writing to the British Ministry that Henry was "a man of desperate circumstances, who had been very active in encouraging disobedience and exciting a spirit of revolt among the people from many years past."[29]

The disapproval of the Royal Governor was hardly surprising, but it is also clear that a number of other "respectable" people were not altogether pleased by Henry's activities. The Governor's Council, which up to this time had been able to steer a course somewhat independent from either Dunmore or the Virginia Convention, now was forced to support the Governor, expressing its "abhorrence and detestation of that licentious and ungovernable spirit that is gone forth and misleads the once happy people of this country." Council members like John Page, who opposed the seizure of the gunpowder, were soon purged and the membership of the Council was monopolized by future Tories such as Richard Corbin and Ralph Wormeley.[30]

Henry was obviously sensitive to some of the criticism directed at him and was particularly upset by the disapproval of men like Pendleton and Nicholas, whom he respected despite his frequent disagreement with them. In a letter to Francis Lightfoot Lee, he attempted to defend himself, claiming that it was only "for the sake of the public tranquility, as well as of justice," that he had taken such bold steps. Afraid that the members of the Virginia Convention might go so far as to actually censure him, he asked Lee to defend his actions for him while he was away at the Second Continental Congress.[31]

While many of the political leaders of Virginia may have been disturbed by Henry's incautious behavior during the gunpowder episode, it is clear that the action had only enhanced his popularity among his constituents. As Henry left Hanover en route to Philadelphia in May, he was frequently stopped by bands of people applauding his conduct. A group of citizens from Hanover, King William, and Caroline Counties personally escorted him across the Potomac, taking leave of him, according to a newspaper account of the time, with "repeated huzzas."[32]

Henry took his seat in the Second Continental Congress on May 18. Once again, his role in that Congress would seem exceptionally subdued for a man of his reputation for boldness and flamboyance. According to Jefferson, who joined the Congress when Peyton

Randolph went back to Virginia to serve as President of the Virginia Convention, Henry was "a silent and unmeddling member in Congress." At the beginning of the session, when subjects of a general nature were discussed, Henry was "in his element, and captivated all by his bold and splendid eloquence," but after the Congress got down to the daily business of coordinating the many complex activities of the thirteen different colonies, Henry "had the good sense to perceive that his declamation . . . had no weight at all in such an assembly as that. He ceased therefore, in a great measure, to take part in the business."[33]

Although Henry remained in Congress until its adjournment on August 1, he seems to have made little impact on its deliberations. He was probably impatient with John Dickinson's draft of a petition to the King—dubbed the "Olive Branch Petition"—because of its conciliatory tone, but he, like most of the radical members of the Congress, was willing to support it simply out of deference to the character and intelligence of Dickinson. It is also likely that Henry, once again in opposition to Pendleton, supported the efforts of John and Sam Adams to make George Washington commander-in-chief of the Continental army. The Adamses, hoping to unite the Southern colonies to New England's increasingly violent struggle with England, pushed for the appointment of Washington while Pendleton and many of the more cautious members of the Virginia delegation initially supported Artemus Ward of Massachusetts in order to avoid a commitment by Virginia to the radical course of New England.[34] Henry, both out of respect for Washington and by his now known sympathy with the plans of the Adamses, was almost certainly one of Washington's most vigorous supporters.

The rest of Henry's activity in the Congress seems to have been purely routine. Although he served on several committees, few were indicative of any significant role in the important business of the Congress. It was perhaps with some relief that he left the oppressive summer heat of Philadelphia for Virginia some time around August 1.

Henry's departure from Philadelphia would mark the end of his political career on the continental scene. He would gain a reputation as one of the principal figures of the Revolution in Virginia, but unlike Washington, Jefferson, or the young James

Madison, his reputation would be made as a spokesman for Virginian, and not American interests. As Washington's and Jefferson's subsequent careers on a continental and even an intercontinental level would further diminish their attachment to provincial interests, so too would Henry's exclusive involvement with state and local politics serve to increase his attachment to a localist political philosophy and to heighten his distrust of central government at all levels. In fact, perhaps one does not have to go beyond the element of immediate experience to explain the increasing divergence in the political world views of Henry and Washington and Jefferson. Henry's successes had all been achieved at the level of colonial politics. He had not disgraced himself at the First and Second Continental Congresses, but except for brief flashes of his oratorical skill, neither had he distinguished himself in these assemblages of exceptionally distinguished men. His principal abilities were, after all, rhetorical and emotive. Those talents were better appreciated on election day at the county court or in the more informal atmosphere of the House of Burgesses than in the decidedly businesslike setting of the Continental Congress. Jefferson, by contrast, had little of the oratorical skill that was so important to Henry's rise to fame on the provincial level, but he possessed precisely those extraordinary literary and administrative talents that would be in demand by the new Continental Congress. As a consequence, Jefferson would make a nationwide reputation for himself before he had reached full power in the politics of his own colony. And of course Washington, now occupying a post that demanded that he operate on an intercontinental level, would become the symbol of a new nation, not of a state or a region.

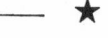

So Henry returned home to Virginia, to an arena with which he was more familiar and to a group of country squires that valued his abilities more highly. On August 5, the Virginia Convention, presumably impressed by his exploits as leader of the Hanover volunteers in the dispute over the gunpowder, elected Henry colonel of the first of two Virginia regiments and commander-in-chief of all regular forces in Virginia. The vote was close, with Henry actually finishing second to Hugh Mercer of Fredericksburg, 40 to 41, but in the runoff Henry was elected by a narrow margin. There was consternation over the choice—consternation from both the more cautious Tidewater delegates who would have preferred one of their own men and from delegates representing all sections who would have preferred the selection of a man with more military experience.[35] Nonetheless, though many would come to regret the choice, it was a testimony to Henry's growing influence in the Revolutionary movement in Virginia.

Henry had little time to reflect on the honor bestowed on him, for he found himself almost immediately at odds with many of the men who had been dubious about his selection in the first place. Executive authority in the colony had essentially vanished when Lord Dunmore fled with his family to a ship lying off York on June 7. The Virginia Convention, stepping into the void left by Dunmore, selected a Committee of Safety that was relatively evenly weighted with conservatives, moderates, and radicals but with Pendleton as chairman. It would be this committee, charged with the exercise of executive authority in Dunmore's absence, with which Henry would have to work.[36]

Henry formally accepted his commission on August 26 and after a few weeks' rest at Scotchtown returned to Williamsburg to begin to organize his regiment. The recruiting of men, at least at this early stage when the colonial militias were not forced to compete with the Continental army for enlistments, did not present much of a problem, as the spirit of resistance among Virginians was high. By late September Henry had picked his campsite, somewhere "behind" the College of William and Mary, and the recruits started pouring in, with over 1,000 volunteers present by mid-October.

While Henry initially had no difficulty rounding up recruits, the problem of obtaining adequate supplies with which to feed and equip his troops was another matter. The combination of the "Association," which enforced the nonintercourse agreement of the Continental Congress, and Lord Dunmore's fleet of ships lying off Norfolk harbor, made it extremely difficult for the colonists to receive any supplies, either from other colonies or from abroad. Food, particularly beef and salt, was scarce, and even more important, it was proving virtually impossible to get sufficient arms and ammunition. Although Henry had received a bill of exchange in payment for the captured gunpowder, that was about all he had received. The colony was nearly out of gunpowder and it proved extremely difficult to purchase more.[37]

Amidst these difficulties the threat of actual combat with the British mounted. In late October, fearing an attack on Norfolk, the Committee of Safety ordered Colonel Woodford, commander of the Second Regiment, but nominally Henry's subordinate, to Norfolk. On route to Norfolk Woodford and his troops thwarted an effort by Lord Dunmore to burn the town of Hampton, an engagement that, in the words of Pendleton, the chairman of the Committee of Safety, in some measure redeemed "the bleeding Honour of Virginia."[38] But in achieving this first small taste of military success Pendleton had obviously ruffled the feelings of his commander-in-chief. He had passed over Henry and given his orders directly to Woodford, simply informing Henry that he should not delay in helping to carry out the committee's order.

On November 6 Lord Dunmore, still on board his ship in Norfolk harbor, increased pressure on the colony by declaring a state of martial law, pronouncing all able-bodied men who refused to fight for the king traitors, and reiterating his offer of freedom to all slaves and indentured servants who would leave their masters and fight for the Crown.[39] The result of Dunmore's proclamation, however, was not to frighten the Virginians into submission but rather to cause them to increase once again security precautions relating to slaves and to strengthen their determination to fight the British. If there was one event which pushed the Tidewater planter aristocracy into the Revolution it was not the bold actions of Henry or the example of noble Washington, but rather the sheer terror evoked by Dunmore's proclamation.

To meet the challenge posed by Dunmore the Committee of Safety once again turned to Woodford, ordering his regiment to Norfolk, leaving Henry in Williamsburg to guard the town. In fact, Woodford was actually given power to "give notice" to Henry if he should need additional troops from Henry's regiment.[40] On December 9, at Great Bridge near Norfolk, Woodford, following closely his instructions from the Committee of Safety and devising what was acknowledged even by Henry's partisans as excellent strategy, won an impressive victory over Dunmore and some 500 British troops. Equally important for the long-range success of the colonists, the black troops used by Dunmore, having had virtually no training before the encounter, suffered heavy casualties and proved generally unreliable in battle.[41] This one bad experience with the freed blacks as soldiers, an experience that was quite clearly the fault of Lord Dunmore for not taking the time to train them before throwing them into battle, would mark the end of any serious attempts to persuade slaves to join the British side and therefore would mark the end of the most serious threat to their supremacy that the master class of Virginia had ever faced.

Those responsible for the decision to bypass Henry in favor of Woodford must have been pleased when they received word of the successful outcome of this first major military engagement with the British on Virginia soil. Public criticism of the treatment Henry had been receiving had been mounting. By the week before the battle Henry himself was beginning to show discernible signs of pique at Woodford's independent attitude. Woodford, of course, was only following the dictates of the Committee of Safety, but there is no question but that he enjoyed his new status and was not bending over backward to defer to Henry.

The Virginia Convention, which had gone into session on December 1, indirectly took up the whole matter a week after Woodford's victory at Great Bridge. In the election of the new Committee of Safety, Henry's supporter Dudley Digges received the highest number of votes and Pendleton, who had received the most votes the year before, finished fourth in the balloting. Pendleton was hardly on the way out; soon after that vote the Convention unanimously elected him President, to succeed Peyton Randolph, who had died in October.[42]

The Convention nevertheless made some attempt to uphold Henry's commission as commander-in-chief. On December 22 the new Committee of Safety passed a resolution stating that "Colonel Woodford, although acting under separate and detached command, ought to correspond with Colonel Henry, and make return to him at proper times, of the state and condition of the forces under his command; and also that he is subject to his orders, when the Convention, or the committee of safety is not sitting, but that while either of those bodies are sitting, he is to receive his orders from one of them."[43] Thus, the committee drew Woodford's attention to the fact that he had been less than tactful in his dealings with Henry and advised him to consult with his nominal commander more frequently, but at the same time it reiterated its right to go over Henry's head and deal directly with Woodford.

At the root of the controversy over whether the committee's dealings with Woodford and Henry were proper is the interpretation of Henry's initial commission. If Edmund Pendleton's most able biographer is correct in concluding that Henry's commission as commander-in-chief of all Virginia forces was valid only when the two regiments were specifically ordered by the Committee of Safety to join forces, and that in all separate actions the two regiments were to be considered as independent units, then it seems, at least technically, that neither Woodford nor the Committee of Safety can be faulted for impropriety. The question then simply becomes: did the committee choose the best commander of military operations when it selected Woodford over Henry? Of course, Edmund Pendleton thought he had, going so far as to write Woodford: "Believe me, sir, the unlucky step of calling that gentleman [Henry] from our councils, where he was useful, into the field, in an important station, the duties of which he must, in the nature of things, be an entire stranger to, has given me many an anxious and uneasy moment." And even George Washington, writing to Joseph Reed some three months later, expressed the feeling that his "countrymen made a capital mistake, when they took Henry out of the Senate to place him in the field; and pity it is that he does not see this, and remove every difficulty by a voluntary resignation."[44]

By the time Washington wrote those lines, Henry had realized that others besides Pendleton were questioning his abilities as a military commander. On February 13, 1776, the Continental Congress merged the First and Second Virginia Regiments into six continental regiments representing all the thirteen colonies. The Congress reappointed Henry as colonel and commander of the First Virginia Regiment, but he was now put explicitly under the command of two Brigadier Generals, Robert Howe and Andrew Lewis, men who had previously been under his command when the Virginia regiments were operating autonomously. At this stage, with it becoming increasingly clear that the leaders of the American military effort no longer had full confidence in his abilities as a soldier and with friends from Virginia urging him to return to civilian life where his influence might be felt with more effect, Henry declined the commission in the Continental army, thus ending his participation in the military operations of the American Revolution.[45]

The controversy would continue, however, with Henry's supporters using the public prints to vindicate their hero, charging that the Committee of Safety was motivated by envy in undercutting his role and Pendleton's supporters avowing that the committee had not exceeded its authority.[46] There is no evidence that the Committee of Safety played any formal role in depriving Henry of the commission as brigadier general, although it is also clear that individual members of the committee, Pendleton included, had ample opportunity to express their opinion informally of Henry's ability to the members of the Continental Congress.

It was probably a good thing for both Henry and the American war effort that he was forced to suffer this, his first important public failure, for the truth is that, while he did not disgrace himself as a military commander, neither had he shown any great talent for the martial life. His departure from the army would give him the opportunity to return to that theater where he was most effective; and when the Virginia Convention opened in May 1776, he would be in the vanguard of those pushing the colony closer toward a complete separation from the mother country.

Richard Henry Lee, aware of the importance of the upcoming session of the Virginia Convention, had written Henry in April, venturing: "Ages yet unborn, and millions existing at present, must rue or bless that Assembly, on which their happiness or misery will so eminently depend. Virginia has hitherto taken the lead in great affairs, and many now look to her with anxious expectation, hoping that the spirit, wisdom, and energy of her counsels, will rouse America from the fatal lethargy into which feebleness, folly and interested views of the Proprietary governments . . . have thrown her most unhappily."[47] Lee's view of events from the vantage point of the Continental Congress, where leaders of the proprietary colony of Pennsylvania were dragging their feet on the question of independence, was much different from the perspective of the representatives to the Virginia Convention. In fact, Robert Carter Nicholas, the treasurer of the colony, seemed to be the sole member of the provincial elite who was not reconciled to independence. The armed clashes with British troops near Norfolk, together with Dunmore's appeal to the Virginia slave population, caused even the most timid Virginians to recognize that reconciliation with the mother country was now out of the question. Thus, when the Virginia Convention opened on May 6, every one of the 128 delegates was aware of the nature of the business that was about to be transacted.

Actually, the House of Burgesses, the official legislative body of the colony, was scheduled to meet before the Virginia Convention convened, but, its name now associated with royal government, it failed to attract a quorum when it was called into session in October 1775 and March 1776. When it met on May 6, 1776, the keeper of the Journal was forced to note: "Several members met, but neither did proceed to Business, nor adjourn, as an House of Burgesses." With that, the oldest representative body in America passed out of existence, to be replaced by the extralegal Virginia Convention.[48] It is interesting to note, however, that the members of the Convention were repudiating only the symbol of the House of Burgesses and not its form and substance. The structure of the Convention was nearly identical to that of the House of Burgesses, with the President of the Convention taking over the same duties as the Speaker of the House and with the committees in the two bodies performing the same functions and being staffed with the same men.

There were a few new faces in attendance at the Convention. Representing Orange County, just a few years out of Princeton, was twenty-five-year-old James Madison. Serving as an alternate for George Wythe from the town of Williamsburg was twenty-three-year-old Edmund Randolph who, in a ritual symbolic of one generation's commitment to America and an older generation's attachment to the mother country, had stayed behind in Virginia as his father, John Randolph, attorney general of the colony, sailed for England in the late summer of 1775. And Richard S. Taylor from King William County would replace one of the stalwarts of the Virginia political elite, Carter Braxton, who was evidently repudiated by his constituents because of his reluctance to countenance independence. In spite of these changes, however, the more cautious members of the Convention retained their hold over most of the important positions in the new assembly. Edmund Pendleton was once again nominated for the presidency of the Convention, and although Thomas Johnson nominated Thomas Ludwell Lee,

Richard Henry Lee's brother and a partisan of Henry, Pendleton won the contest easily.[49] Henry himself opposed the challenge to Pendleton, but it is doubtful if the insurgents would have been capable of unseating Pendleton even with Henry's support. Most of Virginia's political leaders were coming around to support Henry's position with respect to the need for staunch resistance to England, but Pendleton, by dint of his past service and prestige, remained the man to whom they entrusted the reins of government.

From May 6 to May 14 the Convention was occupied with many of the practical concerns of waging an undeclared war with England—the safeguarding of surplus provisions, the overseeing of the slave populations in Norfolk and Princess Anne Counties, the manufacture of saltpeter, salt, and gunpowder, and the dispatching of troops to aid neighboring North Carolina. On May 14 the Convention dissolved into a Committee of the Whole to discuss the general state of the colony, and it was at this time that the question for independence was officially introduced.[50]

According to Edmund Randolph, the sentiment in the Convention was very much in favor of allowing "Mr. Henry . . . to crown his political conduct with this supreme stroke," but surprisingly, Henry initially held back. Randolph claimed that Henry "thought that a cause which put at stake the lives and fortunes of the people should appear to be their own act, and that he ought not to place upon the responsibility of his eloquence, a revolution of which the people might be weaned after the present stimulus should cease to operate."[51] It is even more likely, however, that in holding back briefly from the "supreme stroke," Henry wanted to use the prevailing sentiment for independence to obtain a commitment from his fellow Virginians to press both for a firmer union among the colonies and for aid from foreign nations such as France. Henry had recently been impressed by a letter from Richard Henry Lee on those subjects and, while there is absolutely no sign that he was having second thoughts about the wisdom of independence, it is clear that he was beginning to think about some of the steps necessary to cope with the broader ramifications of that momentous step.[52]

At this stage in his career, Henry was quite willing to resort to a union of the states, even a tightly centralized one, if that was what was necessary to obtain independence. Union of course was not an end in itself, but rather was only a means to protect the provincial interests of Virginia. Over a decade later, when Henry so vigorously opposed a stronger union, he was once again guided by his view, and at times it was an exceptionally narrow one, of what would best serve the particular interests of Virginia.

Actually, there were three sets of resolutions for independence introduced into the House at that time, with a fourth, compromise set ultimately adopted. One set, drafted by Meriwether Smith of Essex County, was the most equivocal. While it proclaimed "the government of this colony . . . dissolved," and recommended that a committee draw up a new plan of government, it did not make any reference to a general American move for independence and presumably could have left the door open for reconciliation. A second set of resolutions, most often attributed to Pendleton, went much further. After a brief but vigorous indictment of Parliament and the King, the "Pendleton Draft" resolved "that the union that has hitherto subsisted between Great Britain and the American colonies is thereby totally dissolved, and that the inhabitants of this colony are discharged from any allegiance to the crown of Great Britain."[53] This was clearly more decisive than anything contained in Smith's resolutions.

Patrick Henry's resolutions, which were introduced by Thomas Nelson in what seems to have been a conscious attempt by Henry to downgrade his role at this, the climax of his efforts for the past decade, were somewhat more far-reaching. Prefaced by a denunciation of the British acts that had led America to this point, they next proclaimed Virginia free of all allegiance to the Crown and called for such "measures as may conduce to the good and happiness of the *united* colonies," thus emphasizing Henry's increasing concern for intercolonial unity. And finally, Henry did not want merely to leave the matter with the Virginia Convention. He asked "that our delegates in Congress be enjoined in the strongest and most positive manner to exert their ability in procuring an immediate and full Declaration of Independency."[54]

The compromise resolutions that were ultimately adopted, prepared by Edmund Pendleton and approved by the Convention the next day, were, for Henry, "not quite so pointed as I could wish," but they nevertheless embodied most of the points contained in his own resolutions and yet were moderately worded enough that even Robert Carter Nicholas, the one man in the Convention who was known to be dubious about independence, was persuaded not to record his opposition to the step, thus allowing the vote on independence to be recorded as unanimous.[55]

The Virginia Resolutions of May 1776, which would provide the stimulus for the Continental Congress's move toward independence, would, alas, not win any awards for literary grace. In the words of David Mays, Pendleton's generally admiring biographer, "It is a pity that in his anxiety to wipe out the King's authority, he took such liberties with the King's English."[56] The principal difference between Pendleton's and Henry's drafts was that, while Henry's had Virginia unilaterally declaring herself independent, the Pendleton draft only instructed the Virginia delegates to the Continental Congress to propose American independence to that body.

Although he had not penned the final product, Henry could with some justification take much of the credit for the decisive step the Virginia legislators had just taken. One is not exaggerating Henry's importance in asserting that he, more than any other individual in the colony, was responsible for leading public sentiment toward the position of independence. Beginning with his debut in the House of Burgesses in 1765, he had always been just a bit bolder than any of his contemporaries in calling for resistance to British authority. While his attention seemed occasionally to be diverted from the constitutional struggle with England during the years 1766 to 1773, this could be said of nearly everyone in America. With the possible exception of Sam Adams, Americans in the 1760s and early 1770s were unwilling to respond vigorously to the British unless their interests were directly threatened. When British policy did begin once again to threaten Virginian interests—as they did in the form of the Coercive Acts and in Lord Dunmore's frequent proroguing of the House of Burgesses—Henry quickly resumed his bold stance of 1765. Although he seemingly faltered for a few days between the opening of the Convention on May 6 and May 14, that hesitation was due to a concern to draw attention to other necessary steps to secure independence and was not an excuse to avoid taking that crucial step. And, by the time the topic was formally introduced into the Convention, Henry was once again the man urging the most decisive course.

It is difficult to explain why Henry, or indeed any Virginian, should have exerted such forceful leadership in the movement for independence in America. There were few outward signs of British "oppression" in Virginia during the 1760s and 1770s. Boston, New York, Philadelphia, and Charleston all saw and felt the effects of British policy more than any town or region in Virginia. There were, after all, few British soldiers or customs collectors stationed in Virginia. Yet Virginians, along with the citizens of Massachusetts, were far ahead of citizens from other colonies at each stage in the struggle with England.

One plausible explanation for this fact has been suggested by historian Jack P. Greene, who interprets the struggle between England and America as primarily a dispute between royal government and the lower houses of assembly.[57] The two assemblies with the greatest traditions of autonomy and independent accomplishment were in fact those of Massachusetts and Virginia. The anger within those two colonial assemblies was therefore particularly intense when the British Parliament began to claim power over areas of legislation—finance, defense, parliamentary procedure—in which the colonial assemblies had traditionally exercised power. Moreover, the anger between assembly and royal government was not long confined merely to disputes over authority. As royal governors gave angry lectures to colonial assemblies, and ultimately used their power to prorogue them, the struggle soon became an intensely personal one. Some within the Virginia provincial elite—those who had enjoyed many years of cordial relations with royal governors in the past—were initially anxious to preserve harmony with royal officials. Patrick Henry, who had never been included in the circle of those favored by the governors, was much less likely to be moved by those considerations. By the end of Lord Dunmore's first year in office, many of the former friends of the royal government in Virginia had come around to Henry's position. They possessed, after all, a long and honorable tradition as responsible legislators, and Dunmore's contempt for their authority as legislators represented not only a violation of the principles embodied in the British Constitution but a direct assault on their prestige and honor as well.

Increasingly, as Bernard Bailyn has demonstrated, American provincial leaders interpreted these assaults on their rights and their honor as a deliberate and conscious conspiracy to destroy their liberties.[58] Accustomed to viewing their own political process as virtuous and that of England as corrupt, they transformed the struggle with England from that of a serious but not momentous difference of opinion over the limits of parliamentary power in America to one where the basic liberties of all Americans were at stake. It is within this increasingly emotional—indeed, some would term it paranoid—style of political discourse that Lord Dunmore issued his call to the slave population of Virginia. This act gave added substance to the fears of every member of the provincial elite, no matter how close his ties to the royal government may previously have been.

It was at this stage that men who had previously abhorred Henry's harsh rhetoric toward the Crown began to endorse the substance of his position. This is not to say that Henry led the colony into the Revolution singlehandedly. Men like Richard Bland, Edmund Pendleton, and even that extremely reluctant revolutionist Robert Carter Nicholas, members of the upper strata of the provincial elite, agreed with the essence of Henry's proposals, but were left with the task of moderating them, making them more palatable for those who were more timid. As we will see, Henry was no radical when it came time to build a new social and political order in Virginia, but he was, when compared to the class of men who had traditionally dominated the House of Burgesses, at least a somewhat more impetuous and less tradition-bound member of that ruling class. It is in some ways a tribute to the wisdom and flexibility of the leaders of the Virginia ruling elite that they were able to expand their ranks, albeit grudgingly, to admit a man of such obvious talents as Patrick Henry. They were hardly admitting a member of the "vulgar herd" to their number, as Henry certainly had enough advantages to qualify him as an important man within the somewhat smaller world of his home county, but he was not yet in 1776 a man of the same lofty social and economic position of the other leaders of the Virginia provincial elite.

When some of the citizens of Williamsburg, on hearing that the Virginia Resolutions for independence passed the Convention unanimously, raced to the top of the Capitol to lower the Union Jack, substituting for it a "Continental" flag, they were not signaling the end of the divisions that existed among the members of the provincial elite. For those divisions would continue at least into the

1780s, when Henry himself would acquire the economic power and social prestige that would render him indistinguishable from the Pendletons and the Nicholases. While the action of the Virginia Convention may not have ended all divisions within the colony, it did, insofar as America's destiny as a nation was concerned, mark the beginning of a new era.

5

A Local Politician

Henry was building a reputation as an important force to be reckoned with in the local politics of the colony at the same time that he was gaining recognition as a vigorous spokesman for his colony against the policies of the imperial government. It was in fact his attachment to localist traditions of government, and to concrete economic and political interests within his own region, first in the Virginia Piedmont and later in the far southwest, that guided his conduct throughout his political career, whether that career led him to the county court, the Assembly, or to the governor's mansion.

Hanover County, the constituency which Henry represented during the years leading up to the Revolution, was located in the eastern Piedmont and possessed a population of close to 10,000 in 1776. The county was rural even by the standards of agrarian Virginia. It had no newspapers, no post office, and in fact as late as 1800 had no town or hamlet within its boundaries possessing even fifty houses. Its economy was not, however, a subsistence one, as more than half its population was composed of African slaves, a sure sign that at least the economic elite of the region was engaged in the cultivation of an export crop. Historically the county had been one of the first regions in Virginia to feel the effects of the Great Awakening, and one of Henry's continuing strengths within his home county was his ability to retain the confidence of both dissenters and the gentry who controlled the Anglican vestry.[1]

Henry's attachment to local interests was apparent in his very first appearance in the controversy surrounding the Parsons' Cause. Although frequently represented as a stand by a united Virginia against royal tyranny, the case was, as we have seen, characteristic of the relatively weak state of the Anglican clergy and a typical example of the way in which the backcountry residents sought to avoid tax payments. The desire of the Hanover County residents was particularly strong in this case, as that county was a center of strength for dissenters and as such could be expected to favor any steps which might lessen their financial obligation to the Anglican clergy.

Henry's second major recorded public stand—an action that occurred just a few days before his celebrated Stamp Act speech—provides us with an even clearer glimpse of the local politician at work. In this case, unlike that of the Parsons' Cause, Henry's defense of local interests put him squarely at odds with many of the principal figures within the provincial elite. On May 24, 1765, four days after he had taken a seat in the House, a bill to establish a public loan office was introduced on the floor of the Assembly. The bill called for the creation of a fund of £240,000 to be borrowed in Great Britain at 5 percent interest and to be paid back by yearly taxes on tobacco exports and by a poll tax. The purpose of the loan office was twofold: it was intended to redeem the approximately £100,000 worth of paper money issued during the French and Indian War and to provide for a £140,000 fund to be lent out on permanent security (land, slaves, etc.) at an interest of 5 percent. Thus it was intended not only as a way of eliminating the public debt but as a future source of capital as well.

The plan seemed like a good way to improve the supply of liquid capital in specie-poor Virginia, but, although the details were not made fully public in 1765, there were some questionable aspects underlying the scheme. In particular, it seemed to some as if the Speaker of the House and treasurer of the colony John Robinson was interested in using the loan fund to bail himself and many of his Tidewater friends out of debt. Robinson, discovering that a substantial number of his friends within the Virginia ruling elite had gone deeply into debt as a result of the combined effect of several bad tobacco crops and the expenses of the French and Indian War, was generous enough to loan money to his friends to help them out of their temporary financial embarrassment. A magnanimous gesture indeed, the only trouble being that the money loaned to those gentlemen—a group including such illustrious names as Edmund

Pendleton, Carter Braxton, Peyton Randolph, and Benjamin Harrison—came straight from the public treasury.[2] Apparently John Robinson and the Tidewater provincial elite had decided that not only political office and personal prestige were their private domains, but the public monies as well.

Robinson's manipulation of the public accounts did not go entirely unsuspected. Richard Henry Lee, a persistent and prestigious opponent of Robinson from the time he first became a burgess in 1758, had already begun a campaign to make certain that the treasurer's activities were supervised more closely. By 1763 Lee had warned that the deficit in the treasury was "sufficient to alarm not the merchants of Britain only, but every thinking person." According to the later testimony of Thomas Jefferson, the loan office plan would have guaranteed that "the debts due to Robinson . . . [on the treasury money loaned to his friends] would have been transferred to the public, & his deficit thus completely covered."[3] Thus when the House of Burgesses began consideration of the plan, there were probably a number of burgesses who were suspicious of the motives of the supporters of the bill, even though the precise details of Robinson's financial dealing were not yet fully known by anyone in the House. At the going rate of exchange, the £100,000 of the loan aimed at redeeming the remainder of the colony's paper currency deficit would just about cover the debts of Robinson's friends, making it necessary for them to pay only a few pennies on the dollar toward their accounts. The £140,000 loan fund, a fund that was accessible only to those men of substantial enough property to be able to put up large amounts of "permanent security," would also have benefited primarily those wealthy and well-born men in Robinson's circle of acquaintance.

Although Richard Henry Lee was absent from the 1765 session, Henry, newly elected and at this time sharing few of the interests of wealthy Tidewater magnates like Robinson, Archibald Carey, and William Byrd, was present in his stead. He urged the House to defeat the bill, exclaiming: "What sir! Is it proposed then to reclaim a Spendthrift from his dissipation and extravagance by filling his pocket with monies?"[4] When one recognizes that this rhetoric was undoubtedly viewed not simply as an abstract statement on the evils of extravagance but rather as an explicit attack on the leadership of the Assembly, then one is no longer surprised at Henry's sudden emergence as an important insurgent figure in the House of Burgesses. His attack on the grandees of the provincial elite—a group whose members were concentrated in the Tidewater but who were tied to one another more by family and personal influence than by geography—would be followed just a few days later by an attack on royal authority, thus identifying him nearly immediately as a rallying point for two kinds of opposition—to the control by the Tidewater elite of the political machinery within Virginia and to the policies of the royal government in London.

Henry soon discovered, as he often would during his early years as a burgess, that he was outnumbered in the Assembly, but this time the Governor's Council, realizing that "to tax the People that are not in debt to lend to those that are is highly unjust . . . ," killed the measure anyway.[5] It was after the defeat of this measure, which most of the burgesses thought was the major item of business of the session, that many of the most prominent members of the House left for their homes. And it was the departure of these men that allowed Henry to push his Stamp Act Resolves through a half-filled House.

John Robinson was to die the following year, and when his lawyers examined his estate they would discover the details of his generosity. The total sum owed to Robinson amounted to £250,000, a fabulous sum of money by eighteenth-century Virginia standards. Pendleton, an administrator of Robinson's estate as well as one of the men in debt to that estate, was probably the first to discover that more than £100,000 of the money Robinson had loaned out had indeed come from the colony's treasury. Moreover, it was obvious that some officials had been at least vaguely aware of the impropriety all along; Archibald Cary, for example, had audited the treasury accounts in 1765 and had claimed that they were in order. The fact that he owed Robinson £3,950 himself may have been a factor in his overlooking the slight deficit of £100,000.[6]

When the Virginia House of Burgesses convened in November 1766, there were two related problems confronting the ruling elite. The first was the simple need to avoid scandal by preventing the details of the affair from being made public. Second, Robinson's supporters wanted to thwart attempts to separate the offices of the speaker and the treasurer, a move that might have the effect of dividing their power. The proponents of the separation of the two offices now had a concrete example of the potential for conflict of interest inherent in Robinson's dominance of both posts.

The logical choice as successor to Robinson was Peyton Randolph, a man who, in the eyes of the Royal Governor, had the same "good qualities of his late most intimate Friend."[7] It is perhaps not too much to say that, had the supporters of Randolph succeeded in elevating him to both the speakership and the treasurer's office, they might have been able to suppress nearly all talk of scandal in association with Robinson's name. The Assembly, on the opening day of the session in 1766, quickly moved to elect Randolph speaker, but Robert Carter Nicholas, a long-standing rival of the Randolphs, stole the initiative from Randolph's supporters by mounting a vigorous campaign for the office of treasurer. In his "campaign," Nicholas actually took the unusual step of writing to every burgess soliciting his vote, intimating in his communications that there were improprieties in the way in which Robinson had fulfilled his duties and implying that the offices of speaker and treasurer should be separated in the future to avoid conflict of interest. He even went so far as to defend his bid for the treasurer's office publicly, announcing in the pages of Purdie's and Dixon's *Virginia Gazette* that he suspected mismanagement of the treasury and affirming his belief that the combination of the offices of treasurer and speaker gave too much influence in the legislature to the speaker. And finally, he let drop the fact that the treasury had a deficit of some £80,000 to £90,000. In short, the private preserve of the Virginia ruling elite had suddenly been opened to the public for inspection.[8]

When the Assembly met in the first week of November, the public mind was thus inflamed not only with the threat posed by British royal authority but also by the peculations of their former speaker and treasurer. In fact, in some counties the usually apathetic citizens actually instructed their representatives to vote for the separation of the offices of speaker and treasurer. Instruction of representatives, although common in Massachusetts town meetings, was a device rarely utilized in Virginia, where constituents regularly deferred to the judgment of their representatives. It seems clear that Robinson's abuse of power, along with the implication that others may have shared in that abuse, resulted in a sudden awakening of a long dormant interest in the behavior of the power holders of the colony.

This reawakening assumes particular importance when seen in the context of the impending crisis with England; at a time when the colonists were rejecting the British principles of virtual representation and demanding that America's interests be directly represented in Parliament with respect to issues of taxation and finance, the cavalier attitude of Virginia's representatives toward the question of the internal finances of the colony could hardly escape notice.

The ruling elite was forced to give ground. Although Peyton Randolph was elevated to the speakership with virtually no opposition, Robert Carter Nicholas's campaigning paid off in the contest for treasurer. In addition to his election as treasurer, Nicholas teamed up with the supporters of Richard Henry Lee, whom Nicholas had long been at odds with on other political questions, to voice publicly their objections to the combination of the offices of speaker and treasurer. In this endeavor they were aided by Henry, who not only was called upon to second the resolution condemning the combination of the two offices but who also spoke eloquently against what he termed "the dangerous system" of multiple office-holding. And for once, the Tidewater elite failed to rally enough burgesses to their side, as the resolution put forward by Nicholas, Lee, and Henry was passed 68 to 29.[9]

The Tidewater elite was thus forced to yield some power to a principally western and slightly less prestigious insurgent group. It is incorrect, however, to interpret this as a victory for a "democratic" or "liberal" faction over an entrenched, "conservative" party. The opposition factions in Virginia were never sufficiently cohesive to be united under any one label and never stayed together long enough to threaten to displace the Tidewater ruling elite. The faction that challenged Randolph and Pendleton at this juncture was composed of such diverse people as Nicholas and Richard Bland, both reluctant Revolutionists in 1776, and, at the other extreme, Richard Henry Lee, a man who spent most of his life opposing Nicholas and his supporters, and of course Henry, who was not yet fully accepted even by the likes of Bland and Nicholas. There was simply no way that these men could agree with enough consistency on the wide range of issues confronting the colony to constitute a cohesive party in the Assembly.

It was not solely the weakness of the opposition forces that contributed to the continued dominance of the Tidewater elite, for that elite was always responsive and resilient. Never in their history did the members of that elite remain obstinate to change or reform. Faced with opposition to the continued combination of the offices of speaker and treasurer, many of Pendleton's and Randolph's supporters temporarily joined that opposition. Moreover, even those who continued to advocate the retention of the old system were not so dogmatic about it that they lost credibility with their former supporters. Men like Pendleton and Randolph were in the end exceptionally flexible and thus, when it came time to constitute a committee to investigate the past conduct of the treasurer's office, they managed to dominate the group charged with the task. The opposition was also represented—both Lee and Henry were appointed to the eleven-man committee—but the presence of Pendleton, Archibald Cary, and Landon Carter was indicative of the continued strength of the Tidewater elite. Nor did these men betray the trust that had been placed in them. When they issued their report on December 12, they did not attempt to hide the fact that Robinson's estate was in debt to the colony for over £100,000.[10]

The entire episode, the repercussions of which were felt even after the Revolution, was indicative of the interlocking character of Virginia politics. It was, or at least it should have been, clear after the report of the committee that Robinson's popularity among the burgesses rested on more than his personable manner. Indeed, Robinson, through the powers of his offices, had extraordinary political leverage at his disposal to maintain or even enhance his power. Doubtless he would have been surprised by the fuss over the state of accounts after his death. He most likely hoped to pay the treasury back and would have considered any public questioning of his conduct a violation of the gentlemanly code upon which the burgesses operated. He probably would have particularly resented the fact that an upstart like Henry, with little experience and little tangible accomplishment in life, should question the integrity of people of means and stature like himself, Pendleton, or Randolph. To complete the irony of Robinson's fall from grace, Henry would later purchase Robinson's magnificent Scotchtown plantation in Hanover County, there to enjoy at least a part of the bounty that the former speaker and treasurer had claimed.

The Robinson affair, though hardly a watershed in Virginia political history, did at least mark the beginning of a trend. From that point on, men like Henry would find the ruling elite a bit more vulnerable; they would defer to the judgment of the members of that elite less and less until, by the eve of the Revolution, they actually came to share power with them. It is important to note, however, that they would come to *share* power with them and *not* overthrow them. For, as we have emphasized all along, the diversity of the opposition, combined with the flexibility of the established, provincial elite, made impossible and perhaps unnecessary a total repudiation of the personnel and policies of the traditional ruling class.

Henry's position on other issues of local concern at this time is best glimpsed from a fragment of a manuscript drafted by him sometime between 1765 and 1770. It is seemingly one of the few extended pieces of writing he ever indulged in, or at least one of the few he saved; though incomplete, it provides us with some indication of his views on a number of matters important to the colony.

Henry's thoughts on the wisdom of an established church—a subject that consistently divided the predominantly Anglican Tidewater and the more heterogeneous west, occupied the most space in the fragment and, given his position on the question just a few years later, is worth noting. At this stage in his career Henry was convinced that the best way to ensure the maintenance of public morality was through a "virtuous" clergy, not an established church. Although he granted that "much learning hath been displayed to shew the necessity of establishing one church in England," he was convinced that the situation in the colonies was considerably different. His concern for religious toleration seems to have been not so much philosophical as it was practical. He was worried about what he considered to be the retarded state of development in Virginia. He noted with the certain eye of the land speculator that lands in Pennsylvania were worth five times those of Virginia; the reason, according to Henry, was that "Pennsylvania is the country of the most extensive privileges. . . ." It had the fewest slaves and "a Dutch, Irish or Scotch emigrant finds there his religion, his priest, his language, his manners, and everything, but that poverty and oppression he left at home." This influx of free white immigrants to Virginia, immigrants who would bring them the skills necessary to stimulate the development of manufactures in the Old Dominion, was for Henry the key to a healthy, prosperous society. He opposed those schemes which offered bounties to prospective manufacturers on the ground that no amount of effort or money would achieve the desired result without the necessary pool of skilled labor. And immigration provided the means to secure that pool of labor.[11]

Henry's views on the established church placed him at odds with the overwhelmingly Anglican, Tidewater-based leadership in the House of Burgesses. But Henry would find, shortly after the Revolution, that a substantial number of the members of the Tidewater aristocracy would prove flexible on the issue of separation of church and state and ultimately would cast their votes in favor of disestablishment. In fact, it would be Patrick Henry, suddenly more concerned with the maintenance of morality in his home state and not with freedom of religion for prospective immigrants, who would become one of the most outspoken advocates of state-supported religion.

The same uneasiness with respect to Virginia's economic development shaped Henry's thinking on the subject of slavery. It is possible in the case of Henry, as it is with most prominent Virginians in the eighteenth century, to unearth a few statements indicating moral disgust with the institution of slavery. There is no question but that he viewed with alarm the possibility that his country was becoming the "gloomy retreat of slaves." The major cause for his alarm, however, was not a sympathy with the plight of black bondsmen but rather the belief that Africans could never attain the skills necessary to bring Virginia beyond its rude agrarian state. Moreover, it is likely that Henry, like most Americans, believed that the Africans' shortcomings extended beyond the realm of economic efficiency. At the core of eighteenth-century "country whig" ideology lay the notions that the ownership of land was the primary source of an individual's independence and that the only means of ensuring the maintenance of a virtuous, republican society was to be certain that such a society be principally composed of free, propertied men, capable of defending their rights in a "well-regulated militia." That ideology did not preclude the ownership of slaves— indeed, most Whigs took for granted the existence of a servile, unpropertied class in almost every society—but it certainly did point in a most explicit fashion to the dangers inherent in a society overloaded with unfree and unpropertied members.[12] Dunmore's proclamation offering freedom to those slaves who deserted their masters and fought with the British would bring those dangers into dramatic relief. Had Dunmore's "sable regiments" been given more time to train themselves, the very social order of the Old Dominion could have been turned on its head.

Henry's own political world view harmonized nearly perfectly with the "country whig" ideology; his concern for the maintenance of virtue in society was one of the few constants in an otherwise erratic political philosophy. In one sense, of course, his concern about the effects of slavery on virtue was a highly moralistic one, but that morality was related mainly to the welfare of whites, not African slaves.

This is not to say that Henry was totally unconcerned with the morality of involuntary servitude in its own right. In a letter to Quaker leader Robert Pleasants acknowledging receipt of an anti-slavery tract by the Quaker philanthropist Anthony Benezet, Henry could do nothing but "wonder . . . that this abominable practice has been introduced in the most enlightened ages." He was particularly appalled by the fact that Virginians, at precisely the time at which they were fighting for liberty against the British, were embracing "a principle as repugnant to humanity, as it is inconsistent with the bible, and destructive to liberty." Like most of his Virginia neighbors, however, Henry equivocated on his sense of outrage over the institution. In that same letter Henry exclaimed: "Would anyone believe I am the master of slaves of my own purchase! I am drawn along by the general inconvenience of living here without them." Nor was he altogether sanguine about the ultimate abolition of slavery. The only hope he could offer was to "transmit to our descendants, together with our slaves, a pity for their unhappy lot, and an abhorrence of slavery. If we cannot reduce the wished-for reformation to practice, let us treat the unhappy victim with lenity. It is the furthest advance we can make toward justice."[13]

We find in Henry, then, a man who readily confessed to the barbarity and immorality of slavery, but who, when faced with these facts, could only affirm that he would strive to be more lenient in his treatment of the victims of that immorality. Indeed, we find Henry, in the years after he penned those sentiments, progressively adding to his guilt by the purchase of even more slaves.

Was it simply hypocrisy, this uttering of pious sentiments to

Quaker antislavery advocates while at the same time purchasing slaves for his own use and comfort? If it was not hypocrisy, then it was at least self-deception on a grand scale. But the explanation for the gap between Henry's rhetoric and the reality of his slave purchases cannot merely stop there. As Winthrop Jordan has so ably demonstrated, the complex overlay of preexisting racial and religious prejudice, the subsequent need to rationalize the existence of the institution, and the potent strain of guilt—both religious and sexual—that flowed from the contradictions between doctrine and practice in America all combined to make men like Patrick Henry extraordinarily ill-equipped to see their inconsistencies in dealing with the "peculiar institution."

Although at least one Henry biographer has labeled his subject "courageous" for his denunciation of slavery to Benezet, that condemnation in fact went no further than those of most prominent Virginians.[14] It was not until the 1830s that it became inexpedient for Southerners to condemn the slave system and, in the unlikely event that his private expression of sentiment to Benezet was ever made public, Henry would have found that most of his political opponents from the Tidewater shared his uneasiness over the institution. And like Henry, they too would act to buttress rather than weaken the institution when faced with the reality of the slave system in their capacity as legislators. In addition to enacting legislation restricting assemblies of blacks, establishing monthly patrols to investigate the security systems of the plantations, and regulating closely the movements of individual slaves, Virginia's legislators would ultimately move to erect new obstacles preventing the attainment of freedom by legal means.[15]

It is generally customary to move from a discussion of Henry's position on the important issues of the day to an analysis of his "democratic" or "liberal" political and social philosophy. What seems most clear after studying those issues, though, is that the categories of "liberal" versus "conservative" or "democrat" versus "aristocrat" do not adequately account for the range of interests and ideas that seemed to be motivating Henry either in his career as a spokesman for the interests of his county in the affairs of the colony or in his role as a defender of the rights of his colony in the affairs of the British empire. Henry's challenge to the traditional ruling elite in Virginia—a challenge based both on his own very different economic and regional orientation and on his impatience with the timidity of men like Pendleton in the constitutional dispute with England—was not the outgrowth of any fundamental difference in political philosophy.

Admittedly, Henry, though hardly from an underprivileged background, did represent a new and different type of politician in Virginia, a politician without the refinement or the extraordinary economic power of the most prominent burgesses in preceding generations. In that sense his rise to prominence did signal a small change in the political structure of the Old Dominion. But there is little evidence that Henry's rise to power opened the floodgate to allow other, less prominent men into the political leadership. Recent studies of Virginia politics in the last decade of the eighteenth century indicate that the people who controlled the business of the independent state were virtually indistinguishable in wealth and prestige from those who controlled the business of the colony before the Revolution.[16] In Henry's own case he simply increased his wealth and prestige until he too had a legitimate claim to the economic power, with its consequent social elevation, that was the prerequisite for political power.

Henry's rise to eminence, if it did not signify a democratization of Virginia politics, did at least represent the strengthening of one elite group at the expense of another, more established elite. The elite which Henry represented—younger, western, more responsive to dissenting religious groups and less attached by sentimental or political ties to the mother country—would play an ever-increasing role in Revolutionary Virginia. To best understand the strengths and the limits of the "radicalism" of this new group, we must turn now to the role played by Henry in the internal affairs of Virginia in the years immediately following the Declaration of Independence.

6

Patrick Henry as Revolutionary Statesman: The Limits of Virginia Radicalism

When Virginia declared itself independent on May 15, 1776, it also declared null and void all those English laws, charters, and ordinances upon which the citizens of the Old Dominion had based their political and legal institutions. Virginians, along with Americans from the other twelve colonies, had made a gradual philosophical transition during the years 1774 to 1776. No longer were they relying merely on a legalistic argument based on their interpretation of the English Constitution; by the eve of independence they were, by necessity, using the natural rights philosophy to justify their refusal to consent to the unconstitutional acts of the English King and Parliament. According to the tenets of that doctrine, the Virginians were no longer bound by English laws after their declaration of independence but rather were thrust back into a society of virtue, without laws or political institutions.

Nearly all Virginia's political leaders probably accepted the basic precepts of the natural rights philosophy, although their comprehension of the implications of that philosophy varied drastically. But if nearly all Virginia's leaders used the natural rights philosophy as their central justification for independence, virtually none of them felt comfortable about the idea of staying in a state of nature any longer than was absolutely necessary. Once independence was achieved, the potential dangers of the natural rights philosophy were made manifest. If the people had the power to reject the authority of the English King, then they also possessed the authority to cast aside their representatives at home. Until a new frame of government was drafted to replace the old colonial charter, any institutions used by the old provincial elite to govern the new independent state were not strictly legal ones, but rather temporary, ad hoc mechanisms without permanent legitimacy. It is not surprising, then, that all the members of the Virginia ruling class agreed on the necessity of moving quickly to draft a new constitution for their independent state, a constitution that would take their society out of a precarious state of nature and place it back into a society of law.

It was this act of constitution making that has given historians one of their best glimpses of the possibilities for social and political reform inherent in the American Revolutionary movement. For if the leaders of the Revolution in America considered themselves genuine social reformers, they would never have a better opportunity to implement their ideas for reform. In the act of constitution making, they had given themselves the chance to make a completely fresh start in formulating the institutions under which their society would operate. If there ever was a potential for the expression of an authentic radicalism in the American Revolution, the opportunity for the fulfillment of that potential came during the period of the framing of the independent state governments.

Given the background and character of the men who found themselves in control of the situation immediately after independence had been declared, it should not be surprising that a major social revolution did not accompany the separation with England. With the notable exception of the recent encroachments on their power by the King and Parliament, the members of the provincial elite in Virginia had benefited from the structure of government under their old colonial charter. The undemocratic county court system had given them a strong base of power at the local level, and through that control they had monopolized access to the House of Burgesses, where they had dominated the internal affairs of the colony. Not surprisingly, a great many of Virginia's political leaders desired only to eliminate the influence of the Crown in the affairs of their colony and to leave the structure of provincial politics untouched.

A closer examination of the crucial months following the Declaration of Independence—a period that saw Patrick Henry elected as the first governor of the independent state of Virginia, a new state constitution drafted and approved, and the formulation of a Declaration of Rights—gives us a somewhat clearer picture of both the political ideology of Patrick Henry and of the nature and consequences of the Revolution in the Old Dominion.

The thirty-two-man committee appointed to draft a Declaration of Rights and a constitution was, according to George Mason, "overcharged with useless members."[1] Mason would not have placed Henry in that category, but it nevertheless was Mason, not Henry, who deserved most of the credit for drafting both documents. The Declaration of Rights, which would later serve as the principal source for the Bill of Rights of the United States Constitution, was an important statement of intent, but it would mean relatively little without accompanying legislation to implement the principles which it enunciated.

The very first sentence of Mason's proposed draft of the Declaration caused a division in the Virginia Convention. According to Ludwell Lee, "a certain set of Aristocrats" in the Convention, led by Robert Carter Nicholas, opposed the opening line of the Declaration, which read: "that all men are created equally free and independent and have certain inherent and natural rights, of which they cannot, by any Compact, deprive or divert their posterity; among which are the enjoyment of life and liberty, with the means of acquiring and possessing property, and pursuing and obtaining happiness and safety." Nicholas and other conservatives in the Convention feared that the phrase might be a "forerunner . . . of civil convulsion," as there was one significant class of people in Virginia—the entire slave population—that was systematically denied precisely those rights. Nicholas, far from arguing that slaves *should* enjoy those rights, wanted it spelled out as clearly as possible that they should *not* possess them. An amendment offered by Pendleton, affirming that all men possessed equal rights *"when they enter into a state of society,"* eliminated the source of contention between Nicholas and Mason, Henry, and their supporters. Since all Virginians steadfastly refused to consider the slave population as a part of their own society, Pendleton's phraseology permitted the framers of the Declaration of Rights to exclude that population from the protection of their laws and constitution.[2]

One must ponder the sentiments of men like Henry at this juncture. If there was ever a point in Virginia history that was propitious for at least the amelioration of some of the harshest features of the institution of slavery, this was it. The conservatives had made the contradiction between the libertarian doctrine of the Declaration of Rights and the inhumanity of involuntary servitude explicit. Yet when faced with that contradiction, the "radicals" in the Convention—even those like Henry who had previously expressed their abhorrence of the institution in private—merely acquiesced to a change of wording in the Declaration that simply defined the black population right out of the body politic.

Winthrop Jordan has brilliantly elucidated the ever-deepening cycle of racial guilt and fears in eighteenth-century America that prevented Virginians, indeed prevented all Americans, from abandoning their racism and extending the black man the same liberty for which they so bravely fought in the Revolution; but to understand the psychological forces is not to absolve Virginians of the brutal effects of them.[3] Patrick Henry had several times in the past decried the evils of slavery; indeed he had specifically called for the amelioration of some of the harsher aspects of the institution. Yet when an opportunity was offered to speak out in favor of that amelioration—to extend some legal rights to the slave or to place some curbs on the master's total control over his life and limbs, for example—Henry, like nearly every other Virginian, remained silent.

If the Declaration of Rights offered no comfort for slaves, it did at least lay down some important guarantees for the white population. The fifth resolution, asserting the principle of separation of powers; the eighth and eleventh, guaranteeing trial by jury; the ninth, prohibiting unlawful search and seizure; and the twelfth, upholding the principle of freedom of the press, were all important restatements of rights that Virginians had supposed were previously protected under English law. That Virginians thought it necessary to spell out those rights explicitly marked an important theoretical step, for as Gordon Wood has noted, Americans came to believe that constitutions differed from mere legislation and that it was the function of those constitutions to guarantee the fundamental liberties of the people against encroachments from future governors or legislators.[4]

The sixteenth and last resolution was perhaps of the most immediate importance. It stated

> that religion, or the duty which we owe to our Creator, and the manner of discharging it, can be directed only by reason and conviction, not by force or violence: and, therefore, all men are equally entitled to the free exercise of religion, according to the dictates of conscience.[5]

This affirmation of the principle of religious toleration was in itself an important step in a society which still persecuted Catholics and Jews, but it is a mistake to view it as a wholesale attack on the established church. In just a few years men like Madison and Jefferson would be in the forefront of the move to separate church and state—a move opposed by Henry—but in 1776 the framers of the Virginia Declaration of Rights were taking great pains to assure members of the Convention that the resolution concerning religious toleration was *not* a prelude to an attack on the established church. At this time in his career Henry was closely identified with the dissenting sects, and a number of the delegates to the Convention were concerned that he might use the resolution as a device for disestablishment.

Indeed, the resolution would materially aid the forces for separation of church and state, but it would not be from Henry that the challenge to the established church would come. When the proponents of disestablishment achieved their final victory in 1786, Henry, increasingly concerned with the preservation of morality and virtue in his society, would find himself an advocate for state-supported religion. At this early stage, however, all the members of the Virginia Convention were prepared at least to endorse the broad principle of religious toleration, and that resolution, along with the other provisions of the Declaration of Rights, was unanimously accepted by the Convention on June 12.[6]

The committee charged with drafting the Declaration had an

even more challenging task ahead of it. It was one thing to formulate a lofty but generally accepted set of abstract principles and quite another to agree on the specific details of a new frame of government. While the Convention members were willing to delegate to George Mason the task of drafting a Declaration of Rights, there were too many special interests at stake to permit any one man to dominate the business of drafting the specific provisions of the new constitution.

There has been considerable debate as to the source of inspiration for the Virginia constitution. Some claim that the document conforms to the outline sent to Henry by John Adams in the spring of 1776, and it does seem that Henry himself played some role in arranging for the *Virginia Gazette* to print a version that was similar both to Adams's and the one ultimately adopted by the Convention. We also know that Carter Braxton offered an exceptionally conservative plan that bore little resemblance to the form of government finally ratified by the delegates.[7] What seems to be the most obvious source for the Virginia Convention, however, is seldom mentioned by historians: it is plainly apparent that the new state constitution most closely resembled in spirit the old colonial charter, with only the power of the King, Privy Council, and Royal Governor stripped away.

The constitution was prefaced by a vigorous denunciation of King George III and a long list of grievances. This section was included at the urging of Jefferson, who sent a draft of his own from Philadelphia, where he was serving in the Continental Congress. The grievances included by Jefferson were nearly identical to the list in the Declaration of Independence, drafted just a few days later.[8] The state constitution then proceeded to define the separate branches of government, with the lower house, renamed the House of Delegates, and the Senate, an enlarged version of the Governor's Council, to constitute the two branches of the legislature. The House members were to be elected annually, with two delegates apportioned to each county; the senators were to serve four year terms and were to be elected from twenty-four senatorial districts.

The balance of power between the Senate and the House was uneven. The House was given the sole power to initiate legislation, and the Senate possessed only the power to accept, reject, or amend legislation except in the case of money bills, when it could only accept or reject. The lower house dominated the executive branch as well. The governor was to be elected annually by joint ballot of the two houses and was instructed to seek the advice of an eight-man Privy Council, also elected by the legislature. He was permitted a maximum of three consecutive terms and was then required to retire for at least four years before being eligible to serve again. The architects of the constitution, mindful of recent proroguings by royal governors, denied the chief executive the power to prorogue or adjourn the legislature. Most important, and again in reaction to the excesses of the royal governors, they stripped the governor of his veto power.[9]

At first glance the strengthening of the popularly elected lower house at the expense of the governor and upper house seems like a significant step toward the democratization of Virginia politics. And ultimately, that may have been an important result of the move. But a desire for democratic government was hardly the motive behind the strengthening of the lower house. There is little evidence in any of the actions of the members of the Virginia Convention, and considerable evidence to the contrary, that they were concerned about the advancement of democratic doctrine. Rather, it seems quite clear that the men serving in the Virginia Convention intended to strengthen the lower house—the agency of government which had, after all, been their traditional base of political power—in order to bolster their own oligarchic grasp on the affairs of the independent state.

By the terms of the constitution, the right of suffrage was to "remain as exercised at present," which meant that a citizen was required to possess at least a fifty-acre freehold in order to be eligible to vote.[10] The reasoning behind this restriction was an old one; only those with a "stake in society" were deemed capable of taking their duties as citizens responsibly. Otherwise, it was feared, the propertyless would pass laws aimed at depriving the propertied classes of their basic rights. Although there has been considerable research indicating that the suffrage in Virginia was widespread in spite of the existence of these restrictions, the very fact that the framers of the constitution did not feel inclined to go on record repudiating the notion of a "stake in society" as an important prerequisite for any voter is evidence of their limited faith in popular government.[11] Any group of men taking the preamble to the Declaration of Rights so lightly as to create separate classes of people in society, with one—the propertied—enjoying full political rights, and the other—the propertyless—facing legal limitations on their role in government, was hardly "democratic."

The cornerstone of the oligarchic political edifice that had ensured the wealthy and well-born members of the provincial elite their political power—the system of local government controlled by the appointive power of existing local officials—was kept completely intact. The county court system, which had provided the Virginia elite with a closed training ground for political service, remained the private preserve of that elite.

There is absolutely no indication that Patrick Henry, one of those often portrayed as being in the "democratical" wing of Virginia's political leadership, made any effort whatsoever to inject a greater measure of popular participation into the state government. On the question of the suffrage there is testimony from Edmund Randolph that not "a hint was uttered in contravention" to the principle that only freeholders could possess a common interest with their representatives.[12] Henry, after all, had achieved his position of prominence in Virginia within the old, oligarchic political framework, and, like his colleagues from other regions of the state, he evidently saw no reason to risk any major change in that framework.

There was one feature of the proposed constitution that Henry was not altogether pleased with, however. Like Jefferson, he was dismayed by the weakness of the executive branch, a "mere phantom," Henry dubbed it. Many of the members of the Convention, had they been so bold as to speak for a stronger executive, would have opened themselves to the charge of favoring a reintroduction of executive tyranny, but Henry, with his record of consistent opposition to the authoritarianism of the royal governors, was in a much stronger position to argue the virtues of a more powerful executive. According to Edmund Randolph:

No member but Henry could with impunity to his popularity have contended as strenuously as he did for an executive veto on the acts of the two houses of legislation. Those who knew him to be indolent in literary investigations were astonished at the manner in which he exhausted this topic, unaided as he was believed to be by any of the treatises of government except Montesquieu.[13]

It was Henry's familiarity with Montesquieu, or more precisely, John Adams's discussions of Montesquieu, that guided his thinking on the subject. Henry was generally unfamiliar with the trends of formal political thought at this stage in his career, so when Adams suggested a rigid separation of powers in the new governments, with a strong executive possessing veto and pardoning powers, he was particularly likely to have an effect on Henry's still unformed thoughts on the subject.[14] When Henry himself assumed the governorship, it would become quickly apparent that he was temperamentally inclined toward strong, vigorous—indeed, sometimes autocratic—action in the executive's post. Such was the hostility to royal government in the Convention though, that Henry's arguments were ignored and the governor's powers remained woefully inadequate to the needs of the independent state.

The new constitution, embodying most of the old concepts that Virginia's provincial leadership found so congenial, was unanimously adopted by the Convention on June 29, 1776.[15] On that moment the goverment of the sovereign state of Virginia came into existence.

At least one Virginian believed that the members of the Convention had exceeded their power by declaring the constitution in full force on their own authority. Jefferson believed that a permanent constitution could be drafted only by a special constituent assembly, elected by the people and specially called for the purpose of drawing up a new political compact. This notion of the "people as a constituent power," which has been termed by historian R. R. Palmer as one of the most significant ideas to emerge from the American Revolution, was apparently lost on most of the people present in the Convention.[16] Most other states, either by calling special constituent conventions to draft their constitutions or by submitting their proposed constitutions to the people for ratification, demonstrated that they were aware of the important role that the popular will must play in the crucial business of constitution making.[17] That the Virginians were not sensitive to the importance of consulting the people in such matters is explained by two factors. First, unlike the representatives to the Massachusetts General Court, who were often instructed by their constituents in the town meeting on how to vote on important questions, Virginia's representatives had a long tradition of independence from their constituents. The job of the voter in Virginia was to elect his representative, not to tell him how to vote once elected. A representative, rather than serving as attorney for his constituents, was thought to have the freedom of action to use his own judgment in protecting and promoting the interests of his district. Second, although in some colonies like Massachusetts the notion of a "constituent power" was widely current by the Revolution, it was, in most colonies, an idea that only slowly came to be accepted as a result of the experience of the Revolution. Virginia was the first state to draft a permanent constitution; others, following her, would profit from her errors.

Henry seems to have shared the ignorance of his countrymen with respect to the notion of the constituent power. He made no distinction between the act of making laws and the act of drafting the frame of government that would determine the boundaries of the lawmaking powers; since the members of the Convention had been vested with the first set of powers, he could see no reason why they should not also take responsibility for the second.

Henry's confidence in the wisdom of the Virginia Convention is not too hard to understand; that Convention had, after all, shown its confidence in him by electing him the first governor of the independent state of Virginia on the same day that the Virginia constitution was adopted. His chief opponent, Thomas Nelson, Sr., the candidate of most of the conservatives, could poll only forty-five votes to Henry's sixty.[18]

There is great temptation to represent this event as a symbolic turning point in Virginia history, as a sign that Henry and his supporters had finally succeeded in overthrowing the conservative dominance of the Pendletons and the Randolphs. In actual fact, however, Henry's election could not have occurred had Pendleton and his supporters been committed to capturing the governorship. The post of the chief executive under the new constitution was, as we have noted, a severely weakened one, bound to frustrate almost anyone who occupied it. The most powerful and prestigious position—that of speaker of the recently strengthened House of Delegates—would be occupied by Edmund Pendleton, who was elected to that office unanimously.[19]

Actually, the governorship would prove to be more important than people had anticipated, at least during the years in which the state was forced to wage its war for independence. The Assembly was in session only a few months each year, and since the exigencies of war were felt all year round, the governor was by necessity forced to act more vigorously than he would have in peacetime. It would be in this fashion, as much as by his ability to win converts to his side with his oratory, that Henry would increase his power in post-Revolutionary Virginia.

Another vital ingredient in Henry's ascendancy to full political power was, of course, his continuing climb up the economic and social ladder of his home state. In June 1777 he would make a proposal of marriage to Dorothea Dandridge, the daughter of Colonel Nathaniel West Dandridge, whose ancestors in Virginia dated back to 1635, when Captain John West served on the Governor's Council. Although much younger than Henry, she was probably considered a good match for the Virginia Governor. Henry, with his rising prestige and wealth, was precisely the person who might revive the fortunes of the socially prestigious but somewhat financially straitened Dandridge family. The courtship would end on October 9, 1778, when Henry, most likely traveling all night from Williamsburg where he had finished with his duties on the Governor's Council, arrived at St. Martin's Parish in Hanover County in time for his wedding.[20]

By 1778 Henry would be the master not only of his Scotchtown plantation but of two farms in Botetourt County and 10,000 acres of land in Kentucky as well. The twelve slaves that Dorothea would bring to her marriage would increase the total of Henry's slaveholdings to forty-two.[21] And despite the financial hardships felt by most Virginians during the Revolution, Henry's wealth and property would continue to grow. In the year of his marriage to Dorothea, Henry would sell Scotchtown and purchase a new 10,000-acre plantation, Leatherwood, in Henry County. At a cost of £5,000, the property was a bargain, and of course there must have been no little pride involved in choosing to live in the county named in one's honor.[22]

As Henry's status in the Old Dominion increased, he would also begin to acquire some of the other attributes of a "gentleman" of Virginia. It was remarked that he was never seen "without a scarlet cloak, black clothes, and a dressed wig." He even drove an expensive carriage, worth some £100. And like most prominent citizens who were forced to be in Richmond part of the year for their political and commercial transactions, Henry would manage to escape from the heat and dirt of the town by renting a plantation, Salisbury, some twelve miles out of the capital in Chesterfield County.[23]

The historian interested in this stage of Henry's career—a stage where Henry reached full maturity both as a statesman and as a private citizen in a society much concerned with economic and social status—searches in vain for a set of clearly defined principles that guided him. Unfortunately, Henry's public actions during this period, both as a governor and as a frequent member of the legislature, offer little evidence indicating that he possessed a coherent view of the ways in which his society should be shaped and reformed. Rather, Henry tended to be guided by three sets of instinctive concerns. The first, and most important, was a vague uneasiness about the decline of virtue in Virginia and a determination to restore that quality to both the public and private life of his state. It was a commonplace among nearly all Americans that virtue was the element that held a republican society together. In a monarchy an elaborate system of titles and ranks, an all-pervasive criminal code, the authority of established religion, and the pomp and splendor of the court all served to maintain public order; in a republic, which possessed few of these mechanisms of social control, the virtue of the citizenry itself was the principal determinant of the stability of the body politic. And, as Gordon Wood has observed, while "everyone in the eighteenth century could have agreed that in theory no state was more beautiful than a republic . . . everyone also knew that it was a fragile beauty indeed."[24]

The spirits of faction, of economic self-interest, and of religious, sectional, and personal animosity were always at work undermining the virtue of a republic, and for Henry those destructive forces seemed to be particularly apparent within Virginia in the years immediately following independence. Within this intellectual framework, which was so much a part of Henry's world view that it never needed to be articulated in a formal ideology, two additional factors, each more closely tied to Henry's own position within Virginia society, were operative. Henry's concern for his prerogatives as a legislator and, in particular, as a governor, would frequently lead him to autocratic action. And, finally, his desire to protect and promote the interests of his own section of the state would often place him once again in conflict with many of his pre-Revolutionary opponents.

Henry nearly missed his governorship altogether. Within a few days of his election he became seriously ill and was forced to leave Williamsburg to go home to Hanover County. He was so sick, in fact, that there was a persistent rumor that he had died, a rumor that so pleased his political opponent Landon Carter that the wealthy and reactionary aristocrat noted in his diary after that item of misinformation: "Particularly favourable by the hand of Providence."[25]

After a long and somewhat uneven recovery, Henry was finally able to return to Williamsburg around the middle of September, just before the first session of the Virginia House of Delegates was to convene. It would be a momentous session, as Thomas Jefferson, who had been absent from the Virginia Convention, and James Madison, whose influence was steadily increasing, would attempt to enact legislation aimed at reforming certain features of Virginia society that went far beyond anything accomplished in the Convention.

The first week of the inaugural session of the House of Delegates witnessed the introduction of petitions from members of dissenting sects, particularly the Baptists, citing the last article of the Virginia Declaration of Rights as proof of the necessity of disestablishing the Anglican church. This was of course precisely what men like Henry were forced to deny during the debates on that section of the Declaration of Rights, but now that the dissenting

sects were prepared to push the issue, an influential group of legislators, led by Jefferson, Madison, and Mason, was willing to lend
support to the dissenters.

According to Jefferson, the majority of Virginia's citizens were
members of dissenting sects by 1776, but the membership of the
legislature was still heavily weighted toward Anglicanism and
would remain so for at least a decade. This is an important fact
to remember, for while most of the steps taken for separating
church and state were initiated by dissenters, the legislation establishing that principle could not have been passed without the
acquiescence of at least a portion of the Anglican members of the
Assembly. In 1776, however, most Anglicans were not yet prepared to accept anything so drastic. It was only after "desperate
contests" lasting through October, November, and most of December that the proponents of disestablishment persuaded the Assembly (1) to repeal laws requiring church membership and punishing
religious unorthodoxy and (2) to pass bills exempting dissenters
from contributing to the established church and suspending for one
year only the taxes for the salaries of the established clergy. In
spite of these steps, the church vestries retained significant power
in their communities, the properties of the church were kept
intact, and most important, the general principle of a state-supported church was not explicitly repudiated.

The 1776 bill, which was principally authored and guided
through the legislature by Jefferson, met considerable opposition
in spite of its moderation. The vote in the House reflected the pattern of denominational strength within the state and provided one
of the few occasions when Henry's views differed from those of his
constituency in the Piedmont and southwest. The eastern, Anglican-
dominated portion of the state tended to oppose Jefferson's efforts;
the west, more heavily populated with dissenters, decisively supported it and provided the margin of passage.[26]

One would suppose that Patrick Henry might have been cheering
Jefferson's efforts from the governor's mansion. He had, after all,
frequently expressed himself as a friend of religious toleration, and
his constituency in Hanover County was heavily weighted with
members of dissenting sects. And of course, his performance in the
Parsons' Cause identified him as an opponent of the extensive privi-
lege of the Anglican clergy. While we have no record of Henry's

view of Jefferson's initial assault on the established church, his actions later in the battle suggest, surprisingly, that he was probably not pleased with Jefferson's proposal in 1776. By 1784, motivated by a concern over what he believed to be a decline in morality and virtue in Virginia, Henry openly championed a bill in the General Assembly aimed at permanently establishing the Episcopal church and imposing a tax for the maintenance of all religious institutions in the state. Although more liberal than the existing law, which taxed the citizens to raise money for the Episcopal church alone, it nevertheless was a step away from the important principle of separation of church and state. In fact, the bill probably would have achieved final passage had not Henry, aided by some of his own political opponents who desired to see his influence in the Assembly diminished, been elected to a fourth term as governor, thus depriving the supporters of an established church of an influential spokesman on the floor of the legislature. In the meantime, Jefferson had prepared a plan in 1779, which had been either defeated or tabled every year until 1786, that was ultimately passed over Henry's protests from the governor's mansion. The bill, "an act for the establishment of religious freedom," was considered by Jefferson himself as one of the three most important contributions of his public life. The vote on the bill was similar to that on Jefferson's 1776 proposal, with the western delegates rejecting Henry's contention that morality depended on state-supported religion, and the Easterners being more evenly divided.[27]

As we shall see in subsequent pages, the very fact that Jefferson was the principal spokesman for the bill for religious freedom may have been a factor in Henry's opposition to that bill, but more than personal pique was involved. Henry was concerned about a number of developments in his home state that he regarded as signs of moral decay. The decline of many Episcopal parishes in Virginia, the flight of Episcopalian ministers from the state, and, more generally, the tendency of many Virginians to ignore their public responsibilities—whether those responsibilities meant paying tithes for the support of the poor or honoring their financial and military obligations to the state—were interpreted by Henry as an indication that some agency to restore and promote the public virtue was much needed. Henry did not feel that the Episcopal church alone should be charged with that task, but he did believe that it was the duty of the state to ensure that its citizens subscribed to some Christian religion.

While Henry's concern for promoting virtue is perhaps laudable, there is little question but that he was lagging behind his contemporaries in insisting that such promotion be done through the agencies of state-supported churches. One did not have to be an advanced deist like Jefferson to see the potential dangers posed to freedom of conscience in state-supported religion.

Jefferson's bill for religious freedom was but one of several reform measures that he and Madison initiated during the late 1770s and 1780s. Henry's preoccupation with the governorship during many of those years provides a partial explanation for his failure to be identified with those two men as a champion of reform on the floor of the legislature, but there is also considerable evidence to indicate that Henry—as in the case of the bill for religious freedom—was actively hostile to some of those measures. Although certainly not of the same conservative temperament as a Landon Carter or Carter Braxton, Henry was nevertheless not an innovator. His youth, his plain appearance, and his impatience with British rule made him seem radical to the pre-Revolutionary provincial elite, but by the time he had reached the peak of his own political power he had acquired a respectability—even going so far as to wear a scarlet cape and dressed wig—that was a more accurate indicator of his habit of mind.[28]

This is not to say that Henry quickly joined forces with his old opponents once he had gained a foothold in the Virginia ruling elite. There remained a series of important state issues—questions turning more on the particular interests of regions and individuals than on lofty theoretical principles—that continued to cause divisions within the body politic and upon which Henry continued to build his reputation as an effective orator and formidable opponent. It was also on these issues that Henry gained a reputation as a maverick who could never be counted upon to give allegiance to any one faction.

During the late 1770s and 1780s identifiable political factions developed in Virginia; Henry, despite his prominence, was never solidly committed to any of them.[29] Instead, he tended to vote in accordance with his own particular view of Virginia society, a view informed by his experiences and frustrations as governor in time of war, by his increasing attachment to the backcountry, and by the bedrock of his political world view—his concern for the preservation of the public virtue. As the years passed, one other factor—the increasing hostility between himself and Jefferson and Madison— would also influence his political behavior.

Henry had already expressed his views on the importance of a strong chief executive in the Virginia Convention, but his frustration over the inadequacies of that office during his terms as Revolutionary governor only reinforced that belief. Henry began to press the House of Delegates for a larger grant of power as early as December 1776, when he requested more freedom of action in the raising and equipping of troops. It was this incident that led Jefferson to recall that "it was proposed, in the House of Delegates, to create a Dictator, invested with every power, legislature, executive, and judiciary, civil and military, of life and of death, over our persons and over our properties." This recollection, written in 1781, after Jefferson's dislike of Henry was well known to everyone, was unquestionably an exaggeration of Henry's true position, but there is no question that Henry's bid for more power was viewed with alarm by many legislators. The result was that the House of Delegates later moved to restrict rather than strengthen the powers of governor and council.[30] This action was not so much a direct attack on Henry as it was indicative of the long-standing suspicion on the part of the Virginia lower house toward the institution of the chief executive, whether the executive officer be a royal official or a former burgess himself. It is likely that Henry would have been more reluctant to yield power to the governor had he spent his entire career as a legislator and avoided the burdens of the governor's office, but his years as governor had left their mark on him, and after he had served his maximum of three consecutive terms and found himself once again a member of the lower house in May 1780, he made himself the champion of a bill to lodge in the chief executive's office sweeping powers in the raising and supplying of troops and in apportioning punishments to those people who hindered the war effort. In fact, Henry would have liked to have gone even further, calling for the appointment of George Washington as a near dictator for the duration of the war. There was, needless to say, instant opposition to the scheme, but Henry nevertheless supported it, claiming that "it was immaterial with him whether the officer proposed was called a Dictator, or Governor with enlarged powers . . . yet surely an officer armed with such powers was necessary to restrain the unbridled fury of a licentious enemy."[31]

This does indeed seem to be strange behavior from the man who was the most conspicuous in his denunciation of executive tyranny before the Revolution. The only way to make his advocacy of the plan seem consistent with his earlier antiauthoritarian rhetoric is to view it as an expression of his own perception of what was necessary to maintain the public virtue. In the year immediately preceding independence Henry, like most Virginians, acquired a heightened sense of the purity and goodness of his own republican society. In contrast to the corruption and avarice he saw in the conduct of British ministers and royal officials, the signs of self-sacrifice and commitment to the public good evident in the actions of Virginians seemed the very symbols of a virtuous society. As a Revolutionary War governor, however, Henry was forced to sit by and watch this initial enthusiasm fade, giving way to public apathy and causing the ranks of troops to be depleted and supplies to dwindle; he was appalled by the profiteering by unscrupulous merchants and by the large-scale speculation in depreciated currency. Like most Americans, Henry blamed these rather predictable developments of a wartime situation on the decline of virtue, a decline which, according to Montesquieu, still the only political theorist Henry had ever read with care, would result in the destruction of republican government. Given this perspective, it is not surprising that he advocated extreme measures.

Other than this one, drastic solution to the problem of the weak executive, Henry showed no inclination to ally with those who wished to remedy some of the defects of the state constitution. When James Madison, who was fast becoming his opponent on almost every question of public policy—currency, British debts, taxation, and religion, to name only a few issues—introduced a plan in 1784 for the revision of the state constitution, Henry was among the opponents. In a speech before the Assembly, Madison pointed to eleven defects in the constitution, defects that Jefferson had earlier remarked on in his *Notes on Virginia*. Those weaknesses included the property qualifications for voting, the unequal apportionment of legislators, the excessive power of the lower house, the ability of the legislature to alter the constitution without calling a constituent convention, and the lack of differentiation between the lower house and senate. Madison's plan, like Jefferson's, called for a special convention to revise the constitution.[32] It was apparently this provision that particularly annoyed Henry, who claimed that such a convention would serve only to disrupt the workings of the government. Evidently a majority of delegates agreed with Henry, as after two days of debate Madison's plan was rejected, with the legislators going so far as to append a declaration saying that the question of constitutional revision could not even be considered until a majority of the citizens of the state had explicitly voted for a new convention to consider changes in the government.[33]

Henry's opposition to Madison's plan remains puzzling. It is clear that he too was not wholly happy with the state's plan of government. Not only was he displeased with the weakness of the governor, but as a representative from the west he should have also been disturbed by the slight underrepresentation of that region in the legislature, a situation that arose because of the difficulty of dividing western counties when their population warranted additional representation in the Assembly. While most historians agree that Henry's opposition to Madison centered around the method of revision and not on the substance of Madison's suggested changes, it is nevertheless difficult to understand why he would oppose the method. It was one thing for the representatives to the Virginia Convention to oppose a constituent convention in 1776, for at that time there were few precedents to follow, but by 1784 nearly all the American states had embraced the notion of the constituent power. Although the calling of special constitutional conventions was a cumbersome business, it was generally considered to be the orthodox method for achieving changes in government.

The reluctance of Virginians to change an old-fashioned and in some cases inequitable constitution would persist for decades. Attempts to reform the constitution would be rebuffed several times in the years following the Revolution. It was not until 1829 that a constitutional convention would finally meet, and the reforms affected at that gathering would only partially remedy the defects of the 1776 constitution.

One of the glaring weaknesses of the state government throughout the Revolutionary period was the paucity of funds in the state treasury, a paucity caused both by an insufficient tax rate and an inability to collect even those existing taxes owed to the common-wealth. This not only hampered the ability of the state government to function efficiently but also created another, more general eco-nomic problem that affected nearly all the citizens in the state: the poor credit rating of the state government caused the paper cur-rency issued by the state to fluctuate wildly, which in turn rendered all financial transactions uncertain. This would be the major prob-lem facing almost every state in the new nation, and the ability to cope with it would be the major test of most state politicians.[34] At least some, like Madison, John Tyler, and Richard Henry Lee, advocated higher taxes in order to strengthen the credit of the state. Henry disagreed, and in actions that won him countless supporters among the taxpayers of the state but which angered and frustrated those Virginians who were attempting to balance the state budget, he consistently thwarted efforts to reform the tax structure. In 1782, a year which probably represented the low point of the solvency of the state up to that time, Henry prodded the Assembly into passing an act commutating the taxes due to the state that year for a period of four months.[35] This move was undoubtedly in the short-range interest of some of the more hard-pressed taxpayers of the state and was particularly welcome to the residents of Henry's region of the state, where specie was exceptionally scarce, but as the anguished cries of state agents poured into the governor's office complaining of the inability of the state to keep the army together, Henry must have had some doubts about the long-range wisdom of the idea.

By the fall of 1784, although the war was over, the finances of the state were still in a shambles. In one more attempt to improve the state's credit, a group of men led by John Tyler, Mann Page, and perhaps Madison introduced a bill into the Assembly propos-ing an increase in the tax rate. The bill seemed likely to pass by a comfortable margin, but just before the final vote Henry once again proved that the power of his oratory had not diminished. He spoke against the bill, evoking images of the hardships of the people of the backcountry. According to Archibald Stuart, "His delineations of their wants and wretchedness was so minute, so full of feeling, and withal so true, that he could scarcely fail to enlist on his side every sympathetic mind." In particular, he took great pains to con-trast the situation of the backcountry inhabitants with that of the people of the Tidewater, whom he pictured as being able to "draw

their supplies at pleasure from the waters that flowed by their doores
. . . peeping and peering along the shores of the creeks, to pick up
their mess of crabs, or paddling off to the oyster rocks to rake their
daily bread." Henry's speech, a combination of pathos and comedy,
was probably responsible for the shift of some thirty votes, a switch
which caused the bill's ultimate defeat.[36]

The divisions in the House of Delegates on the tax questions
were both similar, with the delegates from the Northern Neck portion
of Virginia—usually more closely tied to sources of credit and
large-scale commercial agriculture—supporting a policy of higher
taxes, promptly paid, and the delegates from the Southside, and
from Henry's southwest in particular, opposing that policy.[37]

One would suppose, given Henry's aversion to taxing the citizens of his state, that he would have also supported efforts to pay
off the state debt at a depreciated rate. This at least would have
been consistent with his concern for the burden borne by the taxpayers; it would not be too unusual under the circumstances to
resort to the device used in many other states, that of meeting the
state's fiscal crisis by paying only the "real" value of the obligation
and not the face value. Henry, however, opposed and ultimately
helped defeat a proposal along those lines, claiming that any tamper-
ing with the public credit would violate the sanctity of contracts.[38]

He had taken a similar stand in the Virginia legislature in 1780,
pouring "forth all his eloquence" in opposition to an act of the Continental Congress devaluing its nearly worthless loan office certificates at the ratio of forty to one. Henry actually managed to obtain
a resolution denouncing the Congress's scheme, but a few days
later, after he had left the House of Delegates, the members of the
House reversed themselves and gave their assent to the plan, apparently realizing that no alternative to devaluation existed.[39]

Henry never elaborated on his reasons for opposing devaluation,
but Thomas Jefferson, admittedly not always an objective observer
where Henry was concerned, gives us some indication that Henry
might have had a personal interest in making certain that state and
continental securities were redeemed at full value. In describing
Henry's purchase of a 10,000-acre plantation in Henry County in
1779, Jefferson scornfully claimed that it was paid for "in depreciated paper not worth oak leaves."[40] And it is well known that after
the federal Constitution was adopted. Henry and his partners in

land speculation would find themselves considerably enriched by the federal government's decision to assume at full value the depreciated certificates of indebtedness of the state of North Carolina.

This may simply be a one-sided look at Henry's motivations, for despite the fact that his own speculation with the currency was in some ways evidence of the decline in public virtue that he so much lamented, he nevertheless remained attached to the notion that the sanctity of contracts was a good indicator of the state of the public morality and seemed genuinely horrified by the kind of public irresponsibility displayed by states like Rhode Island, where the government had fostered a policy of drastic devaluation of the currency. Even if Henry believed himself to be sincere in protecting the sanctity of the public debt, however, we must nevertheless question his judgment in pursuing a policy of taxation that was designed to achieve just the opposite result, making it more difficult than ever for the government to meet its obligations.

Henry's attitude toward the question of back debts owed by Virginians to the British is also somewhat surprising in light of his professed attachment to the principle of the inviolability of the law of contracts. Like most Virginians, Henry had favored legislation sponsored in 1777 by Jefferson allowing Virginians to pay debts owed to the British to the Virginia treasury office instead of to their British creditors. This act, which was seen at the time as an important part of the war effort, was an indication of the depth of hostility toward the British as well as of the desire of prominent Virginians, Jefferson included, to avoid their extensive financial obligations to the British. The Treaty of Peace of 1783 explicitly obliged the several states to remove from their books all laws impeding the payment of back debts to the British. In January 1785, Madison attempted to persuade the legislature to repeal those laws conflicting with the order of the Treaty of Peace, but he was opposed by a group of legislators who purposely absented themselves from the chamber, thus preventing a quorum from ever assembling. In the fall of 1785, Madison tried again, the proposal this time being so drastically amended that he never even bothered to bring it to a vote. Henry's position, which was embodied in a resolution passed by the House in 1784 and which remained Virginia policy until the signing of the Jay Treaty in 1795, was that the British should not receive payment until they ceased their illegal occupation of military posts on America's northwestern frontier.[41]

This position would ultimately prove to be an effective one from the standpoint of America's diplomatic dealings with England, but it is clear that Henry, at the time he championed that point of view, was much more concerned with helping Virginians avoid their past financial obligations than he was in strengthening America's diplomatic position vis-à-vis Great Britain. Moreover, the position was a patently unfair one. Henry was not arguing merely that the debts owed to the public treasury of Great Britain be voided; rather, he was arguing that all debts, including those owed to private citizens in England, be canceled. Thus, the action was aimed not only at a hostile British government but at innocent British citizens as well. This was clearly inequitable and contrary to Henry's previous concern for the sanctity of contracts and the preservation of the public virtue. But as so often was the case in Henry's career, the desire to protect the special interests of his constituents—in this case the nearly limitless list of Virginians in debt to British merchants and factors—took precedence over any ideological attachments he might have had.

In spite of his extreme position on the subject of British debts, Henry proved quite willing to be conciliatory toward England when such a posture stood to benefit the citizens of his home state. At the same time that Henry was arguing that Virginians should be allowed to evade their responsibilities to British merchants, he was working for the laudatory goal of improving America's commercial ties with England. Contrary to his bitterly Anglophobic rhetoric on the subject of British debts, Henry realized that the French could not take up the slack left by the British exit from American markets during the war for independence. Although anti-British prejudices died hard in Virginia, Henry was, in May 1783, able to push a resolution through the Assembly calling for a repeal of the act prohibiting trade with England. Nor did Henry's antipathy toward the British Crown carry over to the citizens of Virginia who sided with the British during the Revolution. In the same session that he promoted the resolution for resuming trade with the British, he advocated repeal of a law preventing the return of those tories who had been forced to flee the state during the Revolution. John Tyler, a bitter Anglophobe to his dying day, was dismayed that Henry "above all other men, could think of inviting into his family an enemy whose insults and injuries he had suffered so severely," and apparently there were many in Virginia who shared Tyler's view, as Henry's proposal was soundly defeated.[42] Hostility toward the British, most likely intensified by Virginians' continued fear of slave insurrection—a threat so pointedly raised by Lord Dunmore— would last well into the next century.

Henry's advocacy of the return of the loyalists seems to have been stimulated not so much by any great sympathy for the loyalists themselves, but by his long-standing desire to attract skilled whites to Virginia. Though exceptionally provincial in his thinking on most subjects, he was convinced of the importance of manufacturing and commerce to Virginia's future, and unlike most of his Virginia contemporaries, was unwilling to allow the memory of disputes past to interfere with the immigration policy that he deemed necessary for Virginia's growth and prosperity. It was on this question, in fact, and on few others, that Henry pursued a consistent course.

Henry's steadfast commitment to "his country," which was defined as Virginia, or, increasingly, the even narrower region encompassing western Virginia, can best be seen in his frontier policy while he was governor. Henry enthusiastically supported George Rogers Clark's plan to expel the British from the area between the Ohio and Mississippi Rivers. The plan was carried out successfully in 1779 during Jefferson's term as governor, significantly lowering the threat on the frontier not only from the British but from the Indians as well. On the other hand, Irving Brant, the biographer of Madison and a frequent critic of Henry's conduct during the 1780s, labels the action as one of "state imperialism" and claims that it only increased the already prevalent interstate competition for western lands.[43]

It was Virginia's claim to much of the land between the Ohio and the Mississippi that caused Maryland, many of whose prominent citizens had lodged conflicting claims to the land, to refuse to ratify the Articles of Confederation during the years 1778 to 1781. Surprisingly, though Henry had been vigorous in pressing Virginia's claim to the land, he ultimately proved willing to cede those lands to the Confederation Congress on the condition that Maryland relinquish her claims as well, a move that permitted the new nation to move for the first time toward a rational, centrally administered land policy.[44] It is perhaps unwise to praise Henry too unstintingly for his nationalistic vision, however. There seem to have been other motives involved. All Virginians, including Henry, were beginning to realize that the state might not be able to survive militarily without the help of a stronger continental government. Virginia was faced with the immediate threat of attack from the British in the Chesapeake Bay, and it was recognized by most leaders in the state that a cession of western lands by Virginia would force Maryland to take a similar step, which would in turn eliminate the impasse that had prevented ratification of the Articles of Confederation. Most Virginians had been unwilling to take the first step to end that impasse, but with the threat of British invasion of their own state a reality for the first time, they changed their minds. Moreover, the cession did not necessarily threaten Henry's private interests in lands in that area, as his claims rested with a private company of speculators residing in several states.

Henry's unusual combination of self-interest, state imperialism, and qualified nationalism on the question of western lands can best be seen in his dealings with Spain, a potential ally in the war with England and an open rival on the western frontier. In 1785 John Jay, one of America's most respected diplomats, negotiated a commercial treaty with Spain which, though the best that Jay thought he could obtain, was nevertheless decidedly disadvantageous to western interests. While the treaty granted America some commercial concessions—advantages that would be enjoyed primarily by the Northeast—it denied to America the right to navigate the Mississippi River, a right obviously important to westerners. The seven Northern states in the Confederation Congress all voted to approve the treaty; only the provision in the Articles of Confederation requiring a two-thirds majority for a treaty to go into force prevented it from becoming law. Henry was irate at the terms of the proposed treaty. He wrote to friends urging them to oppose it, even going so far as to say that he would rather part with the Union than with the Mississippi River. This threat to western interests, coming just a year before the Philadelphia Convention, would greatly influence Henry's subsequent attitude toward a strengthened union.[45]

Henry's attitude toward the attempts of some members of the Confederation Congress to secure for the central government the power to levy a 5 percent impost on goods imported into America gives us an interesting perspective on his view of federal power during the Confederation period. The power to tax, which was not granted to the central government by the Articles of Confederation, would have been a significant step toward solving the chronic problem of the Confederation, which was the lack of an independent income with which to pay off the government's debts, stabilize the currency, and provide essential goods and services to the people of the country. The inability of the Confederation Congress to push through an amendment giving the government this all-important power would ultimately cause the demise of the Confederation and would enhance the position of those advocating a new, stronger constitution. But though hindsight makes it easy for the historian to see that the opponents of the impost were paving the way for those who wished to see the destruction of the Confederation government, we should not forget the powerful aversion in America to the very notion of taxation by a centralized government. It was precisely this issue that brought about the American Revolution. If there was any one power that Americans most wanted to safeguard, it was the power over the purse.

Although Virginia had approved the plan for an impost in 1781, it later rescinded it after Rhode Island had witheld the approval necessary to make the vote unanimous and therefore allow passage of the measure in the Confederation Congress. It was not until 1783 that the Virginia Assembly got around to debating the measure again, and by that time the financial position of the Confederation government was desperate. The value of loan office certificates had diminished below the forty-to-one devaluation rate of 1780 and the new bills of exchange that the government had begun printing at that time were nearly worthless.[46] Henry, who was a member of the Assembly that year, was thought to favor the plan, as at this stage his concern over the American war effort was causing him to advocate a stronger government. Jefferson believed that Henry would probably favor the impost, although his intense dislike of his rival prompted him to add, "Henry, as usual is involved in mystery; should the popular tide run strongly in either direction, he will fall in with it. Should it not, he will have a struggle between his enmity to the Lees, and his enmity to everything which may give influence to [Congress]." The tide of opinion, as Madison's biographer Irving Brant has noted, was actually running violently in both directions.

On the one hand the supporters of the impost were pointing to the threat of an army revolt should the funds to pay the continental troops not be forthcoming; on the other, the opponents of the bill were convinced that members of the central government were plotting to steal sovereignty from the states. When Henry arrived in Richmond and discovered that his political rival Richard Henry Lee was opposed to the plan, he immediately announced his support of the impost. Jefferson was overjoyed, claiming that Henry's support would ensure its passage. In fact, Henry even took the lead in championing the plan in the legislature, adding a provision that would allow the people a few months' moratorium on tax payments before the bill was to go into effect, a step likely to win over some of the doubtful delegates.[47]

Henry's support of the impost up to this point was in some ways consistent with his position on taxes. Most of his opposition to statewide taxes had been based on the inability of the people in the specie-poor backcountry to pay them. The federal impost, a tax that would fall on those people importing goods from abroad, would inevitably fall heaviest on the merchants of the coastal areas and those wealthy enough to purchase those imported goods. In this sense, the impost actually represented, from the standpoint of Henry and his fellow residents of the backcountry, a relatively satisfactory solution to the revenue shortage.

Henry's support of the measure began to weaken, however, as soon as a copy of the impost bill itself, along with an address by James Madison defending it, reached Richmond sometime between May 20 and May 24, 1783. Those documents, intended to drum up support for the proposal, actually served to turn opinion against it. In particular, a letter from Alexander Hamilton to the legislature of Rhode Island, claiming that the federal government possessed "absolute discretion" in matters relating to national expenditures, horrified those people who might have wanted to increase the revenue-raising powers of the Confederation Congress in order to meet an immediate financial crisis but who nevertheless remained jealous of the sovereignty of their home states. It seems likely that this was at least a partial cause of Henry's decision to switch sides. Rather than arguing against the bill on a general constitutional basis, however, he publicly opposed it on the grounds that it would work against Virginia's interests. He maintained that Virginia, which supposedly imported more goods than most states, should be given credit for all import duties in excess of its percentage of the national debt. This move, together with the wavering of a number of other supporters of the bill, so muddled the debate that the proponents of the impost were forced to move for a postponement of the subject in order to avoid destroying the entire package. When the question was taken up again in the fall, Henry once again supported the plan, but by this time other states had begun to reverse their previously favorable positions, so the Virginia legislature once again refused to act on it.[48]

It is difficult to know what to conclude about Henry's "nationalism." It is clear, and not surprising, that Henry did not have as strong an attachment to a strong central government vested with broad powers as his younger colleague James Madison. Henry's entire career, except for a few brief and unrewarding months in the Continental Congress, had been spent in the state government; he was quite naturally anxious to protect the powers of that agency of government which had promoted his own rise to political prominence. Madison, on the other hand, had literally been propelled from Princeton College to the Continental Congress where, except for a few years in the Virginia legislature, he spent most of his early political career. The views of both men were conditioned not so much by any conscious intention to protect that agency which was responsible for their own political power but rather by the view of politics that arose out of their experience in those two different environments.

It would be a mistake, however, to assume that Henry's implacable opposition to the federal Constitution in the Virginia Ratifying Convention of 1788 was an inevitable result of a lifelong antipathy to centralized government. There is some evidence that Henry had at least occasionally expressed a desire to strengthen the central government. William Short, Jefferson's private secretary while in France, wrote to his employer on May 14, 1784, after spending some time with Henry, Joseph Jones, and Madison in a Richmond tavern the day before:

> Mr. Henry told them he wished much to have a conference on a subject of importance. The event of it was that Mr. Jones and Mr. Madison should sketch out some plan for giving greater power to the federal government and that Mr. Henry should support it on the

floor. It was thought a bold example set by Virginia would have influence on the other states. Mr. Henry declared that it was the only inducement he had for coming to the present assembly. He saw ruin inevitable unless something was done to give Congress compulsory process on delinquent states, etc.[49]

What this meant, presumably, was that while Henry was not willing to give Congress a broad grant of taxation power such as Hamilton had advocated, he was genuinely concerned about the financial weakness of the Confederation and at least wanted to give Congress the power to coerce the states into meeting their requisitions. This proposal, which was supported by both Madison and Jefferson as being better than nothing at all, was passed in the form of a resolution from the General Assembly urging the other states to agree on such a policy.[50] They would soon discover, however, that mere resolutions were not adequate to support the nation's sagging credit structure. The only way a permanent income could be ensured was through federal taxes, and there were too many people like Henry who opposed that solution to make it feasible.

The failure of the other states to meet their requisitions was not only one of the causes of Henry's qualified support of a proposal to increase the coercive powers of the central government, but ironically, also one of the reasons why Henry ultimately could not bring himself to go even further and support a consolidated, national government. His suspicion of attempts to strengthen drastically the Articles of Confederation was based not so much on a set of theoretical assumptions against centralism qua centralism but rather on a practical-minded view of Virginia's interests. He would later erect an entire states'-rights ideology in his opposition to the federal Constitution, but on the eve of the Philadelphia Convention he had not yet entered that lofty theoretical ground. Rather, his view of the desirability of strengthening the Confederation government was based on his view of what was good for Virginia. As war governor, charged with the near impossible task of waging battle with inadequate troops and supplies, he welcomed support from the continental government and was frequently cited as favoring the strengthening of that government. His early support for a federal impost was unquestionably based on the simple notion that an independent income for the continental government would hasten the end of the war and thus bring peace and prosperity to Virginia sooner. His growing ambivalence over the impost was probably a consequence of both the end of the war, which lessened the threat to Virginia and therefore lessened the need for the state government to rely on any other agency for support, and Henry's recognition that there were some people—and he probably would not have made a distinction between Madison and Hamilton in this case— who wanted not merely to increase the efficiency of the Confederation government but also to increase its power at the expense of the states.

It was at this point that Henry may have come close to thinking ideologically, in terms of state versus national sovereignty; but given his entire range of experience, it seems likely that he would not even have viewed the matter as being debatable. While one might debate the wisdom of delegating certain powers to the central government—such as those relating to limited taxation or the control of interstate commerce—there was simply never a question in his mind that the states should retain their sovereignty.

The one event that most convinced Henry that too large a grant of power to a central government would work against the interests of Virginians—and, in fact, might even work to destroy the sovereignty of the state altogether—was John Jay's negotiation with Spain in 1785. One of the reasons Henry mildly favored strengthening the Confederation government was his concern about the machinations of the Spanish on America's western frontier; he was particularly concerned about keeping the right to navigate the Mississippi open to Americans, a concern that was uppermost in the minds of most people living in the southwest. When Henry discovered that Jay, with the support of seven Northern states, was trying to secure ratification of a treaty giving up the right to navigate the Mississippi, he was furious. Madison, for one, was aware of the danger of losing Henry's qualified support for his plans to strengthen the central government. He wrote Washington in December 1786, describing Henry as "hitherto the Champion of the Federal cause," but predicting that "in the event of an actual sacrifice of the Mississippi by Congress [he] will unquestionably go over to the opposite side."[51]

Even though the Congress ultimately refused to ratify Jay's treaty with Spain, Henry would choose "the opposite side" in the debate over the Constitution. There would be no other cause in Henry's extraordinarily successful life for which the Revolutionary statesman would work so hard and speak so eloquently. Yet ultimately, he would meet defeat. Fortunately for historians, Henry's campaign against the federal Constitution is the one event in his life for which there exists adequate source material; it will therefore be much easier to gauge his motives and actions with respect to the Constitution than with previous aspects of his career.

Before moving on to the story of Henry's opposition to the Constitution, which in many important ways marked a very different phase in his career, it might be helpful to attempt some assessment of his activities during the immediate post-Revolutionary years. Unfortunately, that assessment remains ambiguous. Interests, not ideology, and instinct, not reason, tended to be the forces that guided his conduct. And even when one attempts to sort through the various interests that Henry represented during this period, coherence is still lacking. This is in part simply a reflection of the nature of Virginia politics and not a commentary on the peculiarities of one of the Old Dominion's leading statesmen. For although issues of statewide significance such as those relating to religious freedom, penal reform, western land policy, and the federal impost produced numerous factional divisions in the legislature, they failed to produce any one, dominant faction that voted together on all these issues. Rather, voting blocs would form around particular sets of issues—for example, the western counties would tend to vote in the same way on issues relating to land policy—and then disband once the issue was decided. Henry, in his votes in the legislature and in his activities as governor, behaved in the same particularistic way. It is not possible to link Henry with any one faction or group of interests, a fact which has not only confused those historians who have attempted to describe his political philosophy but also caused his contemporaries no little consternation, as it was always difficult to know which way Henry would jump on most any issue.

Perhaps the only way to typify Henry is negatively, by the men whom he consistently opposed in state politics during the post-Revolutionary period. For Virginia politics, often based on personality and prestige rather than issues and economic interests, frequently turned on the power of individuals or groups of individuals to rally supporters to their banners. It was in the business of commanding personal support that Henry most excelled. Time after time, as in the matter relating to the federal impost in 1784, no one was able to make an accurate prediction on the outcome of a bill until Henry had taken his position on the question. Edmund Randolph described the factions in the legislature during the period:

> It was manifest throughout the last session that H[enr]y had one corps—R.H.L., tho' absent, another, and the Speaker [John Tyler] a third, founded on a rivetted opopsition to our late enemies, and everything which concerns them. The first class, you know, has always been numerous, and will probably remain so. The second has never varied a single point either way for some years. The third is but a temporary bubble contrived [?] to save the trouble of thinking on true national policy. I suspect, however, that these new legislative guests [younger members of the legislature] will want a general to enable them to make head against those of the other parties, who will not fail to impress them with an affection of novelty when they only press the result of liberality and reflection. This renders it probable that our friend of Orange will step earlier into the heart of the battle than his modesty would otherwise permit.[52]

The emerging "Madisonian" faction would be somewhat different from the others because those who supported the young legislator from Orange County did so not out of a sense of personal allegiance but rather because they believed his nationalistic program was in the best interests of their state. By contrast, both Henry and Richard Henry Lee continued to command respect not so much because of their respective ideological stances, which were in fact quite similar in spite of their personal opposition to one another, but rather because of their enormous personal appeal. Madison's brand of politics was the wave of the future, but Henry and Lee were most often powerful enough during the 1780s to win any contest of popularity with the young nationalist. It would be on only the one question of overriding importance—the federal Constitution—that the substance of the issue would prove more important than the personalities and characters of the leaders of the contending parties.

Henry, though he was more often successful than not in these battles of personality in the political arena, has not fared so well at the hands of historians. Because of the personalized nature of eighteenth-century Virginia politics, the participants themselves were likely to describe their opponents in an emotional and often vindictive fashion. Men like Madison and Jefferson, who frequently found themselves on the opposite side from Henry and whose writings were not only more prolific but also better preserved, have left us a large body of material testifying to Henry's character, motives, and style. Written either in the heat of battle or after the men had retired, a time when the old rivalries actually seemed to intensify rather than fade away, these are hardly objective accounts to be taken at face value. But they would be of considerable value if only Henry had written and preserved his side of the story. Unfortunately, Henry was never inclined to write anything down and when he did, his poor sense of his own place in history caused him almost never to make a copy of anything he wrote; as a result, the historian has almost nothing with which to reconstruct Henry's reactions to his political opponents. What we have, then, are countless attacks on Henry and little to offer in defense on those attacks.

Henry's difficulties with Jefferson, which began soon after independence was declared and would have important repercussions for state and national policy all the way up to Henry's death in 1799, were the result of both differing personalities and policies. There was no outward break in relations between the two men between 1776 and 1781, although the two must have begun to realize the differences existing between them even then. Henry, the orator, could speak extemporaneously on nearly every subject, but when it came to the daily work of Congress or the legislature, his talents were far inferior to Jefferson's. The author of the Declaration of Independence, adept at drafting legislation as well as remonstrances to the King, was lacking in that oratorical gift which Henry possessed in such abundance. And if his later feelings about the value of Henry's oratory are any indication, then he must have begun to resent the public attention given to Henry's speeches at a relatively early date. According to Jefferson, Henry's oratory, in spite of its undeniable power, was "without logic, without arrangement." Henry "could not draw a bill on the most simple subject which would bear legal criticism, or even the ordinary criticism which looks to correctness of style & ideas, for indeed there was no accuracy of idea in his head."[53]

The differences between the two men on issues of public policy probably could have been noted by close observers soon after independence was declared. Although Henry's opposition to Jefferson's bill for religious freedom was not formalized until 1784, Jefferson was undoubtedly aware of Henry's sentiments before that time, as the whole question was debated yearly in the legislature after 1776. Similarly, a plan for the revision of the state's laws, for which Jefferson had labored long and hard throughout the 1780s, was also to meet Henry's disapproval; it is likely that Jefferson was aware of that opposition before 1789, when the bill was actually passed over Henry's objections.[54]

The incident that most likely changed Jefferson's feelings toward Henry from disagreement and occasional annoyance to open enmity began in June 1781, when George Nicholas, believed by some to be acting for Henry, stood up in the House of Delegates to ask for an inquiry into Jefferson's conduct as governor while fleeing from Richmond in the face of a British invasion. Nicholas's request carried the clear implication that Jefferson had been less than courageous in his failure to rally defenses for the capital when Benedict Arnold carried out his raid on the city in January of that year. When the Assembly finished its inquiry into the matter, it not only passed a resolution denying the "popular rumours" of Jefferson's cowardice but also voted him its "sincere thanks . . . for his impartial, upright, and attentive administration" of government. In spite of this vindication, which even Henry supported in that December session, Jefferson never forgave Henry. He wrote to Isaac Zane, a Virginia legislator, shortly after the Assembly had upheld his conduct: "The trifling body [Nicholas] who moved the matter was below contempt; he was more an object of pity. His natural ill temper was the tool worked by another hand. He was like the minners which go in and out of the fundament of the whale. But the whale himself was discoverable enough by the turbulence of the water under which he moved." By the next year, writing to George Rogers Clark praising him for his services to his country, Jefferson remarked:

> I was not a little surprised, however, to find a person hostile to you as far as he has the courage to shew hostility to any man. Who he is you will probably have heard, or may know him by his description as being all tongue and without head or heart. . . . That you

may long continue a fit object for his enmity and for that of every person of his complexion in the state, which I know can only be by your continuing to do good for your country.[55]

Thus by the winter of 1782, Jefferson's antipathy to Henry was no longer masked. From that time on, as they continued to clash over one important piece of legislation after another, Jefferson's hostility only increased. Henry's ambivalent position on the impost, while at the time giving Jefferson some hope for its passage, eventually infuriated his rival when the measure was finally defeated, a result that was in some part due to Henry's decision to remain silent on the issue altogether. By 1784, when Henry's opposition to constitutional revision became known, Jefferson abandoned all restraint in his attacks on Henry. Advising Madison to hold off on attempts for constitutional revision until the legislative climate was more favorable, Jefferson added: "While Henry lives another bad constitution would be formed and saddled forever on us. What we have to do I think is devoutly pray for his death, in the mean time to keep alive the idea that the present is but an ordinance and to prepare the minds of our young men."[56] Although nothing Jefferson subsequently wrote about Henry equalled this last letter in sheer ill will, his feelings toward Henry could not have mellowed in the next few years. For in the fall of 1784 Henry was to propose his bill for state support of religion in Virginia, and the next year, though out of the Assembly, he was to oppose Jefferson's cherished bill for religious freedom.

James Madison, even more than Jefferson, found himself pitted against Henry on nearly every major issue of the period. Revision of the laws, religious freedom, taxation, constitutional revision, currency reform, and British debts—Madison and Henry were on opposite sides on all these issues. Henry's stand on the one bill on which Madison had invested the most time and energy, the federal impost, was sufficiently ambivalent to deepen the antipathy between the two men. But Madison, unlike Jefferson, was able to contain his feelings toward Henry. Although his correspondence fairly bristles with his exasperation at Henry's repeated opposition, Madison never resorted to the kinds of personal attacks that Jefferson utilized.

Perhaps as a reward for his forbearance, Madison would eventually have the satisfaction of scoring a clear triumph over Henry in what was to be the most important political battle of the last quarter of the eighteenth century. In Philadelphia, and later in Richmond, Madison's view of Virginia's place in the new American nation would triumph.

7

Defender of Virginia Sovereignty

Henry's opposition to the proposed federal Constitution in the Virginia Ratifying Convention and to the policies of the new federal government in the years immediately following ratification was passionate, articulate, and widely cited by his contemporaries. It is misleading, however, to use his arguments against the Constitution in 1788 as a guide to his views regarding a stronger central government in the years preceding that date. It was not until Henry actually read the document that emerged from the Philadelphia Convention, and probably not even until he had read the arguments advanced by Madison in *The Federalist* defending the Constitution, that he bothered to formulate a rationale for his opposition to a stronger union. That rationalization would amount to one of America's first extended formulations of a states'-rights doctrine, but that still inchoate doctrine was not uppermost in Henry's mind on the eve of the Philadelphia Convention. Rather, Henry would react to the new Constitution on the basis of an unsystematic analysis of past developments in Virginia and an increasing suspicion of and hostility to the Northern states.

Several unrelated factors had combined in 1786 to bring about the movement for the new Constitution. In particular, two recent events outside Virginia had pointed up some of the weaknesses in the Confederation government. In 1786 the New York legislature had vetoed the impost bill of 1785, a bill thought by some to be essential if America was to raise the money to pay back the loans, then falling due, obtained from France and Holland during the Revolution. It is not difficult to understand why New York vetoed the bill; with a lucrative state impost of her own, an impost that would have had to be repealed according to the provisions of the 1785 bill, New York was already enjoying all the revenues collected from ships entering the port of New York City. Why should she be expected to vote for a bill that would almost certainly lower the revenues accruing to her? One cannot blame the state for pursuing her own interests; rather, it was the fatal weakness in the structure of the Articles of Confederation that one state—it had been Rhode Island in 1782 and now New York in 1786—could thwart the will of the remaining states on any proposal to amend the frame of government. What New York's action had shown most conclusively, even to those who would eventually oppose some of the particular features of the new Constitution, was the near impossibility of achieving even a partial revision of the old Articles of Confederation.[1]

At the same time that New York was dealing a death blow to the impost plan, the social structure of Western Massachusetts was threatening to come apart at the seams. In retrospect the men vested with upholding law and order in America had little to fear from the band of angry debtors, unpaid war veterans, and disgruntled farmers who gathered under the leadership of Daniel Shays. And in actual fact the demands of the "rebels" for a reduction in court and lawyers' fees, a decrease in taxes, and a reform in the method of collecting taxes were moderate and reasonable. According to reports circulating at the time, however, the rebellion seemed a precursor of total anarchy. Washington, relying on the exaggerated accounts of Secretary of War Henry Knox, estimated that the rebels numbered from 12,000 to 15,000, all of them believing "that the property of the United States has been protected from Confiscation of Britain by the joint exertions of *all,* and therefore ought to be the *common property* of all."[2] The lesson was obvious to Washington: law and order had to be restored and the best means to that end lay in a "liberal and energetic Constitution." The need to strengthen the arm of the law domestically was brought even more sharply into focus as rumors—again unfounded—spread across the country that the cause of Daniel Shays had been adopted by others in neighboring states. Thus, the localized and feeble attempt of the citizens of western Massachusetts was distorted to make it appear as if all America were in rebellion.

In the midst of these events the Annapolis Convention—a body convened to promote commercial cooperation among the states—was concluding its deliberations. While the Convention was hardly free of differences of opinion, there was nevertheless enough unity of sentiment on the general proposition of the necessity of strengthening the Confederation government that the delegates present recommended that another convention meet in Philadelphia in May of 1787 "to devise further provisions as shall appear to them necessary to render the constitution of the federal government adequate to the exigencies of the Union."[3]

Henry, in temporary retirement at his new home in Prince Edward County, was probably affected by none of these developments. The one issue which had occasionally prompted him to speak in favor of increasing the central government's powers—the necessity of a permanent source of income for the Confederation government—was no longer as pressing to him since he had stepped down from the governorship. As governor, he had been constantly aware of the chronic shortage of funds in both the state and federal governments, but in retirement at Prince Edward, mistakenly holding the belief that Virginia was proving capable of paying her share of the Revolutionary debt, the issue of a permanent income lost much of its immediacy.

Shays' rebellion seemed to hold little threat for Henry. Given the slowness of communications from Massachusetts to Virginia, which was compounded by the difficulty involved in delivering the Richmond newspaper to his home in Prince Edward, Henry was unlikely to have read about the event until long after it had been quelled. Moreover, Henry knew that the situation in the backcountry of Virginia was strikingly different from that in Massachusetts. Indeed, if anyone could claim to be the spokesman for the backcountry and to have the confidence of the residents of that region, it was Patrick Henry himself.

For most people living in western Virginia, the anguished cries of nationalists like Madison or Hamilton must have seemed exaggerated. If one looked at the economy of the region there were unmistakable signs not only of a recovery after the dislocation of the war but of genuine economic boom as well. There was little that a strengthened federal government might do to improve the quality of the lives of backcountry Virginians. The business of the backcountry was farming, and even those areas where commercial agriculture was dominant were more dependent upon market forces and London merchants for their well-being than they were on any agency of government located in America.

It was in part because of this independence that Henry's own ideological inclinations, however ill-articulated, favored a system of localized, decentralized government. After all, the American Revolution had been fought to preserve the power and authority of the provincial leaders in the face of encroachments from the centralized government of England. Given the long tradition of local government in Virginia—a tradition that had proved its efficacy in the past and one in which Henry had made his climb to political power himself—it is not surprising that Henry and most other Virginians like him would be wary of any drastic moves toward centralization. Indeed, it was in part this sense of particularism that had made Henry back away from full support of the much-needed impost bills; his amendment to the impost bill of 1781 stipulating that the revenues collected in Virginia could be applied only to Virginia's portion of the expenses of the Union was a clear indication of the priority which Henry gave to the interests of his state in the affairs of the nation.

All these factors, however, were merely indicators of Henry's possible reaction to a new frame of government; it is quite possible, given his waverings on the issue in the past, that he might have supported a stronger government had there been some concrete benefit to be gained from it by either him or his constituents. As it turned out, precisely the opposite was the case. As Robert D. Meade, Henry's most recent biographer, has noted, John Jay's negotiations with Spain and the willingness of seven Northern states to enter into the subsequent treaty agreeing to give up America's right to navigate the Mississippi River provided graphic proof of how the interests of the Southern states in general, and those of Henry's beloved Southwest in particular, might be threatened by a "consolidated" government.[1] Henry had always been particularly concerned about the interests of the western settlers. Indeed, much of his inclination to strengthen the Confederation government sprang from his desire to protect the western Virginia settlements from intrigue by the Spanish and attack from the Indians. The initiation of diplomatic proceedings to reach an accord with both the Spanish and the Indians and the raising of a military force with which to enforce American policy on these two groups were clearly the responsibility of the Confederation government. Yet through a combination of apathy on the part of the nonwestern representatives in the Confederation Congress and the impecunious state of the continental government, the Congress was unable to do anything to ease the burdens of those living on the frontier. Perhaps an increase in the financial strength of the central government might at least allow for the appointment of additional federal agents on the frontier charged with entering into peace treaties with the numerous Indian tribes of the area. Perhaps. But even while Henry was governor there was considerable evidence indicating that a government dominated by Northerners could not be counted on to look after Virginia interests.

On June 8, 1786, the Virginia representatives to the Confederation Congress replied to Governor Henry's latest request for more federal Indian agents with pessimism. It seemed that opposition in Congress to spending more funds on western defense was considerable. The Virginia representatives opined: "It was perhaps an inconvenience in this instance that so few states have extensive frontiers; as they with reluctance assent to relieving us from difficulties to which they are not themselves likely to be exposed."[5] What better summary of the dangers of consolidated government! Indeed, how was Virginia, with her own distinctive problems and concerns, going to protect her interests in a government where the strength of a primarily Northern and Eastern majority might dominate?

Just a few months later, on August 12, 1786, James Monroe wrote to Henry of Jay's dealings with the Spanish, a communication that changed Henry's view of federal power from one of suspicion to open hostility. Monroe called the whole business "one of the most extraordinary transactions" he had ever heard of; Jay's entire mission was supposed to be devoted to guaranteeing the right of America to navigate the Mississippi, and yet the end result of his labors was a treaty that explicitly yielded that right. It was Monroe's opinion that the seven Northern states in favor of the treaty were so enthusiastic about it that they would try to push the proposal through the Congress by majority vote, against the wishes of the Southern states, even though the Articles of Confederation specifically provided that the approval of nine states was necessary for a treaty to go into effect. Monroe urged upon Henry the necessity of throwing "every possible obstacle" in their way in order to defeat the treaty.[6]

By December 1786 Henry was already perceived to be much less friendly to those advocating a stronger government. Madison, writing to Washington on December 7, was not ready to give up all hope of gaining Henry's support, but he ventured that his long-time opponent was now only a "cold advocate" of the federal cause, and that in the event that Jay was successful in passing his treaty, he would almost certainly join the other side. By March 1787 John Marshall was reiterating the importance which Henry attached to the Mississippi question: "Mr. Henry," Marshall wrote, "whose opinions have their usual influence, has been heard to say that he would rather part with the Confederation than relinquish the navigation of the Mississippi."[7]

Jay's treaty ultimately was not implemented; the seven Northern states, however much they might have benefited from it, were not willing to risk disunion to secure those advantages. Yet the whole affair had provided a disconcerting example of the potential for dramatic conflict of interests between Northern and Southern states. In the short term it is not difficult to see how the Northern states might have been willing to trade the right to navigate the Mississippi for commercial privileges with Spain, but from the standpoint of the Southern states, and in terms of the long-range interests of the nation at large, the proposed treaty would have been disastrous to American interests. That the Confederation had come so close to entering into such a treaty, and that a revised and strengthened central government might make it easier for a bare majority of Northern states to coerce the Southern states into similar schemes contrary to their interests, was a decisive factor in Henry's decision not to support the movement for a new Constitution.

The members of the Virginia General Assembly were no doubt aware of Henry's views when they balloted for their delegates to the Philadelphia Convention, but evidently his feelings on the subject had little effect on the legislators' choices. Washington, known to be a supporter of a stronger Constitution, was unanimously elected; Henry received the second greatest number of votes, followed by Edmund Randolph, John Blair, and James Madison, these last three all favoring constitutional revision. George Mason, considered to be closer to Henry in his views on the subject, was next in the balloting, with George Wythe, a mild supporter of constitutional reform, rounding out the delegation.[8] The composition of the delegation indicates that either the members of the House were themselves not certain of the advantages of a stronger government and thus elected people of diverse points of view, or, more likely, that, following long tradition, they made their selections on the basis of past service and personal prestige rather than on the ideological attachments of the various candidates.

By the time Henry received word of his election to the Philadelphia Convention, he had already retired from the governorship, announced his decision not to seek reelection, and around December 1786, seemingly unable to live in one place more than a few years at a time, moved eastward from Henry County to Prince Edward County, where he hoped to regain some of his declining health and turn his attention to private affairs. Another possible reason for the move may have been the isolation that Henry felt at Leatherwood, 180 miles or about a week's ride from Richmond. Henry had complained that he had "scarcely heard a word of public affairs" at Leatherwood. It does not appear, however, that he was any better informed in Prince Edward. His involvement with the political life of the commonwealth had so lessened by the time of his move to Prince Edward that he failed to receive the letter appointing him a delegate to the Convention until February 1787, two months after Governor Randolph had sent it.[9]

Henry did not elaborate on the reasons for his refusal to serve in his reply to Randolph. Randolph seemed convinced that the attempt to close the Mississippi had been the decisive factor that had turned Henry against the plan for a new government. Madison, on the other hand, was not convinced that Henry had definitely decided to oppose it. Rather, he ascribed "his refusal to attend the convention to a policy of keeping himself free to combat or espouse the result of it, according to the result of the Mississippi." Madison realized, however, that the "Mississippi business" was far from resolved, and therefore he too was pessimistic about gaining Henry's support for a new constitution in the immediate future.[10]

At this stage, however, Henry probably had no firm view of what his opinion on the final product of the Philadelphia Convention would be. Although more suspicious than ever about the dangers of what he termed "consolidated government," he was nevertheless not unaware of the past weaknesses of the Articles of Confederation. On September 24, 1787, just a week after the Philadelphia Convention adjourned, Washington sent Henry a copy of the proposed plan of government. He must have sensed that Henry was not likely to approve it, although he was certain that Henry would recognize some of the beneficial aspects of the plan. Washington admitted that he too wished it "had been more perfect." He added, however, that since the "constitutional door is opened to amendments hereafter," he favored adopting it in spite of its defects. Henry's reply, dated nearly a month later, gave some indication of the deep opposition that he would later display publicly. He forthrightly told Washington that he would not be able to support the Constitution and elaborated only by saying that his concern over the document was "really greater than I am able to express."[11]

A few days later, while serving as a representative to the House of Delegates, Henry would make public his opposition. On October 25, Francis Corbin, a staunch Federalist, introduced a resolution calling for a convention to ratify the proposed Constitution. Corbin was a poor choice as a spokesman for the Federalist cause, as any comparison between Corbin and the man who would become the chief symbol of the opposition to the Constitution was bound to reflect poorly on the Federalists. Corbin's father had been a prominent royal official in Virginia and had quietly gone into retirement during the Revolution, unwilling to join the patriot cause. Francis Corbin, while he had not sided openly with the British, had spent the war years in England obtaining his education. He had returned to Virginia only after the war was over and the outcome decided.

Henry was the first to rise to oppose Corbin's resolution. Although he did not dispute the necessity of calling a convention to debate the Constitution, he wanted that convention to be given the power to amend the document. Both Henry and George Mason steadfastly maintained that they were not opposed to the notion of union altogether but only that they wanted to have the option of amending the Constitution before adding their assent to it. It was left to John Marshall, a man whose devotion to a nationalist vision of empire would ultimately exceed that of any man in Virginia, to propose the compromise that would allow the call for a convention to go forth. He agreed with Henry that the convention should have the power to propose amendments, but he wanted the resolution allowing for such amendments to be free from the suggestion that Virginians were disposed against the new Constitution, a shade of meaning suggested in the tone of Henry's proposal. Marshall's resolution seemed to meet with the approval of everyone and it was immediately adopted unanimously.[12]

Henry was hardly the only Virginian who was suspicious of the proposed Constitution. His chief political rival, Thomas Jefferson, on receiving a copy of the Constitution in Paris where he was serving as American envoy, was not at all pleased with what he saw. He wrote Madison on December 20, 1787, lamenting the omission of a bill of rights and expressing his concern that the inadequate provisions for rotation of office in all three branches of government would open the way for the domination of the new government by a few individuals. In general his attitude was probably more negative than positive, and he admitted, "I own I am not a friend to a very energetic government. It is always oppressive."[13]

Thus, for a brief period Patrick Henry and Thomas Jefferson actually were on the same side of the political fence. But not for long, as Madison, in a number of letters written in the winter of 1788, reassured his friend on several key points with respect to the Constitution, and Jefferson finally came around to favor the proposed plan of union.[14]

Madison was finding it progressively more difficult to suppress his annoyance over the frequency with which Henry opposed measures which he supported. On December 9 he wrote Jefferson that Henry, above all others, was the man most likely to bring about the defeat of the Constitution. Moreover, Henry was simultaneously involved in other controversies with Madison. In the same session of the General Assembly in which the call for a convention had been issued, Henry, no doubt citing his long-standing desire to promote domestic manufactures, had pushed through the legislature a bill prohibiting the importation of foreign rum, brandy, manufactured leather, hats, and candles. Madison was furious, terming the various pieces of prohibitory legislation "mad freakes." Not only did the laws violate Madison's long-standing commitment to free trade, but it was also clear that such a prohibition would never promote domestic industry unless all the other states imposed similar prohibitions, something they were not likely to do.

The efforts of many Virginians to repeal legislation obstructing the payment of back debts owed to the British were also once again thwarted by Henry. His long-standing position—that Virginia would comply with the terms of the Treaty of Peace only after Great Britain had complied—was endorsed by the House almost every year during the 1780s. And as a final straw, Henry continued to oppose the revision of Virginia's legal code, a project dear to the hearts of both Jefferson and Madison.[15]

Henry's opposition to the Constitution remained the greatest source of concern to Federalists like Madison. The young nationalist was able to see that there were not two but actually three groupings of opinion on the subject of the Constitution in Virginia. The first, which included himself, Edmund Pendleton, and John Marshall, favored adopting the Constitution without additional amendments. The second and most crucial group consisted of those, like Governor Edmund Randolph, who generally approved of the substance of the new Constitution but desired amendments safeguarding the rights of the people and the states. The third group, while it spoke in terms of amending the Constitution, desired, according to Madison, to "strike at the essence of the System, and must lead to an adherence to the principles of the existing Confederation . . . or to a partition of the Union into several Confederacies." Henry, of course, fell into this last group. Madison was quite convinced that he would never win the support of the third group; what he was most concerned about was the likelihood that Henry and his supporters would succeed in persuading the members of the crucial second group to cast their votes against the Constitution until a second federal convention could be called to propose additional amendments substantially limiting the powers of the new government.[16]

Henry announced his candidacy for the post of delegate to the Virginia Ratifying Convention at the February session of the Prince Edward County Court. According to Reverend John Blair Smith, Henry gave a passionate speech criticizing the Constitution before a large crowd that had gathered at the courthouse. Smith, the president of nearby Hampden-Sydney College, a supporter of the Constitution, and evidently a long-standing opponent of Henry's on a wide range of issues, arranged for a member of his family to transcribe Henry's speech. A short while thereafter, at a public speaking exercise at which Henry was present, a student delivered Henry's speech and Smith himself offered the rebuttal. Henry was not altogether pleased. He ceased attending services at Blair's church, and in his capacity as a member of the board of governors of the college, he probably had something to do with Smith's dismissal a year later.

Following Henry's victory in the election for delegates to the Virginia Convention, Smith wrote to Madison criticizing Henry's tactics: "That gentleman has descended to lower artifices and management on the occasion than I thought him capable of. . . . It grieves me to see such great natural talents abused to such purposes."[17]

The division across the state on the question of the Constitution reflected Henry's influence. In an analysis that the examinations of modern scholars tend to confirm, Madison wrote that the majority of people in the Tidewater and Northern Neck regions of Virginia supported the Constitution, while those of the central Piedmont and the Southside opposed it.[18] It was of course in the central Piedmont and the Southside that Henry's influence was greatest. He had represented the interests of those areas for over two decades, and the adherence of those people to the principles of antifederalism was in part a reflection of their personal loyalty to him.

It is not likely that the divisions within Virginia on the Constitution were caused by personal influence alone. Professor Jackson T. Main has claimed, for example, that the areas that supported the Constitution tended to be well suited to commercial agriculture, located close to navigable rivers and ports, and dominated by planters with sizable holdings in land and slaves. The Antifederalist areas, on the other hand, tended to be less firmly a part of the commercial-agrarian world. The residents of Antifederalist counties, according to Main, were middle-class Americans who were more dependent upon subsistence or at least limited-market agriculture. Main argues that those favoring the Constitution had much more to gain from it; its centralizing features, together with its implied promise of building up a sound currency and regulating trade more efficiently, would benefit those involved in commercial pursuits more than it would the small subsistence farmers of the Southside, who traditionally feared centralized government and had nothing to gain from the financial and commercial provisions contained in the new frame of government.[19]

To some extent Main's interpretation is helpful in understanding the nature of the debate over the Constitution, but there are a number of areas and individuals that do not fit the analysis. Henry's own Prince Edward County, for example, although sufficiently isolated from the mainstream of communications in Virginia to make its citizens decidedly provincial in their world view, was hardly a subsistence region. Its population, which stood at 8,100 in 1790, was growing more rapidly than nearly any other county in the state. Its slave population, which amounted to nearly half of the total citizenry, is a good indication that a sizable portion of the county's residents were engaged in the intensive cultivation of an export crop. And Henry himself, of course, was hardly a typical member of the Virginia yeomanry.

As Henry's own case suggests, the personality and prestige of the individuals supporting and opposing the Constitution almost certainly influenced the outcome as much as the economic and regional interests of the people involved in the debate over the Constitution. This fact may be hard for the modern reader—accustomed to viewing interests and ideologies in the context of well-organized political parties—to credit, but in the oligarchic, deferential system so prevalent in Virginia, those commodities, together with the powers of persuasion and oratory that Henry possessed in such abundance, were unusually important.

That they were important is attested to by the enormous amount of time that Madison spent worrying about Henry's influence in the months before the Virginia Convention opened. Writing to Jefferson in February 1788, Madison attributed the strong current of opposition to the Constitution to "the influence and exertions of Mr. Henry and Col. Mason." Earlier he had even expressed the fear that Henry's influence would spread to North Carolina and place the Constitution in jeopardy there, too.[20]

Madison did everything he could to overcome this influence; in fact, if Henry, instead of tending to personal affairs in Prince Edward County, had worked as hard as Madison in persuading undecided delegates to oppose the Constitution, the outcome of the Ratifying Convention in Virginia might have been different. In particular, Madison's and Washington's success in winning Edmund Randolph, who had joined in refusing to assent to the draft in the Philadelphia Convention, to the side of the Federalists was a crucial element in the ultimate Federalist victory in Virginia. One of Madison's strategies for converting Randolph was to stir up personal animosity between him and the Antifederalist leaders. He noted to Randolph the "desperate measures" to which Henry was willing to resort in order to defeat the plan of union and reported that Mason was so committed to opposing the Constitution that "he no longer spares even the *moderate opponents* of the Constitution" in his attacks.[21] These were points that must have affected Randolph's judgment on the matter, as he was in basic sympathy with the idea of a stronger union and—unlike Henry and Mason—only wanted a set of amendments that would eliminate a few of the most objectionable features of the Constitution. And of course Randolph must have been particularly disturbed by the mention of Mason's attacks on the "moderate opponents" of the Constitution, as he himself was the most visible of those moderate opponents. In any case, Randolph, who as recently as January 1788 had publicly reaffirmed his opposition to the Constitution, changed his mind by the time the Virginia Convention began its business.[22] In fact, it was Randolph who rose on the Convention floor on the first full day of debate to answer Patrick Henry's attacks on the Constitution. Henry and the other Antifederalist leaders were furious at what they considered to be Randolph's apostasy, with Mason thereafter referring to Randolph as "the young Arnold." They ascribed his conversion to ambition for high office in the new government, which was probably partially true.[23] But as we shall see from our analysis of the Convention debates, there were other, more compelling reasons why wavering delegates such as Randolph would ultimately vote for the Constitution and provide for its narrow margin of victory.

The leaders of both the nationalist and Antifederalist factions in the Virginia Ratifying Convention knew they had a fight on their hands. Madison admitted that "the business is in the most ticklish state that can be imagined." If anything, he felt that the Federalists were a few votes short of a majority. Henry, although he was convinced that the great mass of Virginia's citizens opposed the Constitution, realized that "the numbers in convention appear equal on both sides; so that the majority, which way soever it goes, will be small." In particular, it would be the handful of undecided delegates, particularly those from the western part of the state, who were as yet ignorant of the arguments for and against the Constitution, who would determine the outcome.[24]

By the time the Convention opened for business, the delegates were aware that eight states, including such powerful ones as Massachusetts, Pennsylvania, and South Carolina, had already assented to the Constitution. This fact, which pointed to the likelihood that the new federal union would proceed with or without Virginia, would have great impact on the proceedings.

The Convention began its deliberations on June 2, 1788, and, in a rare display of interest in the political issues of the day, a sufficient number of delegates actually turned up to constitute a quorum on the first day of business. The main item on the agenda that day was the selection of a presiding officer. George Washington would have been the logical candidate for the post, since he had served a similar function in the Philadelphia Convention and was considered by nearly all to be the logical choice for chief executive if the new Constitution was adopted. But Washington, aware even then of the necessity of maintaining the lofty, nonpartisan air that would enable him to transcend partisan struggles in order to achieve the stature of national symbol, declined to attend the Convention for fear that the bitter division over the Constitution in his home state would tarnish his Olympian image. Indeed, Washington's shrewd recognition of his role in American politics—a role that required that he act the part of a monument even while he was still living—was an important reason why he, and not Henry, became the first statesman of Virginia. Henry had simply made too many enemies over his long and illustrious career; he had taken strong positions on too many issues to assure himself a peaceful and controversy-free posterity.

In Washington's absence, the Convention unanimously elected Edmund Pendleton, who of course had experience as a presiding officer dating back to the Revolutionary conventions.[25] At the time of the Revolution, Pendleton's power and prestige had made him the logical person to appoint to a position of that kind; in the intervening years, however, others had eclipsed the aging Caroline

County statesman in power and influence. Nevertheless, it is certain that no one would have thought it appropriate to propose Patrick Henry, no matter how great his prestige and influence, for presiding officer. Henry was too closely identified with one of the two extreme wings in the Convention, and his selection would undoubtedly have drawn opposition from the Federalists. Pendleton, though known to be a Federalist, was considered much more moderate than either Madison or Henry.

On that same day David Robertson, a Federalist-leaning stenographer, was appointed to keep a record of the debate in the Convention, a move unparalleled in the legislative and political history of the commonwealth up to that time. Although a few Antifederalists were later to complain that his partisanship affected his work, historians, grateful for the detailed look at the proceedings that his record provides them, have not found his account intolerably onesided. Biographers of Henry, continually frustrated by the lack of evidence relating to his private or public life, are by necessity particularly grateful to Robertson, for he has given us the first and only full and explicit testimony relating to Henry's political concerns.

In the first full day of debate, George Nicholas, the delegate from Albemarle County, initiated Federalist strategy by defending the proposed plan of union article by article.[26] By proceeding in this manner, the Federalists hoped to keep their opponents on the defensive, forcing them to focus on the specific details of the Constitution rather than on the broad implications of its centralizing tendencies. Henry, who was the first to answer Nicholas, would have none of it. He countered with a broad-gauged attack on the very nature of the new government.

He first expressed wonder at the need for such a radical change in government. He maintained that "a general peace and a universal tranquility" prevailed in Virginia before the Philadelphia Convention; he could not understand the reason for disrupting that harmony. This statement in itself represented a change in Henry's thinking, for as governor of Virginia he had not infrequently been impressed with the disruptive forces he saw at work in society, forces that were in fact a partial result of the weaknesses of the Confederation government. The principal disquieting element in the new plan of government, the one feature that encompassed most of

Henry's specific objections, was the lack of an equitable division of power between the state and federal governments. In fact, Henry rightly concluded, it was not even proper to call the new government *federal*, for it was in fact a *national* government. Otherwise, why else would the framers have prefaced the document with the phrase "We the people" instead of "We the states?" It was axiomatic that the states were the creators of the confederation and thus held ultimate sovereignty. This substitution of "people" for "states" clearly indicated that the new Constitution was not a mere revision of the Articles of Confederation but rather a total repudiation of the principles of federalism upon which that plan of government was based. Such a drastic move would lead, according to Henry, to "one great, consolidated national government, of the people of all the states."[27]

Henry was more than a little displeased over the fact that the members of the Philadelphia Convention had not been more open about their intention to change the locus of sovereignty. He even went so far as to criticize George Washington, "that illustrious man who saved us by his valor," for his role in assenting to such a drastic change.[28] Having raised the issue of "consolidated government," Henry spent much of his time in the Convention pointing to the specific dangers that such a government presented. Although his speeches were seldom confined to any one particular point—indeed, that would prove to be their gravest weakness—it is possible to pick out a few of Henry's principal concerns from among the multitude of criticisms that the Antifederalist leader leveled at the Constitution.

The principal threat to liberty, and the main object of Henry's concern, was the new government's extensive power over the purse. It had been Great Britain's attempts to tax the American colonies that had precipitated the quarrels that eventually led to independence. The power over taxation had been deliberately withheld from the Confederation government and Henry and his Antifederalist colleagues were now determined to strike that power from the Constitution as well. Henry, who had himself complained of the inability of the Confederation government to raise a permanent revenue while he was governor, found himself arguing quite differently in the Virginia Convention. Expressing what were undoubtedly the sentiments of many of his constituents in the west, he objected to the creation of another set of tax collectors, who, he claimed, would not be prevented "from sucking your blood by speculations, commissions and fees." He asserted that the Virginia sheriffs, "those unfeeling bloodsuckers, have, under the watchful eye of your legislators, committed the most horrible and barbarous ravages on our people. It has required the most constant vigilance of the legislature to keep them from totally ruining the people; a repeated succession of laws have been made to suppress their iniquitous speculations and cruel extortions; and as often has their nefarious ingenuity devised methods of evading the force of those laws." Henry was convinced that if tax collectors within the state could not be adequately controlled by the Virginia legislature, then the federal tax collectors would enjoy even greater license to oppress the people. His alternative to a system of direct taxation was a requisition system whereby the state governments would be required to raise a specific sum of money and then turn their revenues over to the federal government.[29] Theoretically this system would differ from that used by the Confederation government: under Henry's plan those states late in their payments would pay additional interest on their debt to the central government. Moreover, the power of the government to coerce the states into meeting their obligations was to be explicitly recognized.

Finally, Henry's objection to the taxation power, like his objection to nearly every feature of the Constitution, was based not on fear of another set of tax collectors or on a preference for a system of indirect rather than direct taxation but rather on a hostility to the notion of centralized power itself. Henry simply was unwilling for Virginia to place herself at the mercy of her sister states. For example, during debate Henry frequently and erroneously reported that Virginia had been diligent in paying off her own state debt while other states had lagged in their payments. He predicted that if the central government were vested with the power to tax the states directly, Virginians would soon find that they were being taxed to pay off the debts of the other, less conscientious states. It was this tendency to endow Virginia with particular virtue, or at the least to view Virginia's situation and interests as significantly different from those of the other states, that made it so difficult for Henry to concede to a transfer of power from the state to the federal government.

Henry's attitude toward the federal government's power over the other major area of authority—defense—was similarly conditioned. Although he had often cursed the inadequacies and inefficiencies of the Virginia state militia system while he was war governor, by 1788, with the immediate pressures of war long past, Henry seemed now more concerned with the dangers of an overly efficient federal militia than he was with the continuing weakness of his own state's armed forces.[30] In some respects Henry was being even more short-sighted than usual, for just a few months earlier he had been lamenting the inability of the Confederation government to provide security for the frontier residents of his state. By June 1788 he may have decided that the central government, no matter how strong its militia, would prove unwilling to help those residents, but it nevertheless seems indisputable that the new federal government provided the only remaining hope for peace on the frontier, as the state governments had proved beyond any doubt their inability to handle the situation.

Henry's attitude toward the new Constitution's provisions respecting the role of the people in the affairs of the government has long been a subject of controversy and confusion. The confusion stems from the insistence by some historians on placing nearly all of Henry's statements in the Convention in just one of two descriptive categories labeled "aristocratic" or "democratic." Thus, we find Cecilia Kenyon, a perceptive but argumentative political theorist, accusing Henry and some of his Antifederalist colleagues of being antidemocratic because of their lack of faith in the ability of the central government to rule effectively and justly over such a large expanse of territory. Conversely, most of Henry's biographers, anxious to prove that their protagonist was a "liberal," have combed his speeches for evidence proving his commitment to democratic forms of government.[31] Indeed, sometimes those labels have some significance in explaining Henry's thoughts on government. Although Henry and probably every other political figure in eighteenth-century America would have angrily denied that their political philosophy was "aristocratic," there were nevertheless occasions when Henry's opinion of the abilities of the great mass of the people to govern themselves was sufficiently low to make him appear to the twentieth-century observer much akin to an aristocrat. And similarly, those historians looking for the "democratic" Henry are not without some evidence to lend credence to their contentions. But one should be extremely careful about reading our modern preoccupation with democratic government into Patrick Henry's late-eighteenth-century speculations on the nature of the division of power between the state and federal governments, for it seems clear that men like Henry most often were unconcerned with such theoretical abstractions. The job of government was to be as efficient and equitable in its operation as possible. Henry's practical experience caused him to believe that local governments best met that ideal, state governments less so, and consolidated governments, located far from the great mass of the citizens they ruled, still less.

One of the things that Henry most despised about the new Constitution was the provision that a mere majority of the elected representatives in Congress could pass a law wholly against the interests of the citizens of Virginia. He was most concerned that the Congress would interpret its power in such a way as to enable itself to dispose of the Mississippi River by a mere majority vote. Since a majority of the states had already gone on record favoring the relinquishment of rights of navigation of the Mississippi in return for commercial privileges from Spain, Henry was quick to denounce the dangers inherent in this majoritarian style of government.[32] It was precisely this attitude that Professor Kenyon has pronounced antidemocratic.

Yet Henry found no difficulty in turning right around to embrace majoritarian principles and condemn those devices designed to thwart the will of the majority when it suited the purpose of his argument. While Henry expressed great concern over the evil that could be accomplished by an overbearing majority in the legislature, he could be equally alarmed over the possibility that a "trifling minority may reject the most salutary amendments" against the will of the majority. On this subject he was explicit in his support of democratic principles, praising the "genius of democracy" and claiming that it could not flourish under the new Constitution.[33]

Of course, Henry was being wholly inconsistent in his praise of majoritarianism on the subject of amendments and his condemnation of it on the subject of specific legislation. One gets the strong impression that had Virginians been the people anxious to enact the Spanish treaty and Northerners in the vanguard for amendments, his arguments might have been exactly the reverse.

What was important for Henry was not the abstract concept of majoritarianism or its opposite but rather the net effect of the system, whatever system, on the people living under it. While Henry did not trust the people of New York to make a reasonable and equitable decision regarding the interests of his state, he continued to have faith in the abilities of the people of the individual counties within Virginia to make their representatives reflect their feelings. In fact, when Governor Edmund Randolph made a passing reference to the great multitude of people at large as a "herd," Henry strenuously objected. Randolph's very use of the word signified to Henry the natural tendency of representatives when serving in a government too far removed from its constituents to ever serve them adequately. He was convinced that the vastness of the new government would "destroy that connection that ought to subsist between the elector and the elected." Because the voters were too often unacquainted with the candidates and the candidates too often unacquainted with the interests of the voters, the mutual set of responsibilities previously accepted by the electors and the elected would disappear: "A common man must ask a man of influence how he is to proceed and for whom he might vote. The elected therefore, will be careless of the interest of the electors. It will be a common job to extort the suffrages of the common people for the most influential characters."[34] Antidemocratic rhetoric? If one expects an eighteenth-century Virginian to foretell the future, a future where party newspapers and, later, television and radio publicize elections to a degree where voters could in fact make their own, informed decisions on candidates residing far from their own homes, yes. But Henry, without the advantage of that extraordinary foresight, was most likely aware of the existing difficulty in persuading representatives and constituents to assume their full responsibilities even in the small world of a Virginia county. Thus the practice of "treating," considered by nearly all Virginia's leaders to be a perversion of the electoral process, continued to play a central role on election day nevertheless. It was not only that some candidates desired to gain an unfair advantage over their less wealthy opponents by serving food and drink to the voters on election day; an equally important factor in the perpetuation of the custom was the apathy of the voters toward the entire electoral process. "I am sorry to observe," lamented Thomas Evans of Accomac County in 1797, "that such is the disposition of my countrymen that nothing will induce them to attend elections of however great importance without being treated." Henry was convinced that far from disappearing when the federal government commenced operation, the problem would only worsen. The voters, less familiar with both the issues and the candidates than ever before, would only become more apathetic; the candidates, driven by the need to rally support, would inevitably further subvert the electoral process. And the successful candidates, with no real sense of their constituents' interests, would be unable to serve those constituents effectively once elected.[35]

As it turned out, Henry's diagnosis would be nearly completely incorrect. The partisan divisions that were to occur over questions of federal policy in the 1790s were of such moment that they would lead to the formation of political parties with an ability to reach great masses of citizens on subjects relating to their interests and ideologies to an extent never before achieved in American history. In effect, the distant and impersonal central government, by its very excesses, actually succeeded in rousing the voters out of their apathy in ways that Henry had never foreseen.

Henry can hardly be blamed for not perceiving these future developments. Even the supporters of the new government, Madison in particular, talked of the evils of permanent political parties; literally no one in America in 1788 could have seen hope for democracy coming from that unlikely corner.

As we have seen, the specific event that caused Henry to perceive a strong central government as a threat to Virginia's interests and which therefore was primarily responsible for the subsequent development of Henry's entire states'-rights ideology was the attempt by the Northern states to barter away the right of the western regions to navigate the Mississippi. Henry, both because he was genuinely appalled by the prospect of losing the Mississippi and because he ardently desired the votes of the undecided delegates from Kentucky—the one area most threatened by the Spanish treaty —was to spend considerable time in the Convention speaking to that point. He was convinced, although he never was able to produce the arithmetic to prove his point, that the proposed treaty with Spain was more likely to be thwarted under the Articles of Confederation than under the new Constitution. How he reached this conclusion is unclear, since, as Madison pointed out in reply, the

Constitution required the approval of two-thirds of the members of the Senate *and* the approval of the President, which in fact made it even more difficult for a bare majority to push through a treaty against the interests of a minority. But Henry persisted, arguing not in arithmetical terms but rather simply stressing the inherent differences between the Northeast and the Southwest that led the Northeastern states to agree to the transaction with Spain in the first place.[36] In this line of argument Henry was coming perilously close to disagreeing not only with the particular details of the proposed plan of union currently under debate but also with the very concept of union. In fact, when Henry's arguments against the Constitution are analyzed closely, it becomes clear that his constitutional objections to excessive power in the area of taxation and defense, his dislike of the length of senators' terms, and his lengthy discourses on the manner of electing representatives were merely side issues. He may have sincerely held these objections, but they were in themselves not enough to cause him to oppose the Constitution. Rather, they were further justifications for his fundamental concern about the dangers of a strong union in any form.

Henry best summed up his concern over the change in the locus of political sovereignty and all his fears over Virginia's fate should she agree to be consolidated into the Union in his first lengthy speech to the Convention, when he exclaimed: "This government is not a Virginian, but an American government. Is it not, therefore, a consolidated government?" Henry believed that it was indeed a consolidated, American government and that Virginia could profit better outside it.[37]

The only occasions on which Henry ever approached the heights of his pre-Revolutionary oratory in the Convention were those when he departed from his wide-ranging assault on the specific provisions of the Constitution and appealed to his fellow delegates' sense of pride and history. He asked the delegates to think back to the Revolution, when

the Genius of Virginia called on us for liberty—called us from our beloved endearments, which, from long habits, we were taught to love and revere. . . . On this awful occasion did you want a federal government? Did federal ideas lead you to the most splendid victories? I must again repeat the favorite idea, that the genius of

Virginia did, and will again, lead us to happiness. To obtain the most splendid prize you did not consolidate. You accomplish the most glorious ends by the assistance of our country.[38]

That country, be assured, was Virginia, not America. And that country was, according to Henry, if anything even stronger after the Revolution than before. This last observation was unquestionably that of a man in different circumstances in 1788 than in 1780. For in 1780, plagued by the inability of the state government to fight the war efficiently, Henry was reported to have been willing to establish a dictatorship in Virginia in order to strengthen the defenses of the state. By 1788, with the war safely past, the virtues and strengths of his country were much more apparent to him. And Henry was convinced that those virtues and strengths would continue to allow Virginia to steer an independent course.

One of the principal arguments of Henry's Federalist opponents had been that the ratification of the Constitution by eight states prior to the opening of the Virginia Convention had made a union, with or without Virginia, inevitable. They contended that while Virginia might well be as strong and independent as any single state in America, she could not hope to compete with a consolidated phalanx of states by herself. Henry vehemently rejected this notion. He not only pointed to the general increase in prosperity within the state following the signing of the Treaty of Peace but also praised the strength of the state government, "a government suitable to the genius of the people."

For all the weaknesses that Henry had himself lamented in the past, it is not surprising that he should feel that sense of attachment to the "genius" of his state's political system. In spite of the oligarchic nature of that political system, or perhaps even because of it, Henry had been allowed to rise rapidly to prominence within it. The ruling elite in the colonial assembly, although they had been suspicious of the "radicalism" of the young burgess, had proved flexible enough to yield power to him. Recognizing that Henry had succeeded in rallying the support of his constituents, those influential and more conservative burgesses, while hardly bowing to democratic impulses, were not inclined to thwart actively the wishes of a substantial portion of the colony's citizens. And so it had been throughout the course of the Revolution. The General Assembly, although occasionally sluggish in responding to the needs and wishes of the people, ultimately did respond. The members of the Assembly, because they were in close contact with the people—they were, after all, elected annually and usually lived within the counties in which they were elected—were virtually unable to avoid serving the interests of at least a good portion of the people they represented. In fact, because of the close physical proximity between representative and constituent, it was quite likely that the interests of the two would naturally coincide. How different things seemed in the proposal for the new government! Representatives were elected every two years and senators every six, and the districts from which they were drawn were so vast that the proximity that had usually guaranteed responsible representation in the state government would be all but destroyed.

Henry ultimately was to prove unable to convince a sufficient number of his fellow delegates of the strengths of their own government and the grievous defects of the federal plan of union. The Federalists, partially because of the effectiveness of their own strategy and because of some serious tactical weaknesses in Henry's assault on the Constitution, were able to win over those crucial ten or fifteen delegates who had come to the Convention uncommitted. The Federalists knew they could count on a solid core of support from those areas of the Northern Neck and central Tidewater, where the commercial interests of the residents would be aided by a stronger government with the power to regulate trade and bolster American credit abroad; they knew too that the delegates from the Virginia Southside and the central Piedmont, whose economic interests made it less likely that they would need a strong central government and whose personal ties to Henry were close, would principally oppose the Constitution. The crucial delegates, those from the far west, had good reason to be more confused about the new plan of government. On the one hand they tended to share the distrust of most Virginians toward centralized government. On the other, the state government of Virginia had not always been as responsive to the needs of their region as it might have been; in particular, the ability of the state to provide them defense against hostile Indians had not proved impressive. The combination of a scarcity of funds and the unconcern of many of the eastern members of the legislature made it impossible to raise and equip a militia force adequate to the task of quelling the Indians. Federalists like Madison and Marshall made much of this fact, promising the western delegates much-needed federal aid in solving the frontier problem. Henry countered arguments of this sort with the quite justifiable assertion that the central government under the Articles of Confederation had consistently shirked its responsibilities to the frontier residents and there was no reason to believe that things would be any different under the new Constitution.[39]

Henry had undoubtedly not forgotten his last days as governor of Virginia, when he attempted to get aid from Secretary of War Henry Knox, only to be rebuffed. On that occasion he was told by Congressman James Monroe that the representatives in the Continental Congress from the Northeast, having no frontier problem of their own, were simply unwilling to vote for expenditures relating to defense.[40] Thus Henry, with history on his side, was able to assure the western delegates that however inadequate the state's defenses had been, they could expect considerably less from a federal government that was largely unconcerned with the particular interests of western Virginia. It was of course this same disregard for Virginia's and Kentucky's interests that had caused the Northeastern states to attempt to peddle the Mississippi River to Spain, an effort that would surely continue under the new Constitution.[41]

If Henry had focused his attacks on just a few themes—the proved cases of the indifference of the Northeast to Virginia's interests would have been the most effective of those themes—then perhaps his efforts at winning delegates to his side might have been more successful. He failed to do that, however, and instead wasted his oratory, and tried the patience of his audience, on too many indiscriminate, scattershot attacks on nearly every specific provision of the proposed Constitution. In his first full speech before the Convention, for example, Henry spoke out against the inadequate separation of power between state and nation in the Constitution, discoursed loosely on the general subject of liberty and public virtue, launched into a defense of the accomplishments of the Articles of Confederation, criticized the inadequacy of the system apportioning representation in the House of Representatives, returned to his discourse on liberty, denounced as unworkable the provision laying out the amendment process, issued a warning with respect to the new government's power to raise a standing army, drew parallels between the liberties enjoyed in America and the tyrannies imposed in Europe, condemned the power of direct taxation, emphasized the differing interests of Northern and Southern states, painted horrible pictures of hordes of rapacious tax collectors descending on Virginia, warned that the President would attempt to make himself a king, decried the fact that Congress could set the time and manner of federal elections, claimed that the Senate— being vested with the treaty-making power—could easily injure Virginia's interests, digressed on the histories of Switzerland and Turkey, complained of the inadequacies of Virginia's representation in Congress, and finally apologized for having "hurried on, from subject to subject" in his discourse![42]

This approach, in addition to weakening the effectiveness of his most important objections by giving nearly equal time to the trivial ones, also led Henry into a number of logical contradictions. Thus, he could denounce the majoritarianism implicit in the legislative powers of Congress but find fault with the Constitution for not providing for majoritarianism in the amending power. In criticizing the new plan of government for requiring the approval of two-thirds of the states for amendments, he would disregard the fact that the Articles of Confederation had actually required unanimous support of the states for ratification of amendments. Similarly, he would find fault with the system of checks and balances on the grounds that it removed the government from the direct influence of the people, and then he would turn around and condemn one branch of government for its excessive influence over the others.

Just as Henry, with his long service in the state government, and young James Madison, with most of his brief career in the service of the continental government, best represented the two extreme wings in the Convention, so too did Governor Edmund Randolph, wealthy, well born, and well respected, seem to speak for the undecided delegates. Randolph delivered the final speech before the vote on ratification took place; in that speech he voiced the motives and the misgivings of nearly all who ultimately decided to cast their ballots in favor of the Constitution in spite of their many reservations about some of its provisions. Randolph reaffirmed the public opposition he had expressed to the Constitution in the Philadelphia Convention, explaining, "*I refused to subscribe; because I had, as*

I still have, objections to the Constitution, and wished a free inquiry into its merits; and that the accession of eight states reduced our *deliberations* to the single question of *Union or no Union*."[43]

This above all others was the one point that the Federalists had been able to impress upon the undecided delegates. Madison and his supporters did not even attempt to persuade the delegates that every feature of the Constitution was unobjectionable. Rather, they simply asked the members of the Convention to choose between two alternatives—no union at all or a partially defective one. It was clear that the old Articles of Confederation would no longer suffice. The defeat of the impost proposal by New York was, to all but the most committed Antifederalists, final proof that it would be impossible for sound and stable government to continue to exist under the old plan of union. Thus the supporters of the Constitution had only to persuade the members of the Convention that the new Constitution was at least preferable to the old Articles and that, whatever its defects, there was probably no alternative to ratifying it, since the other states would almost certainly approve it, leaving Virginia only the choices of joining the Union or remaining outside it and attempting to compete for trade, manufactures, and revenues with those within. In addition, some Federalists earnestly assured the undecided delegates that a bill of rights substantially easing their fears about the excessive power of the new government would be adopted once the Constitution was ratified. Henry, of course, did not trust the Federalist promise of subsequent amendments and devoted part of his arguments in the Convention to proving that Virginia was strong enough to compete with any power on the continent, but for once in his extraordinarily successful lifetime, his oratory failed to carry the day. He must have sensed his failure even before the final vote was taken. In his closing speech on June 25, uttered just before Randolph ended debate with his remarks, Henry apologized for having spoken at such length and in such detail during the preceding weeks. He then added:

If I shall be in the minority, I shall have those powerful sensations which arise from a conviction of *being overpowered in a good cause*. Yet I will be a peaceable citizen. My head, my hand, and my heart, shall be at liberty to retrieve the loss of liberty, and remove the defects of that system in a constitutional way.[44]

He had not yet totally given up the fight. Before the final vote on the Constitution was taken, the Antifederalist forces offered a substitute resolution asserting that a bill of rights "together with amendments to the most exceptionable parts of the said Constitution" should be ratified by the other states before Virginia assented to the new plan of union. This resolution was immediately put to a vote and, in a decision that was a clear indication of the final vote on the Constitution, was defeated, 80 to 88. The roll-call vote on the adoption of the Constitution proceeded similarly, with the supporters of the new government picking up an extra vote, 89 to 79.[45]

It was a momentous decision, but few people greeted it with unmixed emotions. Spencer Roane, Henry's son-in-law, described the mood immediately after ratification:

> The decision has been distressing and awfull to great numbers, & it is generally believed will be so received by the people. The minority is a very respectable one indeed, & made a most noble stand in defence of the liberties of the people. . . . there is no rejoicing on Acct of the vote of ratification—it would not be prudent to do so; & the federalists behave with moderation and do not exult in their success.[46]

James Madison, the man in the Virginia Convention who perhaps had the fewest qualms about the new Constitution, must have at least felt a sense of considerable satisfaction. He had been pitted against Henry in innumerable legislative battles during the 1780s and on only a few of those issues had he enjoyed any success at all. Henry's influence in the Assembly had usually been sufficient to thwart the best-laid plans of the young nationalist. But on this most momentous question, a question debated in a forum that should have given Henry the best possible chance to use his oratorical gifts to their fullest, Madison had triumphed.

Madison's victory was one where organization and ideology were closely related. The Virginia nationalist had been aggressive in rounding up support for the Constitution in his home state; indeed, from the time he entered politics Madison was one of the few prominent Virginians to devote his full energies to a political career rather than divide his time between private and public pursuits. This devotion to public affairs was both a reflection of his belief in the efficacy of a more active central government and an important practical reason for his ultimate success in securing the endorsement from his fellow Virginians for that type of government. By contrast, Henry's opposition to the Constitution was confined principally to orations on the Convention floor; he seems to have made little effort to engage in the politicking necessary to block adoption of the Constitution. Such politicking would have been out of character, for Henry still clung to a more traditional style of political discourse. Inherent in Henry's Antifederalist ideology was a view of politics that required only a part-time attention to public concerns. It was precisely because Virginians were an independent-minded people generally able to guide their own destinies that the reins of government, except in times of public crisis such as the Revolution, needed to be held only loosely. The role of the squire-politicians who governed Virginia society then was a more relaxed one, and Henry's opposition to a stronger central government was perfectly in keeping with his unwillingness to work actively to prevent that government from coming into being.

8

Return to the Assembly

Madison and the Federalists had triumphed, but it was clear that many of those who had cast their votes in favor of the Constitution had misgivings about the new plan of government. On June 27, two days after ratification, George Wythe, chairman of the Federalist-dominated committee charged with proposing amendments to the Constitution, introduced into the Convention a bill of rights designed to protect individual liberties and another twenty amendments designed to strengthen the power of the states at the expense of the central government. The amendments reflected the whole range of the Antifederalists' fears. The western delegates, mindful of Henry's warnings about the future of the Mississippi River, joined in the demand for an amendment requiring the approval of three-fourths of the members of both houses of Congress in order to secure approval of any treaty touching upon the territorial rights of any state. An amendment requiring a two-thirds majority rather than a simple majority for the approval of laws regulating commerce reflected the same fear of the dominance of the commercial North over agrarian Virginia. Similarly, the traditional fear of the central government's power over the sword was manifested in an amendment requiring the approval of two-thirds of the Congress for the recruitment of a standing army during peacetime. Finally, and most important, Wythe's committee proposed an amendment requiring that Congress first requisition the states for funds before levying direct taxes; Congress would thus be prohibited from exercising the power of direct taxation unless a state failed to meet its requisition.

The amendment with respect to direct taxation was the only one to meet any opposition at all, but it too passed, 85 to 65, with twelve of the supporters of the Constitution voting with the Antifederalists.[1] All the remaining amendments passed by voice vote. That such a large majority of delegates was eager to take steps to restrict the power of the new government before it had even begun operation is indicative of the extremely fragile commitment of a great many Virginians to "federalism." And Patrick Henry, when he laid his plans to weaken the new government "in a constitutional way," would be one of the first to attempt to undermine that commitment even further.

Madison was well aware that he would be unable to sit back and savor his victory. Writing to Washington shortly after the Convention adjourned, he referred to Henry's determination to alter the Constitution drastically and fully anticipated that the attempt to do so would come soon and would occur in that one arena where Henry had traditionally enjoyed so much success—the lower house of the state legislature.[2] Madison's assessment was to prove correct, and in the battle for constitutional amendments he would discover that he, too, was under attack from the opponents of the Constitution.

Henry and many of the Antifederalists were not content to trust the new Congress to devise a set of amendments; rather, they desired a second convention, representative of the interests of the states rather than of a small circle of nationalists, to decide the question. In fact, Governor Clinton of New York, a staunch Antifederalist, had written Edmund Randolph on May 8, 1788, proposing a joint conference between New York and Virginia, the purpose of which would be to demand that amendments be a precondition to ratification. Randolph, to the fury of Henry, Mason, and other Antifederalists, did not reveal this until after Virginia had adopted the Constitution. And, of course, Virginia's adoption in turn influenced New York's decision on the Constitution a month later. When New York reluctantly ratified, however, it included with its announcement of ratification a call for a second general convention to consider the subject of amendments.[3]

When Madison heard of the New York plan, he realized immediately that Henry would leap on it as precisely the device he needed to weaken or even destroy the new government. By the time the regular session of the General Assembly convened in October 1788, it was clear that Henry had a sizable majority behind him. Moreover, the Federalist leadership in the Assembly was unusually weak. Madison and Henry Lee were serving in the Continental Congress and Washington was in temporary retirement. Henry, on the other hand, was exceptionally active, so active, in fact, that Washington was later to complain: "The edicts of Mr. Henry are enregistered with less opposition by the majority of that body than those of the Grand Monarch in the Parliaments of France. He has only to say let this be law and it is law."[4]

Henry's opening strategy was to discredit or weaken some of the prominent supporters of the Constitution. The first to face his wrath was Edward Carrington, an aide and informant of both Washington and Madison for several years, who had been serving in the Continental Congress when the news of his election to the lower house reached him in New York. Carrington resigned his post and left for Virginia to serve in the lower house. The Committee on Privileges and Elections recommended that he be seated, but the Antifederalists in the House, led by Henry, insisted that he be deprived of his seat on the ground that he had violated the law prohibiting officials from serving in both the state and continental governments. Because the Antifederalists had a clear majority in the House, they were able to overrule the committee and thus register a rebuke to a representative of Virginia's two most prominent Federalists.[5]

A few days later Henry made his opposition to the new government more explicit. He announced that he would oppose any measure intended to facilitate the operation of the government until specific proposals for amending the Constitution were adopted. On that same day he introduced his plan for a second convention, including in his speech a strongly worded attack on the Federalists. There were, however, few in the House who could answer him. The Federalists tried to soften his proposal by offering a substitute asking that Congress be given the first chance to draft amendments, but their attempt was easily rebuffed.[6]

Henry's next victory came at the expense of Madison. The Antifederalists had deliberately backed Madison as a candidate for the Continental Congress in order to diminish his influence in the Assembly; they now turned his absence to advantage by blocking his election to the United States Senate. On November 8, 1788, in the balloting for the two senatorial posts, Richard Henry Lee received 98 votes; William Grayton, 86; and Madison, 77. Grayson and Lee, two of the staunchest opponents of the Constitution in Virginia, would comprise the only solidly Antifederalist delegation to the United States Senate. Henry took the opportunity of the election to make a direct attack on Madison, claiming that he was "unworthy of the confidence of the people in the station of senator" and that his election would actually produce bloodshed and discord throughout the land.

The next week the Virginia legislature took its final step in asserting its desire for constitutional amendments. In an address to Congress drafted by Henry, the legislature expressed its lack of faith in the "slow forms of Congressional discussion and recommendation" and reiterated its opposition to the Constitution in its present form. The Federalists tried once again to soften the Antifederalist address, but the Antifederalists continued to control the House of Delegates and the Federalist substitute was easily defeated.[7]

Henry had reasserted himself in the 1788 session to an extent perhaps unequaled in his career as a legislator. There had been many instances in the past when his stand on a particular issue had influenced the outcome or when his oratory had swayed a few uncommitted delegates, but never before had he been able to dominate the proceedings from the day the Assembly convened to the moment it adjourned. Tobias Lear, echoing Washington's sentiments with respect to Henry's influence, opined: "In plain English he ruled a majority of the Assembly. . . . And after he had settled everything to his satisfaction he mounted his horse and rode home, leaving the little business of the state to be done by anybody who chose to give themselves the trouble of attending to it."[8]

While Henry's extraordinary dominance in the Assembly was testimony to his continued eminence in the politics of postwar Virginia, it could not have been achieved had not such an overwhelming number of Virginia's elected political leaders been in accord with him on the necessity of combating centralized power. The convenient combination of a respected and energetic politician who was committed to fighting centralized power and the widespread concern of so many Virginians over the new Constitution's tendency in that direction made conditions ideal for Henry's reemergence as the leader of the Assembly.

It is, however, not altogether clear why Henry chose to stake so much energy in this particular fight. His health was steadily declining and it seemed obvious to all that he was happiest when he returned to his plantation in Prince Edward County. Yet he persisted. In fact, he professed to be so worried over the effect of the new Constitution on his native state that he seriously contemplated moving to North Carolina, which had up to that point refused to ratify the Constitution and where, presumably, his liberties would be protected from the horrors of centralized power. Henry was sufficiently determined to make certain that North Carolina continue to be a haven for liberty that in spite of the fact that he had publicly announced his withdrawal from Virginia politics, he explicitly expressed his desire to keep well informed of the tides of political opinion in the Tarheel State. At least some believed that Henry's interest in North Carolina politics was having some effect. James Madison, for one, was convinced that it was Henry's influence that had turned North Carolina against the Constitution in the first place.[9]

Having refused to take part in the operation of the new government himself, there was little that Henry could do after the General Assembly adjourned but go home and wait for reports of the early activities of the First Congress. Before he was to receive those reports, however, he would hear of a series of vicious attacks on his own character. "Decius," who in all probability was Federalist John Nicholas of Albemarle County, initiated a series of attacks on Henry in the pages of the *Virginia Independent Chronicle* that ran for three months in the winter of 1789. The attacks, which embarrassed even some of Henry's confirmed opponents, referred to Henry as being moved by "AMBITION, AVARICE, ENVY, HATRED, AND REVENGE," and included a number of accusations about his private dealings. Henry, commenting about the series to William Grayson, noted that "Decius" had not been "lucky enough to hit upon one charge that is warranted by Truth. How lucky it is that he knows me no better, for I know of many Deficiencys in my own conduct, that I can easily conceive myself an unprofitable servant." He was also certain that the work of Decius had not been planned by responsible Federalist leaders, although he persisted in the belief that they had not gone out of their way to discourage the propagandist.[10]

In spite of Henry's successful efforts to send two Antifederalist senators to the First Congress, the Federalists had a commanding majority in both houses. In fact, seven of Virginia's ten representatives to the Congress were Federalists, although the man from Henry's district, Isaac Coles, was a staunch Antifederalist.

Virginia's "Federalist" congressmen bore little resemblance to Northern Federalists like Alexander Hamilton or Robert Morris, however. They represented, after all, a constituency that had only the most tenuous commitment to nationalism; even James Madison, thought to be the most committed nationalist in the Old Dominion, would depart from the orthodox nationalist position by leading the fight for a set of moderate constitutional amendments in Congress. Although his vision of "moderate" amendments was considerably more limited than Henry's, the very fact that Madison had softened his stand against amendments of any kind was indicative of the continuing strength of Antifederalist feeling in Virginia. Once in Congress, Madison followed the advice of Henry Lee by actually initiating the call for a set of amendments guaranteeing individual liberties while at the same time working to head off attempts to draft amendments drastically weakening the power of the new government. This was a potentially risky course, as there was always the danger that he might alienate his nationalist allies while at the same time failing to appease those who wanted amendments of a more substantial nature, but Madison performed this tightrope act brilliantly.[11]

Not all of Virginia's representatives to Congress were pleased with Madison's congressional amendments. Senator Richard Henry Lee, once again a strong ally of Henry's after years of opposition during the 1780s, wrote to his former rival:

> We might as well have attempted to move Mount Atlas upon our shoulders. In fact, the idea of subsequent amendments was little better than putting oneself to death first, in expectation that the doctor, who wishes our destruction, would afterward restore us to life.

Henry was inclined to agree. He thought that the amendments would "tend to injure rather than serve the cause of liberty" by lulling the suspicions of those who had demanded amendments in the first place without actually removing the cause of those suspicions. Henry believed that just one amendment explicitly limiting Congress's power over taxation would have been more valuable than all twelve of those proposed by Congress.[12]

Henry had also been informed of the attempt in the Senate by Vice President John Adams to bestow titles on the chief executive. The effort was abortive and in the end resulted only in Adams receiving the derisive title of "His Rotundity," but it nevertheless lent some credence to Henry's charge in the Virginia Ratifying Convention that the new Constitution "squints towards monarchy."

Finally, Henry's fears that Southern interests would be sacrificed to those of the North came to take on new meaning. Only the adjournment of Congress and a minor disagreement as to whether the permanent site of the nation's capital should be located in Germantown or on the Susquehanna River had prevented a Northern majority from officially establishing the capital site in Pennsylvania, far from the eyes and the interests of the South. Senator Grayson wrote that the Southern members of Congress, "suppose, with too much reason, that the kind of bargaining which took effect with respect to the Susquehanna may also take effect in other great national matters, which may be very oppressive to a defenseless, naked minority."[13]

This was the situation in October 1789, when the Virginia General Assembly again convened. On the one hand the Federalists could point to the set of moderate amendments as proof that the new government had fulfilled its promise to those states which, like Virginia, had asked for a bill of rights. They could also maintain that nothing had yet been done in the Congress to harm Virginia's interests; the issue of the capital site had been postponed and the attempt to bestow titles had been defeated. On the other hand, some Antifederalists such as Henry were clearly displeased with the congressional amendments, unhappy that the question of titled officers should have come up in the first place, and uneasy over the outcome of the debate over the capital site.

The excuse for a renewed attack on the federal government came in the form of a letter to the Speaker of the House of Delegates from Virginia's two United States senators. In that letter Lee and Grayson apologized for their inability to procure amendments of a more substantial nature and then warned of "the necessary tendency to consolidated empire in the natural operation of the constitution." Henry tried to rally support behind a resolution thanking the two senators for their efforts and reiterating the Antifederalists' dislike for the Constitution in its present form; but in this session, by contrast with the previous one, he could not carry a majority of the delegates with him. He also tried to persuade the House to postpone consideration of the congressional amendments on the grounds that the legislators did not have a clear idea of the attitudes of their constituents toward them.[14] This was a novel argument for Henry to use. Few Virginians, Henry included, had previously shown much concern for the constituent power; nearly all the legislators believed that the very fact that they represented only the small area of their own counties was proof that their interests and views would naturally coincide with those of their constituents.

In any case, Henry's proposal was viewed only as a delaying tactic and was not even brought to a vote. Once the amendments themselves were discussed, Henry received support from an unexpected quarter. Edmund Randolph, while he did not oppose the amendments in their entirety, raised some difficult and time-consuming questions on the wording of the eleventh and twelfth amendments, which would later be combined and adopted as the tenth amendment. Randolph's objections intially led to the outright rejection of those amendments, but finally, on November 30, 1789, the House reconsidered and adopted all twelve amendments. In the state senate, however, the Antifederalists succeeded in persuading a majority to reject the third (freedom of speech, press, and religion), eighth (trial by jury), eleventh, and twelfth amendments on the grounds that their protection was not broad enough. The Antifederalist strategy, it seems, was to reject the most popular of the amendments, thus making it necessary for Congress to take up the whole matter once again. The Antifederalists, of course, hoped that the next Congress might be more favorably disposed toward their more radical view on amendments. The House of Delegates refused to ratify the other eight amendments without the crucial four, and the Senate, in one of its rare displays of independence, refused to add its assent to the other four. As a consequence, Henry and the Antifederalists had won a partial victory when the two houses, after nearly a month of wrangling, decided to postpone action on the amendments.[15] In fact, Virginia, largely through inadvertence, would be the last state in the Union to assent to the amendments.

It is incorrect to interpret Virginia's inaction as a triumph for Henry or the forces of antifederalism. Rather, the delay on the amendments was caused mainly by the inevitable inefficiencies of parliamentary maneuvering. When the Antifederalists attempted to gain approval of an address to Congress denouncing the amendments and asking for the adoption of those proposed by the Virginia Convention, the Federalists, for the first time since the Ratifying Convention, had enough votes to block the effort. In fact, Henry, disgusted with the timidity of the legislature, had already left for his home in Prince Edward when the vote was taken. It was unfortunate for the Antifederalist cause that he did, as the address was defeated only by the tie-breaking vote of the Federalist Speaker of the House Thomas Mathews, and the outcome would have been different had even Henry's one vote been cast for the Antifederalist side.[16]

At least part of the reason for Henry's departure, other than his now constant desire to be away from the heat and filth of Richmond, was the obvious fact, recognizable even to Henry, that the new government had been accepted by most of the people of the state. In short, Henry knew that he had lost still another round to Madison. He was not happy about the fact; indeed, he justified much of his western land speculation during this period on the dubious grounds that the frontier might soon be the only place where one could live free of tyranny. But Henry was not one to continue to fight for lost causes. He realized that the only way to protect the liberties of Americans was for the former opponents of the Constitution to gain office in the new government and try to make the best of a bad situation. This conclusion, while it hardly represented enthusiastic support for the government, did at least end Henry's vocal opposition to the very conception of that government.

-------------------- ★ --------------------

When the federal Congress passed Alexander Hamilton's proposals for funding the national debt and assuming the debts of the separate states at full value, Henry would suddenly find himself cast in the role of prophet, although strangely, he seemed reluctant to take up the challenge too vigorously himself. While most Antifederalists had become less vocal in their opposition to the government in 1789, by the next year that same group of Antifederalists, joined by a substantial group of former Federalists who suddenly began to see the wisdom behind Henry's warnings, would issue forth a series of complaints that would not cease until the election of Thomas Jefferson as President in 1801. The opposition came on two points. Virginians of nearly all political persuasions were unhappy with the provision of the funding proposal that stipulated that all federal security holders, whether they had bought their securities at face value or had purchased them at depreciated prices, would be paid at the face value plus 4 percent interest. They believed that a distinction should be made between original security holders and those speculators who had purchased the securities at depreciated prices. This opposition to funding was mild, however, compared to the reaction to the provision calling for the assumption by the federal government of the debts of the states. Most Virginians were convinced that this was patently unconstitutional. Theodorick Bland, one of the principal Antifederalists in the Ratifying Convention, warned that "our government will have little else to do than eat, drink and be merry" if the federal government was allowed to extend its authority over the debts of the states.[17] And the Antifederalists were not the only ones to complain. David Stuart, Washington's chief aid and informant in Virginia, wrote the chief executive that the assumption proposal contained "a spirit so subversive of the true principles of the constitution [that] . . . if Mr. Henry has sufficient boldness to aim the blow at its existence, which he has threatened, I think he can never meet with a more favorable opportunity." Henry Lee, long an opponent of Henry's and a staunch supporter of the Constitution, wrote Madison:

> Henry is already considered a prophet, his predictions are daily verified—his declarations with respect to the division of interests which would exist under the constitution and predominate on all the doings of the government already have been undeniably proved. But we are committed and we cannot be relieved, I fear, only by disunion.

Lee's mood would improve over the years and he would continue to support the Federalist administration, but at this stage, voicing his alarm over the funding and assumption proposals, he even ventured that disunion was preferable to an existence dominated by "an insolent Northern majority."[18]

Once again, Patrick Henry, serving what would be his last term in the legislature, was the leader of the forces opposing the "consolidating" tendencies of the federal government. But strangely, although he was widely identified and admired as a farsighted prophet who at an early stage had recognized the dangers inherent in federal union, he did not seem as enthusiastic about doing battle with the Federalists as he had on previous occasions.

As leader of the Antifederalist forces in the House, he did introduce a resolution declaring the assumption act "repugnant to the constitution"; but his activities seemed to rest there. On November 22, 1790, the Antifederalists in the legislature proposed an address to Congress that would provide the opponents of the federal government with much of their verbal ammunition over the course of the entire decade. Republican leaders in the federal Congress, when they began to organize in opposition to the Federalists, would lean heavily on the address for their articulation of Republican ideology. It was a powerful document, condemning the resemblance between the Hamiltonian and English systems of finance, claiming that it had been that very English system that had been the principal contributor to the destruction of English liberty. The effect of the Hamiltonian system, according to the Antifederalist memorialists, would be to "perpetuate a large monied interest," which would ultimately result in the "prostitution of agriculture at the feet of commerce" and in the creation of a consolidated government "fatal to the existence of human liberty."[19]

This rhetoric coincided almost precisely with the philosophy that Henry had been articulating over the preceding years. Oddly enough, Henry had already left for home when the address was presented to the legislature. Although he may have contributed something to the content of the address in its early stages, it nevertheless does seem strange that Henry, who was now admired by many former Federalists as well as by Antifederalists for his foresight with respect to the dangers posed by the new government, should drop his opposition at this crucial point. His foes would claim that his own state security holdings caused him to be less vigorous in his denunciation of the assumption proposal than he should have been, but if this were the case it would hardly have been likely that he would have spoken out against Hamilton's scheme at all.[20]

By January 1791, Henry's opposition to the government had slackened to the point where he was advising James Monroe, "as we are one & all imbarked, it is natural to care for the crazy machine, at least so long as we are out of Sight of a Port to refit." He had not, however, been won over to the side of the Federalists, for in stating his determination to keep quiet in the future about the affairs of the government, he admitted that "unless I keep some guard over myself, all I should write or say would be to criminate the late & present proceedings so far as I have knowledge of them."[21] His suspicion of the government had not died, but his determination to carry on the fight against it had almost certainly faded.

The entire text of Henry's letter to Monroe seems to have been written by a man who was ready to retire permanently from public life and to bury those animosities that had been engendered during the long and often stormy years of his political career. He had made no secret of his desire to turn his energies toward augmenting his own private fortune after years of neglect caused by public service; he had always had a reputation as one who enjoyed the pursuit of profit, and he now seemed relieved at the prospect of leaving public affairs and returning for good to Prince Edward County.

His final years as a public servant had been filled with more than his usual share of defeats. His vigorous but in the end unsuccessful battle against the ratification of the federal Constitution, his futile attempts to secure radical amendments, and, finally, his powerlessness in preventing the new government from passing legislation which he believed prejudicial to Virginia's interests were all signs that his personal influence was not sufficient to alter the course of events in the new American nation. Yet in spite of it all, Henry would prove to have surprisingly little rancor toward either the new government or most of the supporters of that government. He would, it is true, develop some bitterness toward Madison in the final years of his life, and the hostility that existed between Jefferson and Henry would continue up to Henry's death. But considering the sheer number of issues upon which Henry had taken a stand during his public career, it seems noteworthy that he was able to view his impending retirement with the degree of equanimity that he so clearly displayed.

Once the decision to retire from the legislature was made, however, he quickly turned his mind toward other concerns. He was interested not only in developing his plantation in Prince Edward

County but in expanding his holdings in the west as well. Henry would make a real effort in his last years, both in his speculation in western lands and in his law practice, to leave his heirs something more than his own good name.[22]

Henry's legal talents were still much in demand. His by then legendary oratorical skills and his fame as one of the foremost political figures in Virginia made him a formidable opponent and powerful ally in any courtroom. His skills continued to be shown to their best advantage in criminal cases where the legal code was most tangled and the ability of a skillful attorney to influence a sympathetic jury given the greatest weight; his practice was, however, considerably broadened during this period to include all manner of civil cases as well. Such was the demand for his services that he had difficulty keeping up with his caseload during the 1790s. Never one who liked the extensive research often necessary to prepare a case, Henry often stipulated that his clients hire additional counsel to prepare the material for him to present in court. The mark of his prominence was that his clients agreed to do so and paid him high fees for his day in court as well.[23]

Nearly all Henry's biographers have devoted chapters to laudatory descriptions by Henry's contemporaries of his courtroom performance. Judging from that testimony, Henry's age and declining health were having little effect on his courtroom manner. He retained the ability to move listeners in almost any direction he chose —to merriment, rage, or sympathy. There is perhaps little to be gained from reviewing all the plaudits showered upon him; a glance at just a few of Henry's most famous cases will suffice to give some indication of the range of his courtroom skills.

By all odds the most important of these cases was that in which Henry, with John Marshall, James Innes, and Alexander Campbell, defended the right of Virginians to continue to evade payment of their prewar debts owed to the British. Although it is clear that the case was not one where Henry was arguing with absolute justice on his side, there is nevertheless considerable evidence that Henry, both by the diligence of his research and the virtuosity of his courtroom performance, laid a quite credible claim to being one of the ablest lawyers in postwar Virginia.

Since the outbreak of the Revolution, British creditors had attempted to collect the debts owed them by Virginians only to be informed that specific state laws, passed with Henry's strong support, had relieved Virginians of their obligation to pay them. The Treaty of Peace specifically upheld the validity of the British debts and implicitly repudiated the legality of the state laws voiding them. Nevertheless, Virginians, under a host of pretexts, continued to refuse to pay the debts.[24]

When a branch of the first federal court opened its doors in Richmond in 1790, the British creditors were given their first real opportunity to press their claims, as the federal courts were the logical places in which to enforce the terms of the Treaty of Peace. For Henry the issue was tailor-made. He had long been identified with attempts to ease the plight of Virginia debtors, and he had in fact been instrumental in erecting impediments within Virginia to the collection of British debts in particular. Henry's argument in one of the first of the British debt cases, which began on November 23, 1791, and continued for three full days, was universally admired in a country in which nearly all the citizens, including political leaders of nearly all ideological inclinations, were looking for legal justifications to avoid payment of the debts.

This was one of the few cases in his legal career for which Henry took great pains to prepare himself; he reportedly shut himself up in his office for days at a time, allowing himself to be bothered only for meals. Even Jefferson, who missed no opportunity to deride any and all of Henry's achievements, admitted that "he never distinguished himself so much as on the question of British debts in the case of Jones versus Walker. He had exerted a degree of industry in that case totally foreign to his character, and not only seemed, but had made himself really, learned on the subject."[25]

As he opened the argument for the defense in that case, Henry appeared to some spectators to be even older than his fifty-four years. (Henry himself evidently made a reference in his opening argument to being "a decrepit old man, trembling, with one foot in the grave.") But his oratory had lost none of its fire. His initial statement was calculated to rekindle his fellow Virginians' long-standing hostility to Great Britain. He argued that while it was desirable in most cases that an individual turn his cheek to his enemies, nations could not afford to live by that dictum. "Forgive as a private man, but never forgive public injuries," he advised. He then proceeded to remind his listeners of the devastation and pain caused by Great Britain during the war. Temporarily leaving the plane of polemics, Henry next cited such authorities as Grotius and Vattel to the effect that war gives the same right over the debts of the enemy as it does over his other possessions, arguing further that it made no difference that the debts were owed to private citizens in England and not to the British government. Yet Henry knew well that the weight of precedent and customary law in Europe was on the side of the position that held that states could not exercise their theoretical power of confiscating debts. Henry countered this by claiming that customary law could only operate in those states that had consented to adopt it; in America, where circumstances were so different and where that aspect of customary law had never been applied, it was quite natural to reject the customary law of England, a nation whose laws had proved so tyrannical, and instead adopt the theoretical principle enunciated by the classical legal scholars.

As impressive as Henry's legal reasoning may have been, it is likely that his evocation of the evils of Great Britain and British rule were the most effective portions of his argument. After citing Vattel and Grotius he returned to that theme, asking the court what the fate of Virginia would have been had she lost the Revolutionary War; he assured his listeners that the British would not have been in any way charitable with American property. Henry was still faced with the fact, however, that the Treaty of Peace specifically recognized the debts as obligations that had to be paid. He got around this point by citing British violations of the Treaty—the refusal of the British to compensate Americans for slaves carried off during the Revolution and the delay in relinquishing posts on the American frontier—and claiming that those violations rendered any advantages that Great Britain might receive from the Treaty null and void.[26]

Henry's oratorical achievements in the case were considerable; everyone who heard him was impressed by his argumentation. One must note, however, that a federal court operating in Virginia, presided over by two Virginian judges, Cyrus Griffin and John Blair, and one Marylander, Thomas Johnson, was not a completely dispassionate forum in which to decide the dispensation of debts owed by Virginians to Englishmen. Indeed, Judge John Blair was himself a debtor to the British.[27]

The panel of judges, for whatever reasons, was impressed with the arguments of the lawyers defending the Virginia debtors; in 1793, when the case was appealed to a higher court, the outcome was again in favor of the Virginians. Although it was generally agreed that Henry's arguments for the defense in the higher court were not up to the level of his performance in 1790, James Iredell, one of the three judges of the 1793 hearing, was nevertheless led to exclaim: "Gracious God! He is an orator indeed."[28]

It would not be until 1796, after Henry had retired from the bar and after the Jay Treaty had once again reaffirmed the obligation of American citizens to pay their back debts to the British, that the Supreme Court would get around to overturning the lower courts' decisions.[29] In retrospect, it is clear that the Supreme Court decision was the more fair and equitable. Henry, had he not been both a lawyer for the defense and a Virginia debtor himself, might have been able to recognize that fact. The importance of the incident lies not in the ethical character of the cause for which Henry was fighting but rather in the unmistakable evidence that Henry was able once again to call forth the passions that had been engendered by the Revolution and use them to his own and his clients' advantage.

Henry's other famous case during this period, his successful defense—with John Marshall and Alexander Campbell—of Richard Randolph on the charge of infanticide, not only confirmed Henry's reputation as the most gifted lawyer in the state but also likely provided many of the residents of the state with enough gossip about one of the most prestigious families in Virginia to last them for years to come. Randolph, it seems, had carried on a love affair with his sister-in-law and cousin Nancy Randolph; the affair, according to Randolph's accusers, resulted in the birth of a child on October 1, 1792. The prosecution contended that Randolph had immediately killed the infant and disposed of the body. Randolph claimed that Nancy was never pregnant and that no murder could therefore have occurred. Although the general feeling was that Randolph was almost certainly guilty, the fact that the one source of testimony that would probably have been the most damaging to his case— that of the slaves on the plantation who had witnessed the events of October 1—was banned under state law made it much easier for skillful lawyers like Marshall and Henry to claim that the Randolphs were the victims of rumors and circumstantial evidence alone. Randolph was acquitted, a fact which no doubt influenced John Randolph of Roanoke, a younger brother of Richard, to praise Henry as "the greatest orator that ever lived," a "Shakespeare and Garrick combined."[30]

One gathers, however, that Henry was more interested, at this stage in his career, in gathering money than fame. It was for this reason, as well as from the nearly instinctive urge of most Virginia planters to acquire more land, that Henry embarked upon an extensive series of land speculations in the last years of his life. William Wirt Henry, a grandson and biographer, described Henry's land dealings in this fashion:

> In making investments Mr. Henry availed himself of the public lands put upon the market, and his selections were made with a discrimination which attested his business capacity. He lived to sell or exchange some of these lands at a considerable advance, and to acquire large tracts in the better settled parts of the country, which he gave to his oldest sons.[31]

One suspects that many of Henry's contemporaries would not have used such dignified prose to describe some of his transactions.

This final chapter of Henry's speculative dealings is an important one, for it was during the last years of his life that he succeeded in coming closer to the aristocratic ideal—the possession of vast amounts of land and slaves and several impressive plantation houses—than nearly any of his Virginia neighbors, the Randolphs and the Lees included. Henry's holdings may not initially have been of the same caliber as those of the Tidewater aristocracy, but ultimately, as the west became more settled and began to resemble the eastern coastal plain in the composition of its population and economic base, they became thoroughly respectable by anybody's standard.

Even before the framing of the federal Constitution, Henry's landholdings, totaling over 22,000 acres, ranked him among the hundred wealthiest men in Virginia. Indeed, in terms of acreage alone, regardless of the per-acre value of those lands, Henry ranked number fourteen. These holdings included a 70-acre tract in Prince Edward (soon to be expanded to 1,689½ acres); 8,000 acres in Henry County; 1,907½ acres in Princess Anne; and a 12,000-acre speculation in Norfolk County. And, of course, Henry did not confine his land purchases to his home state. Most of his speculative activities took place outside the state, in North and South Carolina, Georgia, and Kentucky. Henry's slave holdings, in spite of the fact that he did not appear to make much effort to produce tobacco on his plantations, were considerable as well. By the time of his death, the number of slaves in his possession totaled sixty-five, and in spite of his pious pronouncements on the evils of slavery, he made no move to free them in his will.[32]

Surely the most controversial of Henry's speculations was that involving the Yazoo territory in Georgia, a name that has become synonymous to historians with the notion of corruption in high political office. Henry's part in the Yazoo land speculation began in November 1789, when he and six other Virginians formed the Virginia Yazoo Company and purchased from the state of Georgia a tract of land in the northwest corner of the state totaling 11,400,000 acres. Clearly, Henry had now entered into the big leagues. The total price for the tract was $93,741, or less than 1 cent per acre. Although this seems inordinately cheap even by eighteenth-century standards, there seems to have been no corruption involved—only shortsightedness. The members of the Georgia legislature who voted to sell the tract evidently felt that the state would never be in a position to develop lands located so far away. Thus it turned them over to a group of private investors who might have the energy and capital to make something out of them.

It seems likely that Henry and his partners did not want to cease their speculations there. They evidently wanted to join cause with several other speculative companies in the area and purchase additional land bordering the Mississippi and adjoining their own tract. Included in this area was the land on which Memphis presently stands, a tract that was recognized even then as a likely place on which to establish a commercial settlement. This land was inhabited by hostile Chickasaw Indians, but Henry had exerted great energy in seeing that one of his partners, Joseph Martin, was appointed the federal Indian agent in the region, so there was some hope that the Chickasaws could be made to acquiesce to the settlement of their territory.[33]

Henry's designs received a temporary blow in December 1789, when the North Carolina legislature, which owned a portion of these additional lands, ceded the territory to Congress; but Henry continued to feel that the western settlers living in the area would not go along with the cession and that further speculation might be possible in the future. In fact, Henry made it clear in a series of confidential letters to his partners that he would welcome a secessionist movement by the settlers in the region.[34]

His plans were all to go awry. The activities of the various speculative companies on the frontier threatened to make the already uneasy truce between the United States government and the several Indian tribes in the area even more tenuous. In part to maintain peace on the frontier and in part to supplant private with federal control in the area, the federal government negotiated a treaty returning control over much of the land contained in the Yazoo purchase to the Indians. Henry, never enamored with the federal government, was furious. He wrote to a number of influential Georgians denouncing the action as a usurpation of the rights of a sovereign state and quite obviously tried to persuade the Georgians, including the Governor, to ignore the federal treaty. To make matters worse, however, the Georgia legislature itself began to up the ante on the lands, even though ultimate title to the lands was made doubtful by the federal treaty. Georgia had originally agreed to accept payment in the form of depreciated state loan office certificates, but in December 1791 it began to demand payment in specie. Ironically, this did not initially hurt Henry and his partners too much, for the operation of Alexander Hamilton's assumption scheme, which Henry had so despised, brought the value of their securities up to the level of specie anyway. In fact, it is likely that Henry and his partners, having accumulated a considerable amount of those depreciated securities before the assumption bill was passed, actually realized a healthy profit once the certificates were assumed at full value by the federal government. (Jefferson, for one, actually believed that this fact was the principal reason behind Henry's decision to drop his opposition to the policies of the Federalist administration in the 1790s.) Ultimately, however, the legislature's demand that the speculators pay the balance in specie was disastrous for Henry and his partners, for it is clear that they had counted on being able to buy up state securities at depreciated prices in order to meet their payments on the land. The fact that state securities suddenly became worth their full face value made it impossible to do this, and as a consequence most of the balance due on the lands remained unpaid.[35]

At this stage the combination of federal action and the increased purchase price probably caused Henry simply to discontinue his involvement in the speculation; but if he had any lingering interests, they were probably completely liquidated by late 1794 or early 1795. At that time, several rival land companies, now heavily financed by Northern and European capital, literally purchased the votes of the Georgia legislature in return for a grant to the land that had previously been sold to Henry's Virginia Yazoo Company. Henry and his partners initiated suit in the Supreme Court against the state of Georgia, but by the time the matter was investigated, the passage of the Eleventh Amendment (which prevented citizens of one state from suing another state in a federal court) made it impossible for the company to proceed any further. The entire sordid chapter in American land dealings was brought to a close when a "reform" legislature met in Georgia in February 1796 and declared all the grants made by the 1795 legislature null and void. Although nothing was said of the 1789 grants, it was generally agreed that they too had lapsed.[36]

One cannot feel too sorry for the group of Virginia land speculators. Their initial investment was small, and in fact they probably made some money when they resold the state certificates of indebtedness which they had gathered. While Henry's denunciations of the "tyranny" of federal power were no doubt heartfelt, even he, with the perspective of time, must have recognized that his own self-interest had done much to distort his view on the question. Clearly, the federal government did possess treaty-making powers in that region and the territory in question could hardly be said to have been under the full control of the Georgia legislature. To allow American land policy to develop at the whim of speculative companies and rapacious state legislators was directly against the interests of the nation at large. Henry, as he found suitable alternative investments in subsequent years, may have come to accept this fact.

★

With the exception of his political maneuverings with respect to the Yazoo lands, the aging patriot had made a genuine effort to remain free of the political quarrels that divided his home state during the 1790s. It is no exaggeration to say that the political divisions that split the ruling elite of Virginia in the 1790s were more serious than any which had occurred in the history of the Old Dominion. As Alexander Hamilton exercised his influence over the foreign and domestic policies of the new nation in the first half of the decade, and as the nations of France and England both pursued courses that dragged America into Europe's balance-of-power struggles during the last half of the decade, Virginia's political leaders, rallying around the banners of the Republican and Federalist parties, were polarized as never before.

Henry did everything he could to remain aloof from it all, but as one controversy followed another it became impossible for a man of his eminence to avoid being identified with one of the contending parties. What is most surprising is that it would be the Federalists who would succeed in gaining the allegiance of Virginia's foremost opponent of centralized power.

Attempts to woo Henry to the Federalist side began in the fall of 1795, when Henry Lee and Washington initiated overtures to Henry in order to ascertain his view of the events of the previous years. They were pleased to discover that in spite of his serious misgivings about some aspects of Federalist policy—in particular, he shared the view of most Virginians that the Jay Treaty, recently negotiated with England, was harmful to American interests— Henry was decidedly more sympathetic to the leaders in the federal government than he was to those who were most vocal in their denunciations of federal policy. Henry wrote Washington: "I have bid adieu to the distinction of federal and anti-federal ever since the commencement of the present government and in the circle of my friends have often expressed my fears of disunion amongst the states from collision of interests, but especially, from the baneful effects of faction."[37]

Thus we find Henry, the man who had been most outspoken in the Virginia Ratifying Convention in warning of the division of interests that existed between Virginians and citizens of other states, bemoaning the existence of those divisions and blaming the opponents of the federal government for creating them. Historians have long been puzzled by this sudden concern for "order" and for his decision to blame members of the emerging Republican party rather than the Federalists for creating a spirit of "faction." Henry had, after all, made his reputation as one who challenged the existing order and who valued liberty more than any false sense of tranquility. To the extent that historians do agree on the causes for the change in attitude, the standard interpretation seems to be that the aging patriot was growing more conservative with the passage of time and, repudiating the liberal doctrines that he had formulated during the Revolution, became unwilling to countenance the violent opposition which he feared might tear the nation apart.

Indeed, Henry's attitudes in the mid-1790s did manifest a basic conservatism, but it is all too easy to exaggerate the nature of the change that this new attitude represented. The one unmistakable conclusion emerging from a study of Henry's shifting ideological attachments during the Revolutionary era is that he had precious few consistent precepts to guide him. Certainly he had no radical view of the social order. His moments of radicalism in the pre-Revolutionary struggles with Great Britain were often offset by periods of traditionalism. His advocacy of state-supported religion, his desire for strong executive authority with which to guide and enforce the public virtue during the Revolutionary War—these attitudes might just as properly be cited as "typical" of Henry's ideological bent. In fact, neither was more typical than the other. In each of those cases the specific context of events and characters tended to shape Henry's response. In the pre-Revolutionary years, the interests of Henry and his constituents were threatened by the reimposition of royal authority. Henry seemed radical in comparison to many of the leaders of the Virginia elite only because he had no lengthy tradition of amicable relations with royal governors and crown officials to mitigate his opposition to British policy. After Virginia had risen to the challenge of the British and, not incidentally, after Henry had gained full acceptance by members of the Virginia ruling class, the context became quite different indeed. As Revolutionary War governor, Henry personified the established government; since he generally credited himself with good intentions, virtue, and a concern for the public good, he was quite naturally more reluctant to challenge the traditional order of government.

Henry's swing toward conservatism in 1795 was therefore hardly a major departure from a previously liberal or radical approach.

And once again, the context of events at the time Henry made the choice does much to explain the course he took. First, George Washington was making a concerted effort to woo his support. In the space of a year Henry was offered the posts of Secretary of State, justice of the Supreme Court, and Ambassador to Spain. Although he declined all three offers, his correspondence with Washington indicates that he was immensely flattered by the gestures. Second, and perhaps most important, the leaders of the opposition party were none other than James Madison and Thomas Jefferson. Of Jefferson and Henry it can simply be said that nothing had occurred in the years since they had first clashed on the subject of Jefferson's wartime conduct to eliminate the hostility the two felt toward each other. And Henry had found new reasons to dispute the views of Madison. In his opposition to the Jay Treaty, Madison had claimed that the President and Senate had exceeded their power by declaring the treaty in force; he believed that the House of Representatives had to pass on the treaty too, since some of its provisions dealt with the subject of commerce. Henry was incensed. In a letter to his daughter he admitted that "the treaty is, in my opinion, a very bad one indeed," but added:

> what must I think of those men, when I myself warned of the danger of giving the power of making laws by means of treaty, to the president and senate, when I see these same men denying the existence of that power, which they insisted, in our convention, ought properly to be exercised by the president and senate, and by none other?[38]

In short, in the 1788 Convention both Henry and Madison had fully realized the extent of the President's and Senate's treaty-making power, and only Henry had warned of the dangers inherent in that power. In 1795 Madison, finally realizing the wisdom of Henry's warnings in 1788, was trying to deny the existence of that power which he had endorsed so warmly. Henry was hardly a paragon of consistency in his conduct in public life, but this about-face was too much even for him. Madison's hypocrisy (for that is surely what Henry believed it to be), together with the blandishments of the Federalists, was more than enough to convince Henry that he did not belong in the Republican camp.

Henry continued to resist an active role in politics, however. Several Federalists, uneasy about the unpopularity of John Adams in Virginia, tried to persuade him to allow his name to be put forward as a candidate for the Presidency against Jefferson in 1796, but he wisely refused. As the party battles of the 1790s intensified though, it became increasingly difficult to remain aloof. The Republicans, convinced that the Federalists were subservient to the British and committed to a policy of repression at home, steadily intensified their attacks on Federalist policy. The Federalists, ever more strident in their attacks on the dangers of "French influence" in the affairs of the American nation and steadily more bitter in their assaults on Republican disloyalty, desperately wanted Henry's name and influence to give weight to their warnings. In particular, Henry's support would have done much to quiet those who complained of an undue subservience to the British, as no one in America could outdo Henry in his Anglophobia.

The climactic battle between the two parties in Virginia came during 1798 and 1799 over the issue of the Federalist-inspired Alien and Sedition Acts. The legislation which passed the Congress in the summer of 1798 lengthened the naturalization period for aliens resident in the United States, imposed harsh punishments for aliens acting contrary to the laws of the nation, and, most controversially, imposed fines and jail sentences on anyone who wrote, printed, or spoke "false, scandalous and malicious" statements against any member of the federal government.

The outcry from the Republicans was instantaneous. They claimed that the acts were patently unconstitutional and that they represented a blatant attempt to repress forcibly their own, justifiable opposition to the policies of the federal government. The official response of the Virginia legislature, masterminded by Madison, was not as radical as that of Kentucky's (masterminded by Jefferson), which explicitly declared the laws null and void, thus anticipating by thirty years John C. Calhoun's nullification doctrine; but in vowing to take all "necessary and proper" measures to repeal the unconstitutional laws, the members of the Virginia Assembly had nevertheless served notice that they did not intend to acquiesce to them.[39]

It was at this juncture that Henry, influenced unduly by his enmity toward the Republican leaders and by the pleadings of

Washington to jump into the fray, was impelled to take steps that would at least temporarily tarnish his reputation in the Old Dominion. Henry's first public act was to endorse Federalist John Marshall in a hotly contested election for Congress against Republican John Clopton. In a letter to Archibald Blair, a communication which was intended to have wide circulation in the congressional district, Henry left no doubt about his loyalties. Citing the "calamitous" course of the French Revolution, he expressed his concern that the present attachment of the Republicans to the French would result in the destruction of "the great pillars of all government and of social life: I mean virtue, morality and religion." Henry had returned to embrace fully the principles that had motivated his opposition to Jefferson's bill for religious freedom. His concern over the decline of virtue generally and of religion specifically once again provided his justification for opposing Jefferson and Madison. Henry then proceeded to endorse Marshall warmly, writing to Blair, "Tell Marshall I love him, because he felt and acted as a republican, as an American."[40]

At this stage Henry probably had done little to alienate many of his former admirers. Marshall was generally considered a moderate Federalist (he had not, for example, supported the Alien and Sedition Acts) and had considerable support even among those who were not always friendly to the federal government. Moreover, Henry's fears of French influence, while certain to be denounced by confirmed opponents of Federalist policy like Jefferson, were shared by many Virginians. A few months later, however, Henry would enter even more deeply into the thicket of controversy. Responding once again to the pleas of Washington to use "your weight of character and influence" to stem the tide of Republican opposition, Henry ran for the state legislature himself in March 1799. Much of the account of his campaign in that election is of dubious authenticity and it is unclear whether or not Henry explicitly endorsed the hated Alien and Sedition Acts.[41] His attacks on the opponents of the acts were sufficiently severe, however, to erase any appearance of disinterestedness and nonpartisanship that he might previously have had. His popularity in his home district was still great and he won the election with no difficulty, but he had given his old opponents an excuse to attack him openly. Jefferson's anger by this time knew no bounds. The Vice President, now in temporary exile at

Monticello, snarled: "His apostacy must be unaccountable to those who do not know all the recesses of his heart" and claimed that Henry's talents were so inferior to those of the Republicans in the legislature that his election would make no difference.[42] But Jefferson's very vehemence belied his concern. Henry's presence in the legislature would have been of enormous importance to the Federalists. His reputation as an opponent of the unlawful exercise of power and as a stern critic of the British would have done much to defuse the Republican charges that the Federalists were subservient to England and were abusing the powers granted them by the Constitution.

The final drama was never played out. Henry, critically ill even before he decided to seek election, was never to take his seat in the legislature. Suffering from what was probably a malignancy in the intestines, Henry passed from life on June 6, 1799, at the age of sixty-three.[43]

Alas, Henry's last venture into the political arena would dampen the public testimony and tribute that he deserved. The *Virginia Gazette*, it is true, was extravagant in its praise of Henry in its obituary of June 14:

> Mourn Virginia Mourn! Your Henry is gone! Ye friends to liberty in every clime, drop a tear.
> No more will his social feelings spread delight through his happy house. No more will his edifying example dictate to his numerous offspring the sweetness of virtue and the majesty of patriotism. No more will his sage advice, guided by zeal for the common happiness, impart light and utility to his caressing neighbors.
> No more will he illuminate the public councils with sentiments drawn from the cabinet of his own mind, ever directed to his country's good, and clothed in eloquence sublime, delightful and commanding.
> Farewell, first-rate patriot, farewell! As long as our rivers flow, or mountains stand—so long will your excellence and worth be the theme of homage and endearment, and Virginia, bearing in mind her loss, will say to rising generations, imitate my *HENRY*.[44]

The *Virginia Gazette* was, it should be noted, a Federalist newspaper. Perhaps more typical of the climate of opinion in the state, and indicative of the tragic extent to which partisanship was affecting long-standing friendships among the leaders of the Old Dominion, was the action of the Virginia legislature several months later. When a resolution honoring Henry for his "unrivalled eloquence and superior talents" was proposed, the Republicans, evidently disenchanted by Henry's recent public involvements, defeated it by a substantial majority.[45]

Henry had thrived on controversy since his first entrance on the political stage, and perhaps it is fitting that such controversy followed him to his grave. Yet it is hard not to regret that Henry was deprived of the nonpartisan testimonial that he so deserved. For all his faults, which Jefferson chronicled without compassion, and all his virtues, which William Wirt panegyrized uncritically, he was the man who gave impetus to the movement for independence in the Old Dominion. He reflected, more than any of his equally famous contemporaries, the extraordinary sense of pride that most Virginians felt toward their colony and commonwealth. That pride was often misplaced and parochial, and it too often foreclosed the possibility of a wider vision; but in the much smaller and simpler world of the eighteenth century, it was an important and generally constructive force for unity and social change. There were times, of course, when Henry's attachment to Virginia would itself give way to even narrower loyalties—to the specific interests of his region and to his own not inconsiderable interest in the pursuit of private gain. Those tendencies were not necessarily pernicious, however. Although hardly an impoverished yeoman, Henry could not afford the sumptuous style of life enjoyed by most of those men who dominated the business of the House of Burgesses during the pre-Revolutionary years; nor did he possess inherited wealth sufficient to allow him to devote his time exclusively to public affairs. Although Henry's own political ideology (or lack of it) was not explicitly democratic, his very visible and less affluent presence within that small circle of wealthy men who controlled the political life of the Old Dominion heralded the coming of a political structure more open and responsive than that of the past. And while he invariably led rather than followed public opinion in his Piedmont constituencies, the very vociferousness of the support given to him would do much to alert Virginians to the importance of the constituent power in general and that of the western counties in particular.

And finally, at the end as in the beginning, there was always

Henry's style. The style of the Robinsons, Pendletons, and Randolphs had been subdued; the quiet conference in the committee room or tavern had been their mode of conducting the public business. Henry's style—on the stump at election time, on the floor of the legislature, or in the courtroom—was emphatically flamboyant. Indeed, as Jefferson was quick to point out, Henry's oratorical skills alone were not always sufficient to meet the requirements of creative statesmanship, but that oratory, coupled with a remarkable and consistent ability to comprehend the essential meaning and import of most of the principal political issues of the period, propelled Henry to prominence and ensured his continuation in office as one of the most powerful, effective, and generally constructive local politicians that America had ever produced. As we have seen, Henry was not an ideological innovator; nor did he follow a consistently progressive course. But his very presence within the ruling elite of Virginia helped change the nature of political dialogue within his colony, his nation, and, indeed, the world.

In the words of Edmund Randolph, with whose description of Henry this work began, "for grand impressions in the defense of liberty, the Western world has not yet been able to exhibit a rival."[46]

Notes

Abbreviations

JHB　—*Journal of the Virginia House of Burgesses*

JHD　—*Journal of the House of Delegates*

LC　　—Library of Congress

PMHB—*Pennsylvania Magazine of History and Biography*

VHS　—Virginia Historical Society

VMHB—*Virginia Magazine of History and Biography*

WMQ　—*William and Mary Quarterly*

Notes—Preface

1. John P. Kennedy, *Memoirs of the Life of William Wirt* (2 vols.; Philadelphia, 1856), I, 345.

2. William Wirt, *Sketches of the Life and Character of Patrick Henry* (Philadelphia, 1817). For a perceptive analysis of Wirt's *Henry* see William R. Taylor, "William Wirt and the Legend of the Old South," *WMQ*, ser. 3, XIV (1957), 473–493.

3. George Ticknor Curtis, *Life of Daniel Webster* (2 vols.; New York, 1870), I, 585; Thomas Jefferson to William Wirt, Aug. 5, 1805, in *PMHB*, 34 (1910), 387.

4. Robert D. Meade, *Patrick Henry* (2 vols.; Philadelphia, 1957–1969), I, 52.

Notes—Chapter 1: Beginnings

1. Edmund Randolph, *History of Virginia*, Arthur Shaffer (ed.) (Charlottesville, 1970), pp. 167–168.

2. By far the most detailed account of Henry's Scottish roots is Meade, *Henry*, I, 3–19.

3. For information on John Syme and the Syme family, see *Lyon G. Tyler, Encyclopedia of Virginia Biography* (5 vols.; New York, 1915), I, 334–335.

4. William Byrd, *A Journey to the Land of Eden and Other Papers*, in Louis B. Wright (ed.), *The Prose Works of William Byrd of Westover* (Cambridge, Mass., 1966), p. 376.

5. Ibid.; Meade, *Henry*, I, 23–30.

6. Meade, *Henry*, I, 33, 354n.

7. H. R. McIlwain (ed.), *Journals of the Council of the State of Virginia* (Richmond, 1931), IV, 391, V, 56, 150; C. G. Chamberlayne (ed.), *Vestry-book of St. Paul's Parish, Hanover County, Virginia, 1706–1786* (Richmond, 1940), pp. 148, 151, 197.

8. For the history of education in eighteenth-century Virginia, see Laurence Cremin, *American Education: The Colonial Experience* (New York, 1970), pp. 9–14, 149–150, 455–457, 527–534.

9. Samuel Meredith memo to William H. Cabell, reprinted in George Morgan, *Patrick Henry* (Philadelphia, 1907), p. 432.

10. Ibid.

11. Both Meade, *Henry*, I, 75, and Wirt, *Henry*, p. 7, claim that finances necessitated the decision to forego a college education.

12. Samuel Meredith to William H. Cabell, in Morgan, *Henry*, p. 432.

13. Wirt, *Henry*, pp. 11–12.

14. Samuel Meredith to William H. Cabell, in Morgan, *Henry*, p. 432.

15. Patrick Henry Account Book, 1758–1762, Valentine Museum, Richmond, Va., pp. 91–98.

16. Nathaniel Pope to William Wirt, Sept. 26, 1805, in Misc. Collection, VHS, Richmond, Va.; Thomas Jefferson to William Wirt, Aug. 4, 1805, May 12, 1818, in *PMHB*, 34 (1910), 387, 408.

17. Edmund Winston to William Wirt, in William Wirt Henry, *Patrick Henry: Life, Correspondence, and Speeches* (3 vols.; New York, 1891), I, 20.

18. Daniel J. Boorstin, *The Americans: The Colonial Experience* (New York, 1958), pp. 195–205.

19. Ibid.; Jefferson to Wirt, Aug. 5, 1815 in Paul Leicester Ford (ed.), *The Writings of Thomas Jefferson* (12 vols.; New York, 1904–1905), IX, 476n.

20. Jefferson to Wirt, Aug. 4, 1805, *PMHB,* 34 (1910), 387–388.

21. Ibid.; John Tyler to William Wirt in Wirt, *Henry,* pp. 29–30. There are also accounts of Henry's examination in Memo of George Dabney, Library of Congress; Memo of Spencer Roane, William Wirt Henry Papers, VHS.

Notes—Chapter 2: The Road to Power

1. Henry Account Books, 1758–1762, pp. 102–156; 1762–1770, pp. 1–36.

2. Jefferson to Wirt, Aug. 4, 1805, *PMHB,* 34 (1910), 394.

3. Henry Account Books, 1758–1762, 1762–1770 passim; Meade, *Henry,* I, 101.

4. Henry Account Book, 1758–1762, pp. 102–156.

5. The most helpful analysis of the background to the Parsons' Cause controversy is Rhys Isaac, "Religion and Authority: Problems of the Anglican Establishment in Virginia in the Era of the Great Awakening and the Parsons' Cause," *WMQ,* ser. 3, XXX (1973), 3–36. See also Thaddeus Tate, "The Coming of the Revolution in Virginia: Britain's Challenge to Virginia's Ruling Class, 1763–1776," *WMQ,* ser. 3, XIX (1963), 323–343; Richard L. Morton, *Colonial Virginia* (2 vols.; Chapel Hill, 1960), II, 751–819.

6. Francis Fauquier to Board of Trade, Jan. 5, 1759, Public Record Office, Colonial Office 5/1329: 229.

7. Morton, *Colonial Virginia,* II, 784–808.

8. Ibid., II, 808–809.

9. Ibid.

10. James Maury to John Camm, Dec. 12, 1763, in Ann Maury (trans. and comp.), *Memoirs of a Huguenot Family* (New York, 1852), pp. 418–424.

11. Ibid.

12. Wirt, *Henry,* pp. 40–41.

13. Maury to Camm, Dec. 12, 1763, in Maury, *Memoirs,* pp. 418–424.

14. Ibid.; as Rhys Isaac, "Religion and Authority," p. 20n, points out, the published version of Maury's letter to Camm has apparently been bowdlerized

by the overzealous editor. It omits several phrases in the original version in the Maury Letterbook (American Philosophical Society, Philadelphia). For example, Maury compared many of Virginia's political leaders to "the most seditious Tribunes of old Rome"; his description of Henry as a "little petty-fogging attorney" was also deleted by the editor.

15. Henry Account Book, 1762–1770, p. 29.

16. Morton, *Colonial Virginia*, II, 812–819.

17. Henry Account Book, 1762–1770, passim.

18. Meade, *Henry*, I, 259.

19. Dumas Malone, *Thomas Jefferson and His Time* (4 vols. to date; Boston, 1948–), I, 121–122.

20. *Virginia Gazette* (Purdie and Dixon), May 20, 1773.

21. Henry Account Books, 1762–1770, pp. 132, 169, 178, 195; 1770–1774, passim.

22. Clement Eaton, "A Mirror on the Southern Colonial Lawyer: The Fee Books of Patrick Henry, Thomas Jefferson and Waighstill Avery," *WMQ*, ser. 3, VIII, 520–534.

23. St. George Tucker to William Wirt, 1805, transcript in William Wirt Henry Papers, VHS.

24. Spencer Roane to Wirt, William Wirt Henry Papers, VHS.

25. Wirt, *Henry*, pp. 49–50.

26. Morgan, *Henry*, pp. 113–114.

27. Henry Account Book, 1762–1770, p. 28.

28. Ibid.; Meade, *Henry*, I, 236.

29. Ibid., 1770–1774, p. 7; Henry, *Henry*, 1, 149.

30. Meade, *Henry*, I, 234–235; Thomas Perkins Abernathy, *Western Lands and the American Revolution* (New York, 1937), pp. 114–115, 121–135, 149–161.

31. By 1782 Henry owned sixty-six slaves. Jackson T. Main, "The One Hundred," *WMQ*, ser. 3, X (1954), 368–383.

32. Genealogical information on Henry and his relatives can be found in Henry, *Henry*, II, 633–645.

33. For the best account of the elite-dominated pattern of Virginia politics, see Charles Sydnor, *Gentlemen Freeholders: Political Practices in Washington's Virginia* (Chapel Hill, 1952).

34. Nathaniel Pope to Wirt, Sept. 26, 1805, Misc. Coll., VHS; Charles Campbell, *History of the Colony and Ancient Dominion of Virginia* (Philadelphia, 1860), pp. 538–539.

35. Wirt, *Henry,* p. 43.

36. Campbell, *History of Virginia,* pp. 538–539.

Notes—Chapter 3: Challenge to Authority

1. Jack P. Greene, "Foundations of Political Power in the Virginia House of Burgesses, 1720–1776," *WMQ,* ser. 3, X (1959), 485–506.

2. Ibid.; Sydnor, *Gentlemen Freeholders,* pp. 78–93.

3. St. George Tucker to William Wirt, Sept. 25, 1815, *WMQ,* ser. 1, XII (1914), 252–257. Virtually all of Henry's biographers, including his most recent one, Robert D. Meade, have insisted on dividing Virginia into opposing camps labeled "democrats" and "aristocrats." While it is clear that political divisions existed in colonial Virginia—divisions based on geographic, economic, and ethnic and religious interests—they were far more complex and far less cohesive than those described by Meade and others. See for example, Jackson T. Main, *Political Parties Before the Constitution* (Chapel Hill, 1973), pp. 244–267; and Van Beck Hall, "A Quantitative Approach to the Social, Economic and Political Structure of Virginia, 1790–1810," unpublished paper presented at the annual meeting of the Southern Historical Association, 1969.

4. A photograph of the document is printed in Morgan, *Henry,* p. 100.

5. John P. Kennedy and H. R. McIlwaine (eds.), *Journal of the Virginia House of Burgesses* (13 vols.; Richmond, 1905–1915), 1761–1765, lxiv–lxv.

6. Henry may have been an orator of extraordinary power and effect, but as a draftsman of constitutional pronouncements he left much to be desired. It is hard to imagine any more circumloquacious statement of the principle of "no taxation without representation" than that contained in Henry's third resolution.

7. *JHB,* 1761–1765, lxiv.

8. Carrington's description, contained in a letter to William Wirt, is printed in Henry, *Henry,* I, 86–87.

9. Jefferson to Wirt, Aug. 14, 1814, in Ford (ed.), *Writings of Jefferson,* IX, 470.

10. *American Historical Review,* 26 (1920–1921), 745.

11. Ibid.

12. Jefferson to Wirt, Aug. 4, 1805, *PMHB,* 34 (1910), 389; Jefferson to Wirt, Aug. 14, 1814, in Ford (ed.), *Writings of Jefferson,* IX, 468.

13. Edmund S. and Helen M. Morgan, *The Stamp Act Crisis: Prologue to Revolution* (Chapel Hill, 1953), pp. 120–132.

14. The term "cautious patriot" has been substituted throughout for the more familiar but ideologically loaded word "conservative." Patrick Henry's political philosophy was in many ways "conservative," but his position respecting Great Britain was rarely "cautious."

There is considerable mystery behind the exact process by which the fifth resolution was expunged, but both Jefferson's recollection of the event and Governor Fauquier's letter to the Board of Trade explaining it indicate that the more cautious members were indeed successful in expunging it. Both letters are printed in *JHB,* 1761–1765, lxvii.

15. The sixth and seventh resolutions were first printed in the *Maryland Gazette,* July 4, 1765.

16. Governor Fauquier to Board of Trade, June 5, 1765, in *JHB,* 1761–1765, lxvii.

17. *American Historical Review,* 26 (1921), 745–746.

18. *Newport Mercury,* June 24, 1765; *Maryland Gazette,* July 4, 1765.

19. For the best discussion of the Stamp Act Congress, see Morgan, *Stamp Act Crisis,* pp. 138–154.

20. Wm. Robinson to the Bishop of London, Aug. 12, 1765, in William S. Perry, *Historical Collections Relating to the American Colonial Church* (Hartford, Conn., 1870), I, 514–515.

21. Richard Henry Lee, who would become one of the principal leaders of the Revolution in Virginia and a political rival of Henry, was at this stage so unaware of the significance of the Stamp Act that he initially applied for the job of stamp distributor. Faced with a burst of disapproval from both his colleagues and constituents, he quickly withdrew his application and, ironically, led the movement to force Mercer's resignation. Thaddeus Tate, "The Coming of the Revolution in Virginia," pp. 339–340; Fauquier to Board of Trade, Nov. 3, 1765, in *JHB,* 1761–1765, lxviii–lxix; *Virginia Gazette* (Purdie and Dixon), Oct. 25, 1765.

22. Morgan, *Stamp Act Crisis,* pp. 327–352.

23. *JHB,* 1766–1769, lx.

24. There are several accounts of parliamentary politics at this stage. Among the better brief treatments are L. H. Gipson, *The Coming of the Revolution, 1763–1775* (New York, 1954), pp. 101–115, 170–176; and Esmond Wright,

Fabric of Freedom, 1763–1800 (New York, 1961), pp. 59–60. For a more detailed treatment, see John Brooke, *The Chatham Administration, 1766–1768* (London, 1956).

25. Merrill Jensen, *The Founding of a Nation: A History of the American Revolution, 1763–1776* (New York, 1968), pp. 249–252; David John Mays, *Edmund Pendleton, A Biography, 1721–1803* (2 vols.; Cambridge, Mass., 1952), I, 249.

26. *JHB*, 1766–1769, 79–80.

27. Ibid., 1766–1769, 218; Mays, *Pendleton*, I, 251–254.

28. Mays, *Pendleton*, I, 255. Even New York and Pennsylvania, always the most reluctant to commit themselves to a course of action that might further aggravate relations between England and America, joined the opposition.

29. *JHB*, 1766–1769, 266–277, 233–234. They did, however, continue to support the boycott on tea.

30. Jensen, *Founding of a Nation*, pp. 355–356, 369–370.

31. *JHB*, 1770–1772, 119–140, 266.

32. Ibid., 1773–1776, xii.

33. "The Autobiography of Thomas Jefferson," in Ford (ed.), *Writings of Jefferson*, I, 7–8.

34. St. George Tucker to William Wirt, in Henry, *Henry*, I, 164.

35. *JHB*, 1773–1776, 132.

36. Benjamin Woods Labaree, *The Boston Tea Party* (New York, 1964), is the standard source for the English motives for the Tea Act and for the American reaction to the act. See esp. pp. 58–103, 126–148.

37. Ibid., pp. 170–193; Jensen, *The Founding of a Nation*, pp. 453–460.

38. George Mason to Martin Cochburn, May 26, 1774, in Kate Mason Rowland, *The Life of George Mason, 1725–1792* (2 vols.; New York, 1892), I, 168–169.

39. "Jefferson's Autobiography," in Ford (ed.), *Writings of Jefferson*, I. 9–10; *JHB*, 1773–1776, 132.

40. *JHB*, 1773–1776, xiii–xiv.

41. Ibid., 1773–1776, 138–139.

42. Rowland, *Mason*, I, 168–169.

43. Lord Dartmouth to Dunmore, July 6, 1774, Public Record Office, Colonial Office 5/133.

44. Jensen, *Founding of a Nation,* pp. 456–458.

45. *Virginia Gazette* (Rind), July 28, 1774. The resolutions are also printed in Henry, *Henry,* I, 191–194.

46. The great weight of historical evidence indicates that the hostility of Virginians to the continuation of the slave trade was the result not of a growing awareness of the contradiction between their own struggle for liberty and the enslavement of Africans but rather of increased fears of slave rebellion and of disenchantment with the inflexibility of slavery as an economic system. The Journal of the Virginia Convention is printed in Peter Force (ed.), *American Archives* (6 ser.; Washington, D.C., 1837), ser. 4, I, 686–690.

47. Ibid., 689.

48. Roger Atkinson to Samuel Pleasants, Oct. 1, 1774, in *VMHB,* XV, 356.

Notes—Chapter 4: Rebellion

1. The conference actually never convened, as the British government, fearing further attempts at intercolonial union, prevented many colonies from sending delegates. Henry, *Henry,* I, 148.

2. Meade, *Henry,* I, 316.

3. Lyman H. Butterfield, *Diary and Autobiography of John Adams* (4 vols.; Cambridge, Mass., 1961), II, 113, 119–120, III, 367.

4. Edmund C. Burnett (ed.), *Letters of Members of the Continental Congress* (8 vols.; Washington D.C., 1921–1936), I, 10n; Edmund Burnett, *The Continental Congress* (New York, 1941), pp. 36–38.

5. Butterfield (ed.), *Adams Diary,* II, 125.

6. Burnett, *The Continental Congress,* pp. 36–38; Mays, *Pendleton,* I, 284–285.

7. Burnett, *The Continental Congress,* pp. 42–43.

8. John Adams to Abigail Adams, Oct. 9, 1774, in Lyman Butterfield, Wendell Garrett, and Marjorie Sprague (eds.), *John Adams Family Correspondence* (2 vols.; Cambridge, Mass., 1963), I, 166.

9. Burnett, *The Continental Congress,* pp. 47–51.

10. Ibid., pp. 51–59.

11. See Jensen, *Founding of a Nation,* pp. 515–528, 531–534, 560–561, for a good discussion of the activities of the "Association."

12. Silas Deane to Mrs. Deane, Sept. 10, 1774, in Burnett, *Letters,* I, 28–29.

13. Henry, *Henry,* I, 251.

14. Meade, *Henry,* II, 15–17.

15. *American Archives,* ser. 4, II, 166.

16. Ibid., II, 167; *Virginia Gazette* (Purdie and Dixon), Mar. 11, 1775.

17. *American Archives,* ser. 4, II, 167.

18. Wirt, *Henry,* p. 142.

19. Henry, *Henry,* I, 270.

20. Wirt, *Henry,* pp. 120–123. While there is no direct evidence disputing the fact that Henry actually did utter those words, neither is there any contemporary account available to establish the fact that he did. Wirt claimed that his account was based on testimony from St. George Tucker and John Tyler, who were both present during the speeches. Unfortunately, copies of their accounts have not survived. The only others who were willing to testify to the accuracy of Wirt's text were a Baptist minister, writing many decades after the speech, and Judge John Roane, who, writing fifty-nine years later, verified the correctness of the version that John Tyler had supposedly given to Wirt. Others, like Thomas Jefferson, who did not actively dispute Wirt's account when it appeared, gave at least passive support to the accuracy of Wirt's version. Henry S. Randall, *Life of Thomas Jefferson* (3 vols.; New York, 1858), I, 101–102; Jefferson to Wirt, Aug. 14, 1814, in Ford (ed.), *Writings of Jefferson,* IX, 470; Henry, *Henry,* I, 268–270.

21. Randolph, *History of Virginia,* pp. 212–213. Arthur Shaffer, in his introduction to the *History,* p. xxiv, perceptively analyzes Randolph's views on the importance of oratory. My analysis of Randolph's reaction to Henry's speech follows Shaffer's nearly exactly.

22. *American Archives,* ser. 4, II, 167–169.

23. Mays, *Pendleton,* II, 12.

24. Jefferson to Wirt, Aug. 14, 1814, in Ford (ed.), *Writings of Jefferson,* IX, 469.

25. The best accounts of the gunpowder episode are Mays, *Pendleton,* II, 13–17, and Meade, *Henry,* II, 44–56. The two quite predictably assess the incident differently, with Mays approving Pendleton's more cautious course and Meade applauding Henry's boldness.

26. Jeannie F. Dissette, "Slavery and the Coming of the Revolution in Vir-

ginia" (unpublished paper, University of Pennsylvania), discusses the effect of Dunmore's proclamation on the Virginia gentry. Her paper dramatically demonstrates the depth and intensity of Virginians' fears regarding slave rebellions. For a description of the near-paranoid fear by Americans of a royally imposed despotism, see Bernard Bailyn, *Ideological Origins of the American Revolution* (Cambridge, Mass., 1967).

27. Mays, *Pendleton,* II, 14–15.

28. Charles Dabney to William Wirt, Dec. 21, 1805, in William Wirt Papers, VHS; Henry, *Henry,* I, 282–284; *American Archives,* ser. 4, II, 540–541.

29. *American Archives,* ser. 4, II, 516; Henry, *Henry,* I, 286.

30. *American Archives,* ser. 4, II, 587; Henry, *Henry,* I, 286–287.

31. Henry to Francis Lightfoot Lee, May 8, 1775, in Henry, *Henry,* I, 286–289.

32. Numerous county meetings also passed resolutions applauding his conduct. *American Archives,* ser. 4, II, 529–541.

33. Jefferson to Wirt, Aug. 4, 1805, in *PMHB,* 34 (1910), 393.

34. Mays, *Pendleton,* II, 24–25.

35. *American Archives,* ser. 4, III, 375, IV, 1519–1520.

36. Ibid., ser. 4, III, 418.

37. Henry, *Henry,* I, 319–321; Meade, *Henry,* II, 81–82.

38. Mays, *Pendleton,* II, 53.

39. Dunmore's proclamation is reprinted in *American Archives,* ser. 4, III, 1385.

40. Committee of Safety to Col. Woodford, Oct. 24, 1775, in John D. Burk, *The History of Virginia* (4 vols.; Petersburg, Va., 1804–1816), IV, Appendix 3.

41. Mays, *Pendleton,* II, 71–76.

42. *American Archives,* ser. 4, IV, 76, 87; Mays, *Pendleton,* II, 76.

43. Henry, *Henry,* I, 343.

44. Mays, *Pendleton,* II, 62–65; George Washington to Joseph Reed in John C. Fitzpatrick (ed.), *The Writings of George Washington* (39 vols.; Washington, D.C., 1931–1944), IV, 80.

45. Henry, *Henry,* I, 345–347.

46. *Virginia Gazette* (Purdie and Dixon), March 1, 6, 15, and 22, 1776.

47. Richard Henry Lee to Henry, April 20, 1776, in Henry, *Henry,* I, 379.

48. *JHB,* 1773–1776, 283.

49. *American Archives,* ser. 4, VI, 1510–1511.

50. Ibid., VI, 1522.

51. Randolph, *History of Virginia,* p. 250.

52. Richard Henry Lee to Henry, Apr. 20, 1776, Henry to Richard Henry Lee, May 20, 1776, Henry to John Adams, May 20, 1776, in Henry, *Henry,* I, 378–382, 410–411, 412–413.

53. Ibid., I, 395–398; Mays, *Pendleton,* II, 368n, agrees that Henry and Smith were each responsible for drafts of the resolutions but is not altogether certain that the "Pendleton" draft was in fact authored by Pendleton.

54. Henry, *Henry,* I, 395.

55. Henry to John Adams, May 20, 1776, in ibid., I, 412–413.

56. Mays, *Pendleton,* II, 109.

57. Jack P. Greene, *The Quest for Power; The Lower Houses of Assembly in the Southern Royal Colonies, 1689–1776* (Chapel Hill, 1963).

58. Bailyn, *Ideological Origins,* passim.

Notes—Chapter 5: A Local Politician

1. Van Beck Hall, "Virginia, 1790–1810."

2. Mays, *Pendleton,* I, 174–208, presents a sympathetic treatment of the "Robinson Affair." For a more critical view, see Joseph A. Ernst, "The Robinson Scandal Redivivus: Money Debt and Politics in Revolutionary Virginia," *VMHB,* LXXVII (1969), 146–173.

3. Ernst, "The Robinson Scandal," 150; Jefferson to Wirt, Aug. 4, 1805, *PMHB,* 34 (1910), 388.

4. Jefferson to Wirt, Aug. 4, 1814, *PMHB,* 34 (1910), 397.

5. Ernst, "The Robinson Scandal," 155.

6. Mays, *Pendleton,* I, 180–185.

7. Gov. Fauquier to Board of Trade, June 25, 1765, May 11, 1766, in C.O. 5/1331, quoted in Ernst, "The Robinson Scandal," 157.

8. Ibid., 157–167; Jack P. Greene, "The Attempt to Separate the Offices of Speaker and Treasurer in Virginia, 1758–1766," *VMHB,* LXXI (1963), 11–18.

9. *JHB*, 1766–1769, 24; Ernst, "The Robinson Scandal," 167.

10. *JHB*, 1766–1769, 14, 65–67.

11. The full text of the manuscript is printed in Henry, *Henry*, I, 112–116.

12. The intellectual origins of "country whig" ideology, derived principally from the mid-seventeenth-century writings of James Harrington, are skillfully analyzed by J. G. A. Pocock, "Machiavelli, Harrington and English Political Ideologies in the Eighteenth Century," *WMQ*, ser. 3, XXII (1965), 549–583.

13. Henry to Robert Pleasants in Roberts Vaux, *Memoirs of the Life of Anthony Benezet* (Philadelphia, 1817), pp. 55–57. Also reprinted in Henry, *Henry*, I, 152–153.

14. Meade, *Henry,* I, 299.

15. Winthrop Jordan's provocative and subtle study, *White over Black: American Attitudes toward the Negro, 1550–1812* (Chapel Hill, 1968), esp. pp. 269–429, has discovered some changes in the attitudes of Virginians toward slavery as a result of the Revolution, but he too ultimately stresses the limitations on the development of antislavery thought in the Old Dominion.

16. Greene, "Foundations of Political Power," 485–506; Richard R. Beeman, *The Old Dominion and the New Nation, 1788–1801* (Lexington, Ky., 1972). Jackson T. Main, "Government by the People: The American Revolution and the Democratization of the Legislature," *WMQ*, ser. 3, XXIII (1966), 396, 402–403, has discovered some change in the composition of the Virginia legislature after the Revolution, due principally to the increasing power and affluence of the western delegates, but he too recognizes that this change was not as pronounced in Virginia as it was elsewhere.

Notes—Chapter 6: Patrick Henry As Revolutionary Statesman

1. George Mason to Richard Henry Lee, May 18, 1776, in Rowland, *Mason,* I, 226.

2. Mays, *Pendleton,* II, 121–122; Robert A. Rutland, *The Birth of the Bill of Rights, 1776–1791* (Chapel Hill, 1955), pp. 45–47.

3. Jordan, *White over Black*, esp. pp. 269–429.

4. *American Archives,* ser. 4, VI, 1537; Gordon Wood, *The Creation of the American Republic, 1776–1787* (Chapel Hill, 1969), pp. 273–282, 328–344.

5. *American Archives,* ser. 4, VI, 1537.

6. Ibid.

7. Henry, *Henry*, I, 418–422.

8. Thomas Jefferson, "Draft of Virginia Constitution" (June 1776), in Julian P. Boyd (ed.), *The Papers of Thomas Jefferson* (18 vols. to date; Princeton, 1950–), I, 337–340.

9. *American Archives,* ser. 4, 1598–1600.

10. Ibid.

11. The extent of the suffrage in Virginia has been widely debated by historians. Robert E. and B. Katherine Brown, *Virginia, 1705–1786: Democracy or Aristocracy?* (East Lansing, Mich., 1964), pp. 125–146, have presented convincing evidence that a high percentage of Virginia's free adult male population had the opportunity to vote. They are less successful, however, in proving that the mere right to vote necessarily led to a "democratic" social or political order.

12. Randolph, *History of Virginia,* p. 256.

13. Ibid., p. 255.

14. Eldon G. Bowman, "Patrick Henry's Political Philosophy" (unpublished Ph.D. dissertation, Claremont Graduate School, 1961), demonstrates the influence of Montesquieu on Henry's political thought. He does, however, tend to overestimate the coherence of Henry's political philosophy.

15. *American Archives,* ser. 4, VI, 1599.

16. Thomas Jefferson, "Notes on the State of Virginia," in Boyd (ed.), *Papers of Thomas Jefferson,* 213–239.

17. For the best general survey of constitution making in the individual states, see Elisha Douglass, *Rebels and Democrats: The Struggle for Equal Political Rights and Majority Rule during the American Revolution* (Chapel Hill, 1955); see also Alan Nevins, *The American States during and after the Revolution, 1775–1789* (New York, 1924).

18. *American Archives,* ser. 4, VI, 1601.

19. *Journal of the House of Delegates,* Oct. 7, 1776.

20. Meade, *Henry,* II, 159–160, 162–165.

21. Ibid., II, 165; Henry, *Henry,* I, 618.

22. If Jefferson's charge that Henry paid for the plantation in depreciated currency, "not worth oak leaves," is correct, then it was even a greater bargain. Jefferson to Wirt, Aug. 4, 1805, *PMHB,* 34 (1910), 394; Henry, *Henry,* I, 619–620. It is also worth noting that in spite of the size of his landholdings, Henry apparently did not make his living from the profits of his plantations. Although the plantation was an indispensable symbol of his

place and prestige within the community, it was not his principal source of income. Robert D. Meade has calculated that Henry sold only sixteen hogsheads of tobacco from his Leatherwood plantation in 1785, nine in 1786, and only four in 1787, this last crop bringing him a mere £45 in revenue. Given the fact that the price of just one prime field hand was roughly £50 to £80 at that time, it is clear that Henry's tobacco profits were not adequate to meet the costs of running his plantation, much less to allow him to continue his western land speculation. Meade, *Henry,* II, 320.

23. Spencer Roane memo, in William Wirt Henry Papers, VHS.

24. Wood, *Creation of the American Republic,* esp. pp. 66. 46–70, analyzes the importance of "virtue" with considerable skill. See also Pocock, "English Political Ideologies," pp. 549–583.

25. Meade, Henry, II, 128–131; Jack P. Greene (ed.), *Diary of Colonel Landon Carter of Sabine Hall* (2 vols.; Charlottesville, 1965), II, 1057.

26. The story of disestablishment in Virginia must be pieced together from the accounts of the biographers of the principal participants. See especially Dumas Malone, *Jefferson,* I, 274–284; Irving Brant, *James Madison* (6 vols., Indianapolis, 1941–1961), III, 343–355; Mays, *Pendleton,* II, 133–137; Meade, *Henry,* II, 276–282. Hamilton J. Eckenrode, *Separation of Church and State in Virginia* (Richmond, 1910), is not as helpful.

27. *JHD,* Dec. 9, 1776; Brant, *Madison,* III, 343–350; Hening, *Statutes at Large,* XII, 84.

28. For a good description of Henry at this stage in his career, see Spencer Roane to William Wirt, transcript in William Wirt Henry Papers, VHS.

29. It should be noted that *factions,* not parties, developed. As such, they had no permanence and shifted and disintegrated frequently.

30. *Letters of the Governors of Virginia,* I, 82–83; Adrienne Koch and William Peden (eds.), *The Life and Selected Writings of Thomas Jefferson* (New York, 1944), p. 244; Henry, *Henry,* I, 507–509.

31. Henry, *Henry,* II, 147–148.

32. Brant, *Madison,* I, 260–261, II, 318; Jefferson, "Notes on Virginia," in Koch and Peden (eds.), *Life and Writings,* pp. 236–247.

33. *JHD,* June 21, 1784; Brant, *Madison,* I, 260–271, II, 318.

34. For a superb account of the complicated problems of state finance during the Confederation period, see E. James Ferguson, *The Power of the Purse* (Chapel Hill, 1961), esp. pp. 3–109, 179–220.

35. Henry, *Henry,* II, 175–176; Hening, *Statutes at Large,* XI, 66.

36. Archibald Stuart to William Wirt, in Henry, *Henry,* II, 211–214.

37. Main, *Political Parties before the Constitution,* pp. 250–255.

38. Henry, *Henry,* II, 170–172.

39. Randolph, *History of Virginia,* p. 277; *JHD,* June 6, 1780.

40. Jefferson to Wirt, Aug. 4, 1805, in *PMHB,* 34 (1910), 394.

41. Brant, *Madison,* II, 358–359.

42. *JHD,* May 12, 1783; Tyler to Wirt, quoted in Henry, *Henry,* II, 193.

43. Brant, *Madison,* II, 99.

44. Thomas Perkins Abernathy, *Western Lands and the American Revolution* (Charlottesville, 1937), pp. 217–274.

45. For the best account of Jay's negotiations with the Spanish, see Arthur Whitaker, *The Spanish-American Frontier, 1783–1795* (Boston, 1917); see also Madison to Washington, Dec. 7, 1786, in Gaillard Hunt (ed.), *The Writings of James Madison* (9 vols.; New York, 1900–1910), II, 296–297; John Marshall to Arthur Lee, March 5, 1787, in R. H. Lee, *The Life of Arthur Lee* (2 vols.; Boston, 1829), II, 321.

46. Ferguson, *Power of the Purse,* pp. 116–117, 152–153, 174–176.

47. Jefferson to Madison, May 7, 1783, in Boyd (ed.), *Papers of Thomas Jefferson,* VI, 266; Brant, *Madison,* II, 248.

48. Brant, *Madison,* II, 251–252; see especially Joseph Jones to Madison, May 31, June 8, and June 14, 1783, Madison Papers, LC.

49. William Short to Jefferson, May 14, 1784, in Boyd (ed.), *Papers of Thomas Jefferson,* VII, 253–255.

50. Hening, *Statutes at Large,* XI, 401, 402, 415.

51. Madison to Washington, Dec. 7, 1786, in Hunt (ed.), *Writings of Madison,* II, 296–297.

52. Edmund Randolph to Jefferson, May 15, 1784, in Moncure D. Conway, *Omitted Chapters in the Life of Edmund Randolph* (New York, 1888), pp. 55–56.

53. Jefferson to Wirt, Aug. 4, 1805, in *PMHB,* 34 (1910), 390.

54. See, for example, Madison to Jefferson, Dec. 20, 1787, in Boyd (ed.), *Papers of Thomas Jefferson,* XII, 444.

55. Archibald Cary to Jefferson, June 19, 1781; Jefferson to Nicholas, July 28, 1781; Jefferson to Isaac Zane, Dec. 24, 1781; Jefferson to George Rogers Clark, Nov. 26, 1782, in Boyd (ed.), *Papers of Thomas Jefferson,* VI, 97,

104–106, 143, 205; Randolph, *History of Virginia*, p. 296; Hening, *Statutes at Large*, X, 568.

56. Jefferson to Madison, Dec. 8, 1784, in Boyd (ed.), *Papers of Thomas Jefferson*, VII, 558.

Notes—Chapter 7: Defender of Virginia Sovereignty

1. The best discussion of the relationship between the failure of the impost and the movement for the Constitution is Ferguson, *Power of the Purse*, pp. 220–250.

2. Washington to Madison, Nov. 5, 1786, in Fitzpatrick (ed.), *Writings of Washington*, XXIX, 51.

3. Brant, *Madison*, III, 375–387.

4. Meade, *Henry*, II, 327–328.

5. Virginia Delegates in Congress to Patrick Henry, June 8, 1786, in Henry, *Henry*, II, 357–358.

6. Monroe to Patrick Henry, Aug. 12, 1786, in Henry, *Henry*, II, 291–296.

7. Madison to Washington, Dec. 7, 1786, in Hunt (ed.), *Writings of Madison*, II, 296–297; Marshall to Arthur Lee in Lee, *Life of Arthur Lee*, II, 321.

8. *Senate Journal*, Dec. 4, 1786.

9. Randolph to Henry, Dec. 6, 1786, Henry to Randolph, Feb. 11, 1787, in Henry, *Henry*, II, 310–311.

10. Randolph to Madison, March 1, 1787, in Conway, *Randolph*, p. 65; Madison to Jefferson, March 19, 1787, in Boyd (ed.), *Papers of Thomas Jefferson*, XI, 221.

11. Washington to Henry, Sept. 24, 1787, in Fitzpatrick (ed.), *Writings of Washington*, XXIX, 278; Henry to Washington, Oct. 19, 1787, in Henry, *Henry*, II, 320–321.

12. *JHD*, Oct. 25, 1787; Henry, *Henry*, II, 322–324.

13. Jefferson to Madison, Dec. 20, 1787, in Boyd (ed.), *Papers of Thomas Jefferson*, XII, 438–442.

14. Madison to Jefferson, Dec. 9, 1787; Dec. 20, 1787; Feb. 19, 1788; Apr. 22, 1788, in Hunt (ed.), *Writings of Madison*, V, 62–69, 74–78, 100–104, 120–123.

15. Madison to Jefferson, Dec. 9, 1787, in ibid., V, 62–69.

16. Ibid.

17. Henry, *Henry,* II, 332–334; William C. Rives, *Life of James Madison* (3 vols.; Boston, 1859–1868), II, 544.

18. Madison to Jefferson, Apr. 22, 1788, in Hunt (ed.), *Writings of Madison,* V, 122.

19. Jackson T. Main, "Sections and Politics in Virginia, 1781–1787," *WMQ,* ser. 3, XII (1955), 96–112.

20. Madison to Jefferson, Feb. 19, 1788, Madison to Randolph, Jan. 10, 1788, in Hunt (ed.), *Writings of Madison,* V, 103, 83.

21. It was of course no accident that Madison, the first Virginian to make a profession of politics at the continental level, should prove so conspicuous in rounding up support for the Constitution; nor is it surprising that Henry, whose entire public career was tied to the defense of local interests, would choose to remain in his own locale. Madison to Randolph, Jan. 10, 1788; Jan. 20, 1788; March 3, 1788; Apr. 10, 1788, in ibid., V, 86–88, 113–114, 117–120.

22. Randolph to the Speaker of the House of Delegates, Oct. 16, 1787, in Jonathon Elliot, *The Debates in the Several State Conventions on the Adoption of the Federal Constitution . . .* (5 vols.; 2d ed., Philadelphia, 1876–1881), I, 482–491.

23. Rowland, *Mason,* II, 308.

24. Madison to Washington, June 13, 1788, in Hunt (ed.), *Writings of Madison,* V, 179; Henry to John Lamb, in Isaac A. Leake, *Memoirs of the Life and Times of General John Lamb* (Albany, 1857), 307.

25. Elliot, *Debates,* II, 1.

26. Ibid., 7–21.

27. Ibid., 21–23.

28. Ibid.

29. Ibid., 57–58.

30. Ibid., 52, 410–412, 422.

31. Cecilia Kenyon, "Men of Little Faith: The Antifederalists on the Nature of Representative Government," *WMQ,* ser. 3, XII (1955), 3–43. Among Henry's biographers, Robert D. Meade is only the most recent to be inclined to impose a twentieth-century "liberal," "democratic" framework on Henry's eighteenth-century political thought.

32. Elliot, *Debates,* III, 151–152.

33. Ibid., 49–50.

34. Ibid., 148, 322–323.

35. Thomas Evans to John Cropper, Dec. 6, 1796, John Cropper Papers, VHS; ibid.

36. Elliot, *Debates,* III, 141–142, 151–152, 325–326.

37. Ibid., 55.

38. Ibid., 162.

39. Ibid., 331–332, 345–348, 420–421.

40. Monroe to Henry, Aug. 12, 1786, in Henry, *Henry,* II, 291–298.

41. Elliot, *Debates,* III, 325–326.

42. Ibid., 43–64.

43. Ibid., 652.

44. Ibid.

45. Ibid., 653–654.

46. Spencer Roane to Philip Aylett, quoted in Mays, *Pendleton,* II, 272.

Notes—Chapter 8: Return to the Assembly

1. Elliot, *Debates,* III, 657–663.

2. Madison to Washington, June 27, 1788, in Hunt (ed.), *Writings of Madison,* V, 234.

3. Conway, *Randolph,* pp. 114–116; Elliot, *Debates,* II, 413–414.

4. Washington to Madison, Nov. 17, 1788, in Fitzpatrick (ed.), *Writings of Washington,* XXX, 131.

5. *JHD,* Oct. 23 and 24, 1788; Edward Carrington to Madison, Oct. 24, 1788, Madison Papers, LC.

6. Charles Lee to Washington, Oct. 29, 1788, in U.S. Department of State, *Documentary History of the Constitution of the United States* (5 vols.; Washington, D.C., 1894–1905), V, 101–103; *JHD,* Oct. 30, 1788.

7. George Lee Turberville to Madison, Oct. 27, 1788; Carrington to Madison, Nov. 9, 1788, in *Documentary History,* V, 110; JHD, Nov. 14, 1788.

8. Tobias Lear to Governor of New Hampshire, Jan. 31, 1789, in George

Bancroft, *History of the Formation of the Constitution of the United States* (2 vols.; New York, 1885), II, 488–489.

9. Henry to Caleb Wallace, Nov. 15, 1788, Patrick Henry Papers, LC; Madison to Jefferson, Aug. 23, 1788, in Hunt (ed.), *Writings of Madison*, V, 254.

10. *Virginia Independent Chronicle*, Jan. 14, 28, Feb. 11, 18, and March 25, 1789; Henry to William Grayson, March 31, 1789, in *VMHB*, XIV, 202–204.

11. Beeman, *Old Dominion*, pp. 56–58.

12. R. H. Lee to Henry, Sept. 14, 1789, in James C. Ballagh (ed.), *The Letters of Richard Henry Lee* (2 vols.; New York, 1911–1914), II, 501–504; Henry to Lee, Aug. 28, 1789, Henry Papers, LC.

13. William Grayson to Patrick Henry, Sept. 29, 1789, Henry Papers, LC.

14. R. H. Lee and William Grayson to Speaker of the House of Delegates, Sept. 28, 1789, in *Documentary History*, V, 217–218; Carrington to Madison, Dec. 20, 1789, Madison Papers, LC.

15. For a fuller discussion of this matter, see Beeman, *Old Dominion*, pp. 61–66.

16. *JHD*, Dec. 5, 1789.

17. Theodorick Bland to St. George Tucker, March 6, 1790, Tucker-Coleman Papers. College of William and Mary.

18. David Stuart to Washington, June 2, 1790, in Worthington C. Ford (ed.), *The Writings of George Washington* (14 vols.; New York, 1889–1893), II, 482–484; Henry Lee to Madison, Apr. 3, 1790, Madison Papers. LC.

19. *JHD*, Nov. 3 and 22, 1790.

20. Jefferson, in particular, claimed that Henry softened his stand against the federal government because he stood to gain financially from Hamilton's assumption proposal. Jefferson to Wirt, Aug. 4, 1805, *PMHB*, 34 (1910), 395.

21. Henry to Monroe, Jan. 24, 1791, Henry, *Henry*, II, 459–462.

22. Given the size of Henry's family—he had sixteen children in all—Henry would have had to amass a considerable fortune to keep all his heirs happy. And in fact, he would ultimately fail to satisfy all of them. At least one of his children would file suit after Henry's death, complaining that she had been shortchanged. For more information on Henry's children see Meade. *Henry,* II, 80, 86, 139, 167–168, 213, 305–311, 319, 383, 389. 433–434.

23. Henry, *Henry,* II, 464–465.

24. For a good discussion of the British debts question, see Albert Beveridge, *The Life of John Marshall* (4 vols.; Boston, 1916), II, 186–195; see also Henry, *Henry,* II, 471–476, Meade, *Henry,* II, 403–412.

25. Jefferson to Wirt, Aug. 14, 1805, *PMHB,* 34 (1910).

26. The full text of Henry's speech in the British debts case is reprinted in Henry, *Henry,* III, 601–648.

27. Beveridge, *Marshall,* II, 188; Meade, *Henry,* II, 405.

28. Henry, *Henry,* II, 475.

29. Beveridge, *Marshall,* II, 189–192.

30. W. C. Bruce, *John Randolph of Roanoke* (2 vols.; New York, 1922), I, 106–123.

31. Henry, *Henry,* II, 505.

32. Jackson T. Main, "The One Hundred," *WMQ,* ser. 3, XI (1954), 354–384. Henry's will and inventory are reprinted in Morgan, *Henry,* 455–468. The original is in Hanover County Records, Wills and Inventories.

33. For an excellent account of this very complicated matter, see Thomas Perkins Abernathy, *The South in the New Nation* (Baton Rouge, 1961), pp. 77, 88–91.

34. Ibid., pp. 91–92.

35. Ibid., pp. 91–98.

36. Ibid., pp. 136–168.

37. Washington to Henry, Oct. 9, 1795; Henry Lee to Washington, Dec. 26, 1795, in Fitzpatrick (ed.), *Writings of Washington,* XXXIV, 334–335, 421, 421n; Henry to Washington, Oct. 16, 1795, in Henry, *Henry,* II, 558.

38. Henry to Elizabeth Aylett, Aug. 20, 1796, in Henry, *Henry,* II, 569.

39. Beeman, *Old Dominion,* pp. 184–220.

40. Henry to Archibald Blair, Jan. 8, 1799, Timothy Pickering Papers, Massachusetts Historical Society (also reprinted in Henry, *Henry,* II, 591–594).

41. The principal source on Henry's views on the Alien and Sedition Acts is a recollection of a speech made by Henry at the Charlotte County Court-house on election day by a South Carolinian, John Miller. According to Miller's recollection, Henry did not commit himself either to support or oppose the Alien and Sedition Acts. Henry's opponent in that election was none other than John Randolph of Roanoke, and according to a manuscript in the possession of William Wirt, Randolph was of the opinion that Henry

favored the laws. For a full review of the evidence on the question, see Henry, *Henry*, II, 605–614.

42. Jefferson to Archibald Stuart, March 14, 1799, in Ford (ed.), *Writings of Jefferson*, VII, 378.

43. Meade, *Henry*, II, 452.

44. *Virginia Gazette and General Advertiser*, June 11, 1799.

45. *JHD*, Dec. 13, 1799.

46. Randolph, *History of Virginia*, p. 181.

Bibliographical Note

William Wirt, whose phenomenally popular but frequently mythologistic biography of Henry went through twenty-five editions, was only the first of many who have tried to explain Henry's place in Virginia society. Far more trustworthy than Wirt's creation is the three-volume compilation of Henry's grandson, William Wirt Henry. His work, *Patrick Henry, Life, Correspondence, and Speeches* (3 vols.; New York, 1891), is not only one of the fullest accounts of Henry written to date; it also reprints a substantial portion of the primary source material pertaining to Henry's life. Robert D. Meade, *Patrick Henry* (2 vols.; Philadelphia, 1957–1969), is the most detailed biography of Henry to appear in the twentieth century. Relying heavily on the previous research of William Wirt Henry, but also uncovering some new material relating to Henry's land investments and frontier activities, Meade has attempted to deal at close range with virtually every aspect of Henry's public and private life. The finished product is a useful piece of scholarship, although my own view is that the available source materials are not ideally suited to such an intensive approach. Moses Coit Tyler, *Patrick Henry* (Boston, 1887); George Morgan, *Patrick Henry* (Philadelphia, 1907); George Willison, *Patrick Henry and His World* (New York, 1969); and Eldon G. Bowman, "Patrick Henry's Political Philosophy," unpublished Ph.D. dissertation, Claremont Graduate School, 1961, have also completed book-length studies of Henry. Bernard Mayo, *Myths and Men: Patrick Henry, George Washington, Thomas Jefferson* (Atlanta, 1959), includes a particularly perceptive essay on Henry.

Any biography of Henry is in part a history of the Revolution in Virginia, a subject that has, surprisingly, produced numerous specialized works, but very few synthetic, interpretive books. David John Mays, *Edmund Pendleton, 1721–1803: A Biography* (2 vols.; Cambridge, Mass., 1952), despite demonstrating a strong bias against Henry, is a perceptive account both of Pendleton and of the Revolutionary era in Virginia as well. Thaddeus Tate, "The Coming of the Revolution in Virginia: Britain's Challenge to Virginia's Ruling Class, 1763–1776," *William and Mary Quarterly*, ser. 3, XIX (1963), 323–343; Joseph Ernst, "The Robinson Scandal Redivivus: Money, Debt, and Politics in Revolutionary Virginia," *Virginia Magazine of History and Biography*, LXXI (1969), 146–173; and Rhys Isaac, "Religion and Authority: Problems of the Anglican Establishment in Virginia in the Era of the Great Awakening and the Parsons' Cause," *William and Mary Quarterly*, ser. 3, XXX (1973), 3–36, are especially useful in dealing with some of the political controversies in the immediate pre-Revolutionary period.

Historians are fortunate to have a number of excellent studies of the political and social structure of eighteenth-century Virginia. Jack P. Greene, "Foundations of Political Power in the Virginia House of Burgesses, 1720–1776," *William and Mary Quarterly*, ser. 3, X (1959), 485–506; Charles Sydnor, *Gentlemen Freeholders: Political Practices in Washington's Virginia* (Chapel Hill, 1952); Jackson T. Main, "Sections and Politics in Virginia, 1781–1787," *William and Mary Quarterly*, ser. 3, XII (1955), 96–112, "The One Hundred," *William and Mary Quarterly*, ser. 3, X (1954), 368–383, and *Political Parties Before the Constitution* (Chapel Hill, 1973); and Robert E. and B. Katherine Brown, *Virginia, 1705–1786: Democracy or Aristocracy?* (East Lansing, Mich., 1964), are just a few of the most recent and helpful works published on this subject.

Among other secondary works that touch on Henry and the Revolution in Virginia are Irving Brant, *James Madison* (6 vols.; Indianapolis, 1941–1961); Moncure D. Conway, *Omitted Chapters in the Life of Edmund Randolph* (New York, 1888); Albert Beveridge, *The Life of John Marshall* (4 vols.; New York, 1916–1919); H. J. Eckenrode, *The Revolution in Virginia* (Boston, 1916); Freeman H. Hart, *The Valley of Virginia in the American Revolution, 1763–1789* (Chapel Hill, 1942); Dale Benson, "Wealth and Power in Virginia, 1774–1776: A Study of the Organization of Revolt," unpublished Ph.D. dissertation, University of Maine, 1972; Dumas Malone, *Thomas Jefferson and His Time* (4 vols.; Boston, 1948–); and Kate Mason Rowland, *The Life of George Mason* (New York, 1892).

In recent years several historians have sharpened our perceptions of the ideological impact of the Revolution. My own views on the causes and consequences of the Revolution in Virginia have been profoundly influenced by Bernard Bailyn, *Ideological Origins of the American Revolution* (Cambridge, Mass., 1967); Gordon Wood, *The Creation of the American Republic, 1776–1787* (Chapel Hill, 1969); and, from a different perspective, Jack P. Greene, *The Quest for Power: The Lower Houses of Assembly in the Southern Royal Colonies, 1689–1776* (Chapel Hill, 1963), and "Political Mimesis: A Consideration of the Historical and Cultural Roots of Legislative Behavior in the British Colonies in the Eighteenth Century," *American Historical Review,* LXXV (1970), 337–360.

The primary source materials relating to Henry's life are widely scattered, but there are several collections that are particularly valuable. John P. Kennedy and H. R. McIlwaine (eds.), *The Journals of the House of Burgesses* (13 vols.; Richmond, 1905–1915), and the *Journals of the House of Delegates* (microfilm, Library of Congress) are the most obvious sources with which to begin to examine Henry's legislative career. Similarly, William P. Palmer (ed.), *Calendar of Virginia State Papers, and Other Manuscripts Preserved in the Capitol at Richmond* (11 vols.; Richmond, 1875); William W. Hening, *The Statutes at Large: Being a Collection of the Laws of Virginia from the First Session of the Legislature in the Year 1619* (12 vols.; Richmond, 1875); and Peter Force (ed.), *American Archives, Consisting of a Collection of Authentic Records, State Papers . . . and Other Notices of Publick Affairs . . . [1774–1776]* (9 vols.; Washington, D.C. 1837–1853), also provide important leads to Henry's public career. Jonathon Elliot, *The Debates in the Several State Conventions on the Adoption of the Federal Constitution* (4 vols.; Washington, D.C., 1836), gives an extensive account of Henry's speeches in the Virginia Ratifying Convention.

The precise details of Henry's private economic dealings, particularly his farming activities, remain elusive, but some useful information can be uncovered in his manuscript account books, which are on deposit at the Valentine Museum and the Virginia State Library, Richmond, Virginia.

The newspapers of the period provide the researcher with a glimpse of nearly every aspect of life in Virginia during the Revolutionary era. For the years before the Revolution the [Williamsburg] *Virginia Gazette,* published by a variety of different printers, is an indispensable source. Lester Cappon and Stella Duff, *The Virginia Gazette Index, 1763–1780* (Williamsburg, 1950), is an essential aid in using the *Virginia Gazette.* In the period after the Revolution the number of newspapers in circulation increased dramatically; of the dozen newspapers in the post-Revolutionary period that I have consulted, the [Richmond] *Virginia Gazette and General Advertiser* was the most helpful.

The published correspondence of Henry's contemporaries, while not always conducive to a balanced view of the Revolutionary orator, proved to be of considerable value in assessing Henry's place in the political order. Those that I found most helpful are Julian Boyd (ed.), *The Papers of Thomas Jefferson* (18 vols.; Princeton, 1950–   ); Paul Leicester Ford (ed.), *The Writings of Thomas Jefferson* (12 vols.; New York, 1904–1905); John C. Fitzpatrick (ed.), *The Writings of George Washington from the Original Manuscript Sources, 1745–1799* (39 vols.; Washington, D.C., 1931–1944); Gaillard Hunt (ed.), *The Writings of James Madison* (9 vols.; New York, 1900–1910); and the previously mentioned three-volume compilation of Henry's writings by William Wirt Henry.

The single contemporary source most important to my understanding of Henry is Edmund Randolph, *History of Virginia,* Arthur Shaffer, ed. (Charlottesville, 1970). Randolph, although he frequently had cause to resent Henry's power and influence, nevertheless proved capable of appreciating Henry's talents in ways that eluded many of Henry's most ardent admirers and bitter detractors. Arthur Shaffer's excellent introduction to the *History* makes the volume all the more useful.

Index